k_{RF}	Rate of return on a risk-free security
k_S	(1) Cost of retained earnings
	(2) Required return on a stock
M	Maturity value of a bond
M/B	Market-to-book ratio
MCC	Marginal cost of capital
MIRR	Modified internal rate of return
N	Calculator key denoting number of periods
n	(1) Life of a project
	(2) Number of shares outstanding
NPV	Net present value
NWC	Net working capital
P	(1) Price of a share of stock; P_0 = price of the stock today
	(2) Sales price per unit of product sold
P/E	Price/earnings ratio
PMT	Periodic level payment of an annuity
PV	Present value
PVA_n	Present value of an annuity for n years
PVIF	Present value interest factor for a lump sum
PVIFA	Present value interest factor for an annuity
ρ	Correlation coefficient
ROA	Return on assets
ROE	Return on equity
RP	Risk premium
RP_M	Market risk premium
S	Sales
SML	Security Market Line
Σ	Summation sign(capital sigma)
σ	Standard deviation(lowercase sigma)
σ^2	Variance
t	Time period
T	Marginal income tax rate
TIE	Times interest earned
V	Variable cost per unit
V_B	Bond value
VC	Total variable costs
WACC	Weighted average cost of capital
YTM	Yield to maturity

Hotel Investment & Finance: A Practical Guide for Development and Control

BY

CHOI, JEONG-GIL

BAEKSAN
Publishing Co

First edition 2011

Permissions may sought directly from
Baeksan Publishing in Seoul, Korea
(82)2-914-1621
http://www.ibaeksan.kr

Manufactured in South Korea

Jeong-Gil Choi
Kyung Hee University, South Korea
Hotel Investment & Finance: A Practical Guide for Decision Making

Includes bibliographical references.
ISBN: 978-89-6183-529-9

Price ₩20,000

This book is dedicated to my family, students, and fellow friends
I love you very much.

Preface

Hotel Investment & Finance : A Practical Guide for Decision Making is intended for use in the introductory-investment & finance course. This book is prepared especially for students majoring in hospitality and tourism management in order to provide a practical guide for sound decision making.

The book begins with a broad picture of hotel business development and financing. Subsequent chapters explain how owners and managers conduct feasibility study for investment, ownership formation and operation, and fundamental knowledge of investment.

From the chapter 5 this book focuses on corporate finance including corporation and management, cash flows and measuring their values, risk and return analysis, and valuation.

Chapter 10 and 11 explain how financial managers can maximize the value of their firms by making better decisions in such areas as capital budgeting, choice of capital structure, and working capital management.

The last chapter of this book introduces the franchising and management contracts from the financial manager's perspectives.

Intended Market and Use

This book is intended for use as an introductory text. To emphasize the investment and feasibility study, the instructor will probably spend more time on chapter 1 through 4. In order to pay attention to corporate finance, the instructor will probably cover only selected chapters before chapter 5 and start with chapter 5, leaving the others for students either to examine on their own or to use as references in conjunction with work in later courses.

<Note1> This book is prepared to be used in a one-semester course. A comprehensive set of PPT class lecture material is available to instructors who adopt the text.

<Note2> Appendix P-1 ; Finance Basics in student's hand, is prepared for students who want to study the key concepts & theories at anytime. Students can use this to study in more convenient manner.

Acknowledgements

This book reflects the efforts of a great many people over number of years. Especially, I would like to thank the following professors who taught me in Michigan State University and Virginia Tech: J. M. Tarras, M. D. Olsen, F. A. Kwansa, R. S. Schmidgall. Most of the contents come from my formal college and graduate school class notes. Special thanks are due to authors of finance books with which I could enriched this book: E. F. Brigham, M. Coltman, S. Rushmore, F. R. Lawson. Finally, I would like to express my sincere appreciation to my great students: Akhmedov Armigon, Seong Ae Jeon, Jekaterina Melehova for their proofreading, and to the president and editing staffs in Baeksan publishing company.

Errors in the Text

As a result of error detection procedures, I am convinced that it is virtually free of mistakes. However, I admit there is some possibility that I might have missed. Because I want to detect any remaining errors and correct them in subsequent printings, I hereby offer a reward per error to the first person who reports it to me. (Any errors that follow-through effects is counted as two errors only.) Please report any errors to me at the e-mail address. (jechoi@khu.ac.kr)

I hope that you enjoy this book and enrich your body of knowledge in the hospitality investment and finance.

Appendix P-1 : Finance Basics in Student's Hand

Understanding Key Concepts & Theories

The Time Value of Money and Present Value

A dollar today is worth more today than a dollar to be received in the future. Because capital is productive over time, there is an **opportunity cost** to delayed payments. This simple intuition, known as the **time value of money**, is essential for, among other things, valuing stocks and bonds, determining whether to undertake a new corporate venture, and deciding to buy or lease equipment.

Present value refers to the current value of future cash flows. These future cash flows must be adjusted by an appropriate **discount factor** in order to account for the time value of money. The discount factor so related to the **rate of return** demanded by investors for accepting delayed payment on a particular investment. This rate is often referred to as the **discount rate or cost of capital.**

$$\text{Discount factor} = \frac{1}{(1+r)^n}$$

where r is the appropriate rate of return and n is the number of periods over which the payment must be discounted, assuming simple discounting.

Simple Present Value Calculations

The present value (PV) of a future cash flow (CF) to be received in n periods assuming a simple discount rate of r is calculated as:

$$PV = CF \times (\text{discount factor}) = \frac{CF}{(1+r)^n}$$

For continuous discounting, $PV = CFe^{-rn}$

Similarly, the **future value (FV)** of a current investment (INV) that is expected to return r per period (simple compounding) over n period is given as:

$$FV = INV(1+r)^n$$

–the rule of 72 is a "back of the envelope" method for calculating the approximate number of years(x) it will take to double an investment given an expected return of r per year, assuming simple compounding: $x = \frac{72}{r}$

An **annuity** is a series of fixed payments (CF) to be received each period over a specified number of periods (n). The present value of an annuity is given as:

$$PV = \sum_{t=1}^{n} \frac{CF}{(1+r)^t} p = CF\left[\frac{1}{r} - \frac{1}{r(1+r)^n}\right] p$$

A **perpetuity** is a series of fixed payments to be received each period for an infinite number of periods. The present value of a perpetuity is calculated as:

$$PV = \frac{CF}{r}$$

–For a perpetuity with cash flows growing at a constant rate of g per period after period 1: $PV = \frac{CF_1}{r-g}$,
where CF_1 is the cash flow in period 1.

The present value of a series of different cash flows to be received at different times in the future ($t_1, t_2, \cdots, t_n$) is calculated as:

$$PV = \sum_{t=1}^{n} \frac{CF_t}{(1+r)^t} = \frac{CF_1}{1+r} + \frac{CF_2}{(1+r)^2} + \cdots + \frac{CF_n}{(1+r)^n} p$$

Net Present Value

The Net Present Value (NPV) of a project is the sum of the present values of all cash flows associated with the project over its life, assuming an appropriate discount rate. This includes any current investment (CF_0) associated with the project.

$$NPV = CF_0 + \sum_{t=1}^{n} \frac{CF_t}{(1+r)^t}$$

The NPV method can be used to determine whether a firm should undertake a project. In general, **positive *NPV*** projects (i.e., those with $NPV > 0$, assuming an appropriate discount rate) will increase shareholder wealth and therefore should be undertaken: **negative *NPV*** projects will decrease shareholder wealth and should be rejected.

Estimating Cost of Capital: CAPM

Investors require a higher return for taking on additional risk. While certain risks associated with individual projects or companies can be eliminated through **diversification**(i.e., the certain of a broad portfolio of different projects or companies), there is an underlying **market risk** that cannot be diversified away. In the context of securities, the risk of a diversified portfolio is determined by the market risk of the securities in the portfolio.
The **Capital Asset Pricing Model (CAPM)** is a commonly used model that relates a security's expected rate of return (r_s), and hence its associated cost of capital, to its contribution to the risk of a portfolio comprising the market as a whole-the theoretical **market portfolio**-using its **beta** (β_s), the risk-free rate (r_f), and the expected return of the overall market (r_M).

$$r_s = r_f + \beta_s(r_M - r_f)$$

–**Beta** is a statistical concept that measures the sensitivity of a security's return to the return of the market as a whole.
–The interest rate on long-term Treasury bonds (e.g., the 10-year Treasury) is typically used for the risk-free rate.
–The difference, $r_M - r_f$, is known as the market risk premium. While there is no precise way to measure this value, the market has returned approximately 7~8% above the 10-year Treasury bond on average over the past 70 years.

Debt

Introduction to Debt Securities

Companies periodically need funds to invest in projects and to cover working capital shortfalls. Typically, companies raise capital by issuing one of two types of corporate securities: **debt** (referred to as **bonds** or **fixed-income securities**) and **equity** (referred to as **stocks**).

When a company issues debt, it is essentially borrowing money with the promise that it will ultimately repay the amount borrowed-**the principal**-and make regular **interest payments** in the interim.

- The face value of each bond (typically $1,000) is referred to as the **par value**.
- Interest payments are often called **coupon payments**. These payments are typically made annually or semi-annually. Bonds that repay the face value at a specified future time but do not make any intermediate coupon payments are known as **zero-coupon bonds** or **strips**.

If the company fails to make its payments, it **defaults** on its debt and must turn over assets to repay the debtholders.

A company's interest payments are deducted from its taxable (i.e., before-tax) income; this favorable tax status is sometimes referred to as a **tax shield**.

Debt securities are characterized by a number of features:

- **Maturity** refers to the period over which the bond is to be paid back.
- **Seniority** refers to the liquidation preference of the bond in the event of a default. Holders of **subordinated debt** must wait until the firm's more senior creditors have been paid before seeking claims on the company's assets.
- Assets are sometimes pledged as **collateral** against a loan; holders of a collateralized bond will have first claim on these assets in the event of a default. This type of security is also known as **secured debt**. Unsecured long-term loans are known as **debentures**.
- While interest payments are typically fixed at the time of issuance (e.g., 5% annually), some bonds offer a variable rate that can fluctuate based on another rate (e.g., **prime rate** or **LIBOR**, plus 1%). These are referred to as **floating-rate** bonds.

Debt securities are rated by several ratings agencies according to the likelihood of defaulted.

- **Standard & Poor's scale** runs from AAA (least likely default) to C; **Moody's scale** runs from Aaa to C.
- The highest quality bonds are known as **investment grade** (AAA-BBB for S&P, Aaa-Baa for Moody's). Bonds with lower ratings are commonly referred to as junk or **high-yield bonds**.

A **convertible bond** allows holders to exchange the bond for a specified number of common stock in the firm at a prespecified conversion rate.

Valuing Debt Securities

Bonds are relatively easy to value using simple present value formulas. A bond is essentially a combination of an annuity-the coupon payments-and the discounted value of the face value to be paid back at maturity (the exception here is the floating-rate bond, which can have fluctuating coupon payments). For a nonfloating-rate bond (B) with a given face value (F), periodic coupon payment (C), discount rate (r_B), and total number of periods until maturity (M), the value can be calculated as:

$$V_B = \frac{F}{(1+r_B)^M} + \sum_{t=1}^{M} \frac{C}{(1+r_B)^t}$$

$$= \frac{F}{(1+r_B)^M} + C\left[\frac{1}{r_B} + \frac{1}{r_B(1+r_B)^M}\right]$$

The current price of a bond is often used to determine its **yield to maturity ("yield")**. The yield refers the discount rate at which the present value of the bond is equal to its current market price and represents the rate of return required by investor for this type of loan. Note that for corporate securities, the yield is greater than the **risk-free rate** (i.e., the interest rate on risk-free bonds like U.S. Treasury Bonds); this is because all corporate securities carry some degree of default risk.

Duration is a measure of a bond's effective maturity. It is defined as the weighted- average of the time until each payment, with weights proportional to the present value of each payment.

For a bond with a given yield to maturity (y), periodic coupon payment (C), total number of periods until maturity (M), face value (F), and current market price (P), **Macauley's Duration** (D) is defined as follows:

$$D = \left[\frac{\left(\frac{1C}{(1+y)^1} + \frac{2C}{(1+y)^2} + \cdots + \frac{M(C+F)}{(1+y)^M}\right)}{P}\right]$$

Modified Duration (MD) is a related measure defined as:

$$MD = -\frac{1}{1+y}\left[\frac{\frac{1C}{(1+y)^1} + \frac{2C}{(1+y)^2} + \cdots + \frac{M(C+F)}{(1+y)^M}}{P}\right]$$

Duration can be a useful measure in understanding the sensitivity of a bond's price to changes in interest rates. The percentage change in a bond's price $(\%\triangle P_B)$ with respect to a given absolute change in interest rates $(\triangle IR)$ can be estimated using the following:

$$\%\triangle P_B = -\frac{1}{1+y} D(\triangle IR) = -MD(\triangle IR)$$

This estimation method is only accurate for small, identical changes in interest rates at all maturities.

Equity

Introduction to Equity

Equity represents ownership in a corporation. There are two forms of equity: **common stock** and **preferred stock**. The smallest unit of equity is known as a **share**. **Common stockholders** (or **shareholders**) exercise control over a company by voting for its **Board of Directors** and, in certain cases, by voting directly on major corporate issues (e.g., **mergers**). These common stockholders are entitled to receive whatever assets or earnings are available from the business once its creditors have been paid.

A company distributes its profits to shareholders through periodic **dividend** payments, typically on a quarterly basis. These dividend payments often grow as a company's earnings grow; however, a company can choose to reduce or even eliminate its dividend payments.

- Whereas interest payments are paid out of before-tax income, dividends are paid out of after-tax income; thus, interest payments are tax-advantaged, relative to dividends.

$$-\text{Dividend yield} = \frac{\text{dividend per share of common stock}}{\text{price per share}}$$

$$-\text{Payout ratio} = \frac{\text{dividend per share}}{\text{earnings per share}}$$

Preferred stock is an equity security with certain features similar to debt:

- Like bonds, preferred stock typically offers a fixed dividend; however, payment on a preferred dividend can be withheld without threat of default. All preferred dividends must be paid before a company can pay a dividend to its common shareholders.
- In the event of liquidation, holders of preferred shares line up behind debtholders but ahead of common shareholders.
- Preferred stock often has a conversion feature that allows shares to be converted into common shares.
- Preferred dividends, like common dividends, are paid out of after-tax income.

Valuing Equity Securities

The **dividend discount model** values an equity security based on the future dividends anticipated by holders of that security. These future dividends (Div_1, Div_2 ,...), which represent the cash flows associated with share ownership, are estimated and discounted at the appropriate cost of equity capital (r_E) to give the present value of the security (V_S):

$$V_S = \sum_{t=1}^{\infty} \frac{Div_t}{(1+r_E)^t}$$

If a constant growth rate (g) is assumed for these dividends, this model can be simplified using the familiar formula for a growing perpetuity:

$$V_S = \frac{Div_1}{r_E - g}$$

Another valuation technique, known as a **Discounted Cash Flow (*DCF*)** analysis, seeks to determine the value of the entire firm (V_F), from which the value of a single share can be deduced. In the most common form of this analysis, the company's future **Free Cash Flows (*FCF*)** are estimated and discounted at a rate that takes into account the capital structure of the firm (i.e., its mix of debt and equity) and the tax benefits associated with interest payments. This rate is known as the after-tax **Weighted Average Cost of Capital (*WACC*)**:

$$V_F = \sum_{t=1}^{\infty} \frac{FCF_t}{(1+WACC)^t}$$

The WACC is calculated based on the company's cost of equity(r_E), cost of debt(r_D), market value of outstanding dept (D), market value of equity (E), and marginal tax rate (T):

$$WACC = r_E \frac{E}{D+E} + r_D\left(\frac{D}{D+E}\right)(1-t)$$

- Free cash flows are defined at the cash flows from operating activites that are available for distribution to suppliers of capital.
- In practice, free cash flows are often projected over a relatively short forecast horizon (H), after which they are expected to grow at a modest annual growth rate (g) indefinitely. The present value calculation can then be simplified as:

$$V_F = \frac{FCF(1+g)}{(WACC-g)(1+WACC)^H} + \sum_{t=1}^{H} \frac{FCF_t}{(1+WACC)^t}$$

- Note that the DCF analysis assumes that the firm maintains a constant ratio of dept to equity and has sufficient income each year to realize the tax benefits of interest payments.

Contents

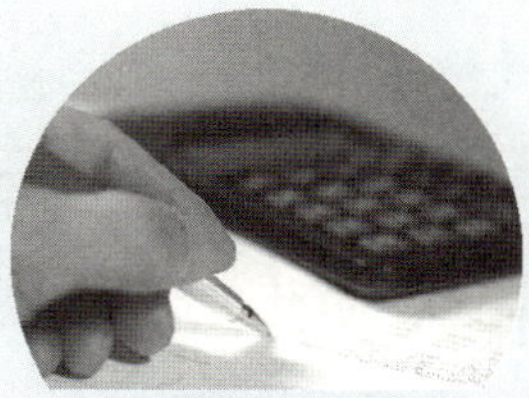

Chapter 01

A Broad Picture of Hotel Business Development and Financing

Chapter 01 A Broad Picture of Hotel Business Development and Financing

1. Hotel Business & Market

The hotel business is the most challenging and rewarding business in the modern era. There are many factors that directly or indirectly contribute to the success of hotel industry; tourism (domestic and international) is one of the most important factors. International Tourism is showing no signs of slowdown in new millennium generating huge demand for hotel rooms.

If the trend continues to grow at the same rate, more and more people will be traveling in the future, hence creating more demand for hotel rooms and attracting more investment and setting up of new hotel properties worldwide.

Hotel business is a rewarding business but at the same time it is also a very complex kind of business. The success or failure of a hotel depends on how well the particular property is managed. It is impossible to teach someone how to "run a hotel" from a book. Only the practical experience can teach a subject so complex. Let's take a look into the basic factors that every hotelier must understand before starting a new project.

1) 3 Important Components of Hotel Business

The first step to learn before starting any business is to understand its basic fundamentals. Hotels are not only just buildings with rooms and restaurants; a hotel can serve numerous functions from a meeting place to a real estate investment. There are 3 important components of hotel business.

1. **People:** Hotel business is people's business. A huge number of people from different walks of life are involved in a single property. A 1,000-room hotel is likely to employ from 700 to 1,100 people, depending on the level of service it provides. If the above mentioned hotel sells all the rooms, it will house approximately from 1,500 to 2,000 guests, each of which with different needs and preferences. The parties involved in a single hotel are employees, guests, managers, stakeholders, shareholders, suppliers, transporters; travel agents etc. That makes a hotel people's business.
2. **Product:** The product, in case of hotel business is the services and facilities that are being offered to the guests. As mentioned above that; guests staying in a hotel might have different needs and preferences, the services and facilities that are going to be offered, must be designed and operated with superior quality, to satisfy the needs and desires of the guests.
3. **Profit:** The ultimate goal of every hotel is to maximize the profit. The success of a hotel can only be measured by the profit earned by it. If a hotel makes enough profit to satisfy all its stakeholders and shareholders that hotel is said to be a successful hotel. Running a hotel that fails to make profit, is wasting time, money and efforts. Moreover profits are required to grow and survive in the market and a good service without profit is called a "Charity" not a "Business Transaction".

2) Demand and Supply Side of the Hotel Industry

It is important to understand that hotels exhibit cyclical characteristics that affect their operation and management. The demand for hotel rooms varies from day to day. During the high or busy season a hotel will run very high on the occupancies; during the off-season it may have half or less the business it enjoyed during the high season. The cyclical nature of demand causes hotel problems because a hotel can do nothing to increase the occupancy in off-season. And in off season there is no need to hire too many people as the occupancy is low that leads to frequent staff fluctuations, but on the other hand, in high season, hotel will have to hire more people. These frequent staff fluctuations, necessitated by cyclical demand, make it particularly difficult for hotels to maintain service standard. Furthermore, the demand is affected by many other factors such as consumer demographics and population trends, including age, gender and marital status. Income and employment trends also influence the consumer preferences. Also the education level of population and the changing culture we live in influence consumer tastes and interests.

The fortunes of the hotel industry are driven by basic supply and demand. It is true in case of hotels that supply of hotel rooms cannot be increased in short run but over the past decades there have been an oversupply of new hotels, as more and more people were attracted to the lucrative business of hotel. Excesses on the supply side have often caused hotel occupancy to drop and have sometimes caused hotel price wars which further depress the average daily rates (or ADRs) on the reduced number of rooms occupied. And ironic part of the story is that, as a hotelier you cannot bar the entry of a new comer in the capitalist market system.

Figure 1-1 shows the unique nature of supply and demand curve of the hotel industry. Please see the note in the figure.

FIGURE 1-1 Supply & Demand Curve of the Hotel Industry

(1) Demand & Supply Curve(In general)

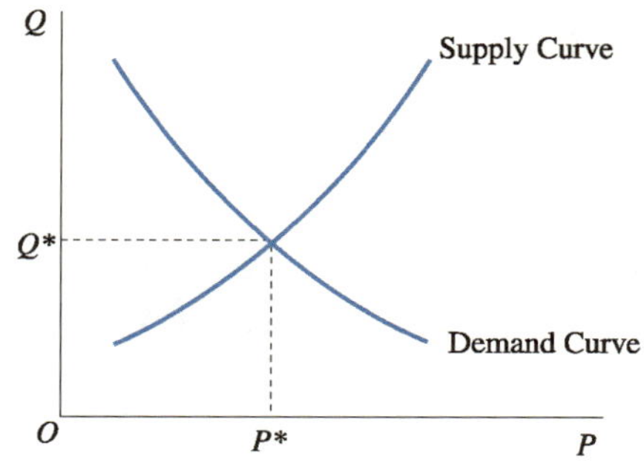

P* : Equilibrium Price
Q* : Equilibrium Quantity
P* × Q* = Total Revenue

(2) Demand & Supply Curve(Hotel Industry)

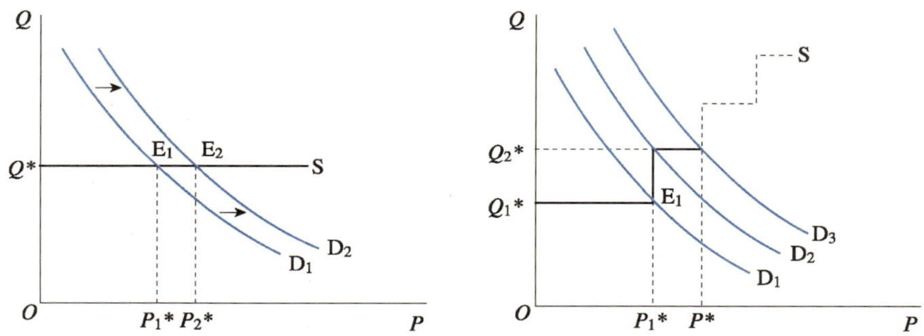

(A) Short Period (B) Long Period

D : Demand Curve
S : Supply Curve

Note:
1. Supply is fixed, but Demand fluctuates overtime.
2. Controlling price is the only way to increase total revenue.
3. Supply may be increased in the long-run according to increasing demand.
4. At some point supply and demand will meet together because customer will resist to continuous price increase.

3) Classification of Hotels

The hotels can be classified according to their location, quality, management, availability of facilities, mode of payment etc. Given are the classifications of hotels.

1. Depending on location:
   Center City Hotels, Resort Hotels, Airport Hotels, Freeway Hotels, Casino Hotels

2. Depending on service type, service quality and price:
   Full Service Hotels (Deluxe, Luxury, Upscale, Mid-Scale), Limited Service Hotels (Mid-Scale, Economy, Budget)

3. Depending on purpose:
   Commercial Hotels, Convention Hotels, Resort Hotels, Apartment Hotels

4. Depending on period of stay:
   Transient Hotel, Residential Hotel, Permanent Hotel

5. Depending on availability of facilities:
   Motel, Boatel, Yachtel, Floatel, Youth Hostel, All-suite Hotel

6. Depending on Management:
   Regular Chain Hotels, Referral Organization Hotels, Management Contract Hotels, Co-owner chain Hotel, Independent management Hotel, Franchise Hotel, Lease Management Hotel, Vacation Ownership

7. Depending on location of industry:
   Metropolitan Hotel, City Hotel, Suburban Hotel, Country Hotel, Airport Hotel, Seaport Hotel, Terminal Hotel, Beach Hotel

8. Depending on the mode of payment:
   American Plan Hotel, European Plan Hotel, Dual-Plan Hotel

4) Guests vs. Services

A hotel makes profit by housing and entertaining guests. Guests are human beings hence they are very complicated to understand. Different guests have different purposes to visit a hotel. So it is very important to understand all the guests and treat different guest differently. We are to make our guests satisfy with good quality services. "Quality service means exceeding your guest's expectations and paying attention to details. Treat customers like guests and manage the organization from the guest's point of view" The art and science of knowing your customers is referred to "guestology". This term was first introduced by Disney.

Every hotelier must always keep in mind that hotels sell "experience" to its guests. Guest Experience has following three components.

- Service Product
- Service Environment
- Service Delivery System

Guest Experience = Service Product + Service Environment + Service Delivery System

We should not underestimate the importance of service, which plays a crucial role in guest satisfaction, repeat business, and a hotel's reputation. It often costs money to improve a hotel's service but improved services create more satisfied guests that lead to repeat business, a better reputation, higher revenues, and greater profits. However, it takes time for the benefits of improved service to be felt, and it is not always easy to measure the effect of good service on revenues and profits.

5) Site Selection

After understanding the basics of hotel business and the guests, it is now time to look for a suitable site to erect a property. The location of a property is very important to the success of the hotel. Imagine you build a 100 million dollar hotel in the middle of nowhere; where it is impossible for the guests to reach! Or you build a multi million hotel in downtown, where you paid exorbitant price to acquire land and the area is already saturated with the supply of hotel rooms. Can you run your hotel successfully? It can not be guaranteed, because first of all you have to lower your price to attract guests in a saturated market and secondly you have to pay more interest on the land acquired. There are lots of things that have to be taken into account before finalizing the site. Table 1-1 below shows some of the important considerations for successful site selection.

Table 1.1 Factors to be considered for site selection.

• Ease and cost • Proximity to airport • Adequate taxi/limousine service • Sufficient parking space • Adequate airport assistance • Adequate number of flights into destination • Seasonality of destination (peak season vs. off-season) • Availability of local attractions • Shopping	• Recreation • Restaurants • Weather conditions • Appearance • Safety of area • Economic health of community • Reputation of area/facility for hosting meetings • Support and services available from local bodies • Availability of experienced suppliers, such as exhibit service contractors, temporary help, and security.

A lot of research is needed to be carried out in choosing the site because once if the hotel has been erected, it is virtually impossible to shift it to another site. Please keep in mind that like a product, every tourist attraction also has a life cycle. Figure 1-2 shows the product life cycle curve.

FIGURE 1-2 Product Life Cycle Curve

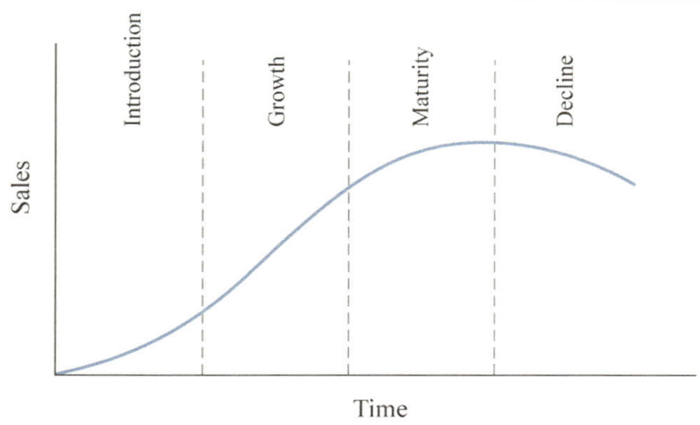

The tourism market in Europe has already passed its maturity stage and new markets like China, India, Middle East and Southeast and East Asia are at their growth stage. With the economic and political conditions that are favorable and government systems that are committed to improve infrastructure and to harness the economic benefits of tourism; it is the right time to consider these countries while selecting sites.

6) Arranging Capital

We have selected the site and now we are ready to build a hotel. Or there can be a case that already operating hotel on the favorable site is on sale. Buying already operating hotel can also be a good idea if the right calculations have been done regarding true market value of the property. It can save lots of time, as it takes 2 to 3 years (depending on the area) to construct a new property. Whether you are acquiring a running hotel or you are building a new hotel; you need money. Millions of dollars! Imagine you don't have that money. You can either seek a bank loan or borrow from a private lender. Getting a loan is a difficult task. Due to seasonality of demand and other risk factors associated with the hotel industry, lenders are sometimes reluctant to finance a hotel project on prevailing interest rates. Their interest rates are sometimes higher than the market rate to cover the risk.

Hotel business is a capital intensive business. You not only need cash to build a property, but also need it to operate the property. Hotels have some large variable costs, most being in the food and beverage departments. Lodging itself, however, is capital intensive; that is, it requires large investments of capital in fixed plant and equipment. And capital costs such as depreciation, interest, insurance, and property taxes are fixed costs. These capital costs must be met regardless of business. And sometimes you might need cash to catch up with your competitors or to respond to a sudden change in the demands of the customers due to a technological invention. For example: imagine the customers prefer new Hi-Definition flat screen LCD TV screens in the room. This is only one problem, there may arise hundreds of them which need immediate solution.

There are two kinds of factors which can influence the financing of a hotel and can determine approval as well as interest rates and overall cost of the financing.

They are called *Controllable Factors* and *Uncontrollable Factors.* Controllable factors are the factors in which you have some measure of influence. These factors can be controllable. On the other hand Uncontrollable factors are the factors in which you have no influence yet these factors are very important when it comes to determining the overall cost of your hotel loan. Given is a table that lists some of the controllable and uncontrollable factors that can determine the financing of your hotel project.

Table 1.2 Factors influencing the financing of hotel project

Controllable Factors	Uncontrollable Factors
• Appraisal of property • Debt service coverage • Income history of property • Length of loan • Loan amount • Loan-to-value ratio • Management experience • Occupancy rate • Personal income/credit history	• Bond market • Current economic conditions (local and national) • Expected future economic conditions (local and national) • Lender portfolios • Market capitalization rate

You should keep in mind that all these factors do not need to be in your favor in order to be approved for hotel loan financing. If you have the controllable factors in order and the economic conditions are fair, you should be able to obtain affordable hotel financing.

7) Decisions Regarding the Management

One of the interesting things about the hotels is that; sometimes the person or the party who builds or owns the property has no knowledge about how to operate the hotel. The owner may lack the technical skills that are required to run a hotel efficiently. In this case the owner can either opt for a Franchising Contract or a Management Contract with the third party. These contracts allow the owner of the property to seek the professional expertise from the people who have better understanding of the market and the customers.

A hotel owner can choose either franchising or the management contract with the company; depending upon his needs and the availability of suitable offer. Both management contract and franchising have their own benefits and disadvantages. More details for franchising and management contract are shown in chapter 12.

2. Understanding Basic Concepts of Investment and Financial Decisions

Making investment and financial decisions require an understanding of the basic economic principles of financial markets. It could be possible to describe a financial market as that makes it possible for individuals and corporations to borrow and lend. As a consequence, financial markets can be used by individuals to adjust their patterns of consumption over time and by corporations to adjust their patterns of investment spending over time. By far the most important economic decisions are those that involve investments in real assets. It does not mean savings decisions, which are decisions not to consume some of this year's income, but decisions regarding actual investments: building a machine or a whole factory or a hotel, for example. These decisions determine the economic (future for) worth of a society. Economists use the word capital to describe the total stock of machines and equipment that a society possesses and uses to produce goods and services. Investment decisions are decisions about whether or not to increase this stock of capital.

The investment decisions made today determine how much additional capital the society will add to its current stock of capital. That capital then can be used in the future to produce goods and services for the society. Some of the forms that capital takes are obvious, like computers. But many kinds of capital assets are things that we never would have thought of as part of a country's capital stock. Public roads, for example, are a form of capital, and the decisions we are making to invest in education is no different in principle from these other investment decisions. Your decision to invest in education is a decision to build your human capital, just as a company's decision to build a new factory is a decision to invest in physical capital.

The investment decision deals with how much money to invest in a firm's assets as well as which specific assets the firm should invest in.

- Creditors and government generally have a higher priority claim to a firm's operating cash flow than the firm's owners.
- When a corporation's board of directors decides to keep the owners' money and reinvest it in the firm, it is implicitly making a new investment for the owners.
- A project creates value for the owners of a firm when it generates an NPV(Net Present Value) greater than zero.
- It is virtually impossible to erect entry barriers in the capital markets.
- The government pays some of the cost of debt financing.

In a sense, finance can be thought of as the study of the following three questions:

1. In what (long-lived) capital assets should the firm invest? This question concerns the left-hand side of the balance sheet. Of course, the type and proportions of assets the firm needs tend to be set by the nature of the business. We use the terms capital budgeting and capital expenditure to describe the process of making and managing expenditures on long-lived assets.
2. How can the firm raise cash for required capital expenditures? This question concerns the right-hand side of the balance sheet. The answer to this involves the firm's capital structure, which represents the proportions of the firm's financing from current and long-term debt and equity.
3. How should short-term operating cash flows be managed? This question concerns the upper portion of the balance sheet. There is a mismatch between the timing of cash inflows and cash outflows during operating activities. Furthermore, the amount and timing of operating cash flows are not known with certainty. The financial managers must attempt to manage the gaps in cash flow. From an accounting perspective, short-term management of cash flow is associated with a firm's net working capital. Net working capital is defined as current assets minus current liabilities. From a financial perspective, the short-term cash flow problem comes from the mismatching of cash inflow and outflows. It is the subject of short-term finance.

3. Investment in Hotel Business

The hotel enterprise can be thought of as a complex organization made up of processes utilizing various technologies that provide both services and products. The investment in these products and services and the technologies to produce them, form the competitive method of the hotel enterprise. The manager must evaluate the investment made in each carefully to be sure that it helps firm's gain competitive advantage which ensures that appropriate returns are achieved.

The evaluation processes require the synthesis of concepts from the field of financial management and strategic management. Strategic decisions are ultimately investment decision, which when taken properly, make use of concepts in finance and strategy.

Every competitive method chosen by a firm requires capital. Capital is supplied by an array of investors ranging from the individual to the largest of institutional investors. When the investor makes a decision to put his/her hard earned dollar into assets, he/she expects a desired return. The return should offset inflation, and compensate for the risk that is being taken. Put differently, the investor seeks wealth maximization at minimum levels of risk. This can be accomplished by achieving the following goals:

1. Investing in competitive methods that give the firm sustainable competitive advantage, which produce growth in turn in the value of the assets of the firm.
2. Making full utilization of the assets
3. Minimizing risk
4. Balancing long-term growth against short-term objectives

In more technical sense, adding value means that management is able to earn from its investment amounts in excess of the cost of capital utilized to create them. This demands that each investment in a competitive method will result in a positive Net Present Value(NPV). If investments of the firm do not meet this criteria, managers fail to achieve their most essential responsibility, which is "Creating Wealth." More details for this subject are presented in chapter 6 for time value of money and in chapter 11 for capital budgeting.

Investment in hotel business is a difficult but interesting and rewarding job. Hotel business is here to stay. But as the time passes it will become more complex and sophisticated. The demand patterns of the customers will change and hotels have to respond according to them. To understand better the future of the hotel industry consider the following questions about the future.

How will the customer be traveling in the future?

How will the customer be communicating in the future?

How will the firm's product be distributed to the customers in the future?

What new customer benefits will be needed to meet future demands?

What competencies will be needed to serve the customer in the future?

What standards will be accepted in the future?

What will the successful hotel firm look like in the future?

What new competitive methods will demand the majority of your resources in the future?

It is very necessary to keep in mind these questions before we start planning a hotel project.

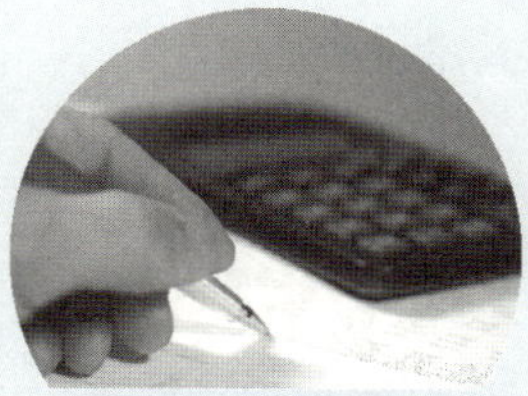

Chapter 02

Feasibility Study for Investment

Chapter 02

Feasibility Study for Investment

1. Understanding Hotel and Grading[1)]

1) Definitions and Standards: Hotels

In most countries a 'hotel' is defined as a public establishment offering travellers and temporary visitors, against payment, two basic services: accommodation and meals. The precise definition of what constitutes a hotel and condition for hotel registration and grading are set out in more than one hundred classification systems worldwide operated by governmental or representative agencies.

National systems of classification vary both in the range of categories and method of designation (letters, figures, stars, crowns and other symbols) and may be compulsory or voluntary.

Circumstances of hotel operation also vary: resort hotels may be operated under exclusive contract to one or more tour operators; they may restrict food service to residents and remain open only during the holiday season. Hotels may also include many different types of accommodation: guestrooms, suites, self-catering units and supplementary apartments using the hotel services.

1) Adapted from F. R. Lawson, Hotels and Resorts : planning, design and refurbishment.

2) Grading

Since 1962 the World Tourism Organization (WTO) - previously the International Union of Official Tourism Organizations (IUOTO) - has sought to develop a universally accepted hotel rating system. Similar proposals have been considered by the International Hotel Association (IHA). The Confederation of National Hotel and Restaurant Associations (HOTREC) of the European Union has devised an alternative system using symbols to represent the facilities without classification.

There are over 100 classification systems in operation, the majority based in the WTO model but customized to suit local conditions.

Systems fall broadly into two groups:

1. *Official classifications* Standards set by governmental agencies - usually the Ministry of Tourism or Regional Tourist Board - either as a compulsory requirement for registration or licensing or as a voluntary scheme.
2. *Independent ratings* Hotels inspected and assessed by associations (such as hotel or automobile associations) or commercial bodies (Mobil and Michelin Travel Guides).

(1) Benefits and limitations

Grading of accommodation offers a number of advantages: the published ratings provide channels for direct promotion, give guidance on the facilities, and reassurance that standards will meet expectations. Grading also sets standards and incentives for improvement of quality and contributes towards an image of reliability for a destination.

Difficulties can arise in introducing or changing a system where there is a large stock of existing hotels. Some schemes allow modified or compensatory standards for existing premises and others exclude traditional forms of guest-houses (such as the Ryokans in Japan).

Other considerations include:

1. *Local infrastructure* - fundamental requirements such as pure water supply, sanitation, ceramic tiles, which are generally assumed, may need to be specified in developing countries.
2. *Overall quality* - some properties, while lacking certain amenities may have outstanding features (history, location, character). Some schemes are based on points awarded.
3. *Factual basis* - all schemes consider tangible factors (space, facilities, amenities, services provided). Qualitative aspects (performance, personal service) which involve subjective judgements tend to be more variable. Some schemes (Korea) provide for two types of awards, others have a combined points system (China).
4. *Location and market needs* - user requirements for resort hotels differ from those in a city. Separate standards may apply (Austria).
5. *Maintenance* - hotel quality depends on standards of cleanliness, upkeep and maintenance which can impair comfort and safety but may be difficult to monitor.

(2) Model Schemes

Table 2.1 indicates minimum standards based on the classification proposed by the World Tourism Organization and is broadly comparable to minimum standards adopted in most countries.

Table 2.1 WTO minimum hotel standards

	1 star	2 star	3 star	4 star	5 star
Physical requirements					
Size	Minimum of 10 letting bedrooms				
Entrance	The hotel must have its own independent entrance		Hotel restaurants must have their own external as well as internal entrances. Separate service entrance		
Staircases	To comply with legal requirements →		Separate service staircase		
Construction	Architecture, design, furniture and decoration should reflect the local style with the degree of sophistication increasing with category →				
Furniture, fittings and equipment	Moderate cost construction, simple, durable equipment and furniture of standard design		Medium cost construction materials and fittings. Custom made furniture	High cost construction and fittings. Custom made equipment and furniture	Top cost construction, fittings, equipment and furniture. Individualized decor
Emergency power supply	Emergency light sources		Stand by generator to supply basic lighting and power up to 24 hrs	Stand by generator to supply energy for lighting, lifts, water treatment, cooking and refrigeration, and heating	
Heating and cooling	Heating of fan cooling when necessary	+ central heating and comfort cooling seasonally available	+ individual heat control in bedrooms. Temperature maintained between 18 and 25°C	+ individual air conditioning control in all rooms. High quality equipment with very low noise emission	
Lift(s) available to match room capacity	Where more than three upper floors	Where more than two upper floors		When more than one upper floor	
Service lift				Separate from main guest lift	
In room	Call bell	Internal only	Telephone connected	Direct dial telephone to	Direct dial telephones

communication		telephone. Telephone available on request	through hotel switchboard	other rooms and for national calls	for national and international calls. Telephone in bathroom
	One externally connected telephone per floor				
Public telephones	Telephone available through reception	Telephone booth in the lobby		Soundproof booth in lobby with national and international connections	
		Telephone available near all public rooms			

Bedrooms					
Size	Adequate for free movement, comfort and safety. Minimum area in square meters (excluding bathroom and lobby):				
Single	8	8	10	12	13
Double	10	10	12	14	16
Triple	12	12	14	16	19
Suites				Some suites available or connecting rooms to make temporary suites	Independent suites of various types and connecting rooms
Single bed minimum size	1900 mm × 800 mm			2000 mm × 800 mm	
Linen/towels	Bed linen changed with each new occupant. Bed linen changed twice a week.		Towels changed with each new occupant and daily → Bed linen changed daily		
Room cleaning	Daily →			Additional room cleaning on request up to 12.00 pm	24 hours additional room cleaning
Storage	Closet or wardrobe with hangers plus shelves or chest of drawers. Increasing in sophistication →				
Seating	Minimum of one chair per person		Minimum of one armchair per person		

Tables	One bedside table per guest →				
		Table in room	Writing/ dressing table	Writing/ dressing table with drawers	
Lighting	Natural light through windows during the day. Artificial light at night adequate for reading. Ceiling light with switches at entrance and bedside. One bedside lamp per person →				
			Reading lamp at armchair/ writing table		
Floor covering	Suitably tiled or covered floors with bedside rugs or carpets where appropriate			Wall to wall carpets or high quality flooring and floor coverings	
In-room entertainment			Radio/central music system controlled by the guest		
			TV available	color TV	color TV with channel
Other room facilities	Window coverings to provide privacy and exclude light →			High quality furnishing	
	Wastebasket. Ashtray (if not non-smoking room). At least one water glass per person.				
	Written information on hotel services and procedures provided in one other languages.		Written information on hotel services and procedures provided in two other languages.		
	Do-not-disturb sign	Fire safety instructions Luggage rack	Local regulations may require display of tariff →		
		Mirror other than in the bathroom or at the sink			Plus full length mirror
			Stationery		
				Mini fridge/mini bar	
Soundproofing	Tolerate for day and night stay		Good to tolerate	High standard soundproofing	
Door	Lockable with individual keys or other means. Easily identifiable from outside. Internal security fastening →				
Bathrooms					
Availability	Sink with a mirror, light,	+ at least 25% of rooms with private	All rooms have private bathrooms		Spacious bathrooms Separate toilet

	shelf, towels, soap and electric socket marked with voltage	bathrooms			
Size	Adequate for free, comfortable and safe movement →				
Standard facilities	Natural or induced ventilation providing at least 3 air changes/hr →				
	Hot and cold running water. color coded. Thermostatically controlled →				Chilled drinking water
	Sink with a mirror, light, shelf, towels, soap and electric socket marked with voltage →				
	Water closet with toilet paper. wastebasket →				
	Shower cabinet or bath with showerhead and curtain or screen			Bath with showerhead minimum 1600 mm long	Bath with showerhead minimum 1600 mm long. Separate shower cubicle
	Minimum of one hand and one bath towel per guest→				
			Bath mats		
			Shampoo provided		Shampoo and other toiletries provided
				Cabinet for personal effects	
					Hairdryer, telephone
Shared bathrooms (minimum)	One bathroom per five bedrooms sharing Two on each floor (one for each sex) Equipped with shower cubicle or bath tub, sink, mirror, toilet (unless separate) and standard facilities				
Shared water closets (minimum)	One toilet per five bedrooms sharing Two on each floor (one for each sex) with a sink and standard facilities				

Public areas					
Public toilets	Separate for each sex. Normally each should have a minimum of two water closets with toilet paper, sinks with hot and cold running water, mirror, soap, towels or hand drier and wastebasket. Separate cubicle for the disabled equipped with appropriate fittings. Suitably sited near public areas with interiors screened from view. Ventilation with at least 3 air changes/hr				
Corridors	Well lit 24 hours a day by natural and/or artificial light. Adequately ventilated. Free from obstacles or hazards. Suitably signposted with emergency exits clearly indicated				
			Carpets wall to wall carpeting or special floor finishes		
Reception area	Seating and appropriate furniture commensurate to hotel capacity. Well lit.				
			Coffee and/or writing tables. Carpets, wall to wall carpeting or special floor finishes. Plants. Music/PA system.		
Parking	Free access by car. Some reserved parking space		Parking space reserved for average number of car-using guests	Exclusive parking or garage to accommodate all hotel guests and casual visitors. 24 hr security	As four star plus basic care servicing available
Green area				Some garden area or terrace with plants	Green area for guest use such as terrace with plants, roof garden, patio or adjoining gardens
Food and beverage, leisure and recreation facilities					
Lounge	Area with lounge seating, music and/or television services.	Lounge area or sitting room with music and television services,	Lounge area or sitting room as before seating at least	Choice of lounge(s) or sitting room(s) as before, plus service of drinks and	Choices of lounge(s) or sitting room(s) as before with 24 hour

	May also be used for breakfast and reception of guests	newspapers and/or magazines	one-third of hotel bed capacity in combination with reception area	refreshments	lounge service
Breakfast	As above or by service to rooms	Provided in hotel or facilities in immediate proximity	Restaurant(s) provided within hotel with adequate seating capacity for breakfast and other meals		
			Breakfast served from 7.00 am to 10.00 am		from 7.00 am to 11.00 am
Room service	The option of self-catering facilities may be provided →				
	Breakfast served in rooms where no breakfast area available		Limited room service may be offered	Breakfast service including newspaper. 24 hour beverage and light meal service	24 hour full meal and beverage services
Restaurant		Restaurant or cafeteria where meals are served at lunchtime and evening or in immediate proximity to appropriate independent facilities	Restaurant or coffee shop where meals are served at lunchtime and evening. Seating not less than half of hotel bed capacity	main restaurant or choice of restaurants serving a variety of meals Private dining or function rooms available. Total seating not less than hotel bed capacity	
				High quality food and beverage services	Highest standards of cuisine and services
Bar			Separate bar	Separate bar(s) and cocktail lounge	
Conference facilities				Meeting and conference rooms with appropriate conference facilities	
Cloakroom			Cloakroom and toilets near public rooms		
Entertainment				Music and public address system	

				Night club, dancing area or discotheque available in hotel or near proximity	
Recreation				Sauna or swimming pool or health club or a combination	Sauna, gymnasium/ health club, swimming pool/jetpool
Hairdresser				Hairdresser/beauty studio	
Services					
Reception services	Reception desk manned throughout the day. Night bell		Permanent reception service. 24 hour check-in		
	Guest luggage handling on request			Hall porters/luggage handling and doorman	
			Paging service/public address system		
Medical services	Emergency medical/first aid service →				
				First aid room	
Cashiers services	Safety deposit →				Individual safety deposit boxes
		Credit cards accepted			
			Currency exchange service	24 hour currency exchange service	
Postal services	Service to include mail delivery and dispatch and sale of postage stamps and stationery →				
			Dispatch of telex or telefax	Dispatch and receipt of, telex and telefax	
Tourist and travel services	Taxi on call			Taxi service	taxi and rent-a-car service
				Hotel minibus available if isolated location	Free hotel vehicle if isolated location

Rental services			Sale of newspapers, books, postcards, tobacco and photographic supplies		
				Sale of cosmetics and souvenirs	Sale of cosmetics, souvenirs and flowers
Language services	Adequate knowledge by reception staff of one key international language		Working knowledge of two key international languages by customer staff	Good knowledge of two key international languages by customer contact staff	Good knowledge of two key international languages by management positions and very good knowledge of three such languages by customer contact staff
Conditions	Buildings, grounds, equipment, fittings and furniture maintained in clean, safe and sound condition, in good working order and free from detects which could impair use →				
	Public and guest cleaned at least daily, maintained in good decorative order and provided with clean furnishings in good sound condition. Attention given to defects with minimum of delay			Exceptionally clean and in excellent decorative order and condition. Rapid response to any matter requiring attention	
	Full compliance with legal and licensing standards in respect of fire, means of escape and other safety precautions, hygiene, conditions for places of work and habitation, hotel insurance and other stipulated requirements →				

Notes → General requirements which apply to all hotels
Column requirements apply to hotels of the grade indicated and above

3) Hotel Categories

(1) Identification

Hotels may be described by their locations, standards of quality, operation as a chain or independently and extent of specialization (Table 2.2).

Table 2.2 Hotel identification

Identified by	Examples	Characteristics: emphasis
Location	City center, provincial town Resort, country house Airport, motel	Business travel, urban visitors Vacation and conference users Transient and staging needs
Quality	Official or voluntary grading systems denoted by 1 to 5 stars, crowns, diamonds, etc.	Standards of space, facilities and services appropriate for hotels of that grade
	Company tiering or sub-branding of products to serve differentiated markets.	Budget, mid-markets and luxury hotels distinguished by brand names, specific design features and range of services offered
Operation	Large hotel companies operating as a chain or group of company-owned, managed or franchised properties	Similar standards of quality, facilities and services. Branding is usually adopted to provide a recognizable and consistent product at a common national tariff
	Individual hotels which may be fully independent or associated with a marketing consortium	Emphasis is often placed on the distinctive character of the hotel and personal service
Specialization	Hotels offering particular facilities and services, e.g.:	
	Resort hotels	Orientated around resort and leisure attractions
	Convention hotels	Including extensive facilities for meetings and conventions
	Spa hotels	Providing medical, paramedical, fitness and convalescence services
	Casino hotels	With gaming rooms, spectacular entertainment and public facilities

(2) Sizes

The stock of hotel accommodation in most developed countries is characterized by a high proportion of small family-run hotels, inns and guest houses. New hotels are generally in the mid- to large size range to justify commercial investment and group operation. The optimum for efficient staffing is usually around 200 rooms (120 rooms for budget/mid-tariff hotels) while larger units can provide savings in property operation and advantages in marketing. In prime locations (city centers, resort prominence) the high cost of site acquisition will usually dictate the minimum size and grade to achieve a viable cost/room ratio (Table 2.3).

Table 2.3 Characteristics of various sizes of hotel

Size range	Characteristics
Fewer than 25 rooms	Typical guesthouses, farmhouse and cottage conversions, small private hotels and traditional inns and lodges. Usually family run and individually owned. This form of small-scale dispersed tourism development is actively encouraged in many rural tourist areas.
50-80 rooms	Includes the smaller independent hotels and country houses and luxury conversions of stately houses, Paradors (Spain). Hotels of this size are large enough to employ a separate manager and may be operated independently or as part of a company or marketing consortium
80-120 rooms	Most new budget hotels, inns, lodges and motels are in this size range providing standard rooms with an independent restaurant. Depending on location the development may include a small outdoor swimming pool and children's play area
120-200 rooms	New provincial hotels in Europe tend to be in this size range. The number of rooms allows for better utilization of space and facilities - which usually include some business meeting/private function rooms, a separate coffee shop and restaurant and health-fitness center
200-300 rooms	Typical size for resort hotels supporting more extensive dining areas, lounges and recreational facilities. This size is also representative of mid-scale city center hotels and many airport hotels
150-250 rooms	Luxury hotels in resorts and spas. Hotels of this size can retain a personal service while offering a wide range of exclusive facilities (private beach,

	golf-course, speciality restaurants, remedial treatments)
300-500 rooms	High grade hotels in city center, downtown and prime resort locations. Invariably these provide more than one restaurant, a health-fitness club including an indoor pool and extensive business facilities. This size is also necessary to support more extensive convention facilities.
300-800 rooms	Most integrated resorts, holiday centers and club complexes have a large capacity to support extensive recreational and entertainment facilities and marketing costs
800-1000+ rooms	Mega city center hotels where economies of scale can allow spectacular designs and cost savings in construction and operation. This includes the larger convention hotels and casino hotels

2. Competition Analysis

This important section focuses on the competition and its likely impact on the proposed property.

The developer should pay close attention to the total hotel and rooms inventory that currently exists in the market area. It must also be learned if any other properties are scheduled to be built or are likely to be built in the near future.

The competition is analyzed by segments (i.e., those of similar size and class, and those in the same location). The consultant may personally inspect competing properties, review travel rating guides, and interview local hotel managers. The consultant should consider the following factors when analyzing a competing property; location, room rates, market segments, facilities and services, physical condition, chain affiliation, and perception of guests and the surrounding community.

Exhibit 2-1 contains a model competitive summary for a hypothetical city. Note how the quality, service facilities, and price/value rankings are rather subjective. The reader of the feasibility study must examine these factors closely to test the consultant's assumptions in arriving at the rankings.

Future projects by competitors may be more important to the economic health of the proposed hotel than the existing properties in the area. The hardest projects to analyze are those in the early planning stages. Although it may be impossible to determine with any certainty whether a proposed hotel will be completed or not, the consultant should provide the developer with as much information about it as possible.

An often overlooked subject is the subsequent retirement of hotel properties from the market because they are no longer competitive with newer facilities. Also, an analysis should show any properties that may be downgraded in the foreseeable future.

If the developer's proposed hotel includes food and beverage facilities, the report should analyze the supply of and the demand for similar types of eating facilities in the area. This analysis should cover (1) location, especially in relation to competitors that exist or will exist; (2) type of restaurant; (3) menu prices; (4) number of seats; (5) liquor availability; (6) entertainment; (7) perception of guests and the community; and (8) impact of private, social, and fraternal clubs and organizations.

EXHIBIT 2-1 Example of a Competitive Summary

Hotel	Rooms	Year Opened	* Quality Rating	* Service Facility Rating	* Price/ Value Rating	Current Quote Rates		Guest Occupancy	Current Average Daily Rate (ADR)
						Single	Double		
1. Holiday Inn	200	2113	5	7	7	$65	$72	68%	$52
2. Ramada Inn	220	2115	6	6	5	$63	$70	66%	$49
3. Hilton Inn	250	2116	7	8	7	$70	$80	69%	$60
4. Howard Johnson's	250	2117	7	7	9	$60	$69	73%	$58

*Rating 1-Worst 10-Best

4. Demand Analysis

Demand analysis is used to determine whether the area of the proposed hotel will support it. Demand analysis attempts to answer the following questions: (1) Is the present demand greater than the present supply of rooms? (2) Is the present supply of rooms inferior in quality to the needs of the present market? And (3) Can existing supply meet a new market segment? The sections previously discussed are often considered an introduction to this section of the feasibility report.

There is no hard and fast rule about how detailed the demand analysis should be or how many market segments should be reviewed. Generally, the following markets are analyzed by the consultant: (1) single/commercial; (2) group/convention; and (3) tourist/transient.

The developer must examine closely the data used and the consultant's assumptions in interpreting that data. The data used for demand analysis can be obtained from the Department of Commerce, local Chamber of Commerce statistics, lodging reports, visitor and convention bureaus, local hotel managers, charge card statistics, and hotel sales tax figures. The developer should ensure that the data used in timely and applicable to the area being studied.

Based on the data, the consultant will determine the compound growth rate. He or she will also determine the estimated average daily room demand and the percent of the total it represents among the various segments. Exhibit 2-2 below is an example of a typical hotel market with estimated average daily room demand and the portions of the total controlled by each segment.

In most markets, the commercial demand represents the largest segment of demand. However, commercial and convention demand will occur

Sunday through Thursday in many markets, limiting the potential-room night demand and the occupancy rate a typical hotel can hope to achieve. Depending on the market, the tourist/transient demand will more likely occur on the weekends and during the week in peak vacation months.

The next step is to analyze the market demand growth in terms of daily supply and demand for all lodging properties within the market being studied. The growth rates determined in Exhibit 2-2 are applied to the supply of rooms for the next three to five years. Exhibit 2-3 shows growth rate in room supply over the next five years for a hypothetical hotel. Notice how the additional planned rooms in the market change the room occupancy percentage over the years.

The market demand is more complicated than just a plot of the anticipated growth rate of each segment. The consultant must consider the impact of other hotels coming into the market as well as the deletion of competing properties. Also, the report must take into account average daily additions and deletions to the supply of rooms when properties in the area close all or a portion of their facilities for major renovations. Exhibit 2-4 above shows additions and deletions that are available to the consultant. A major assumption in this exhibit is that the consultant has incomplete information about all hotel additions and deletions. After all, hotel companies do not share development plans with each other.

EXHIBIT 2-2 Example of Daily Room Demand By Market Segment

Market Segment	2111 Estimated Average Daily Rooms Demand	portion of Total
Single/Commercial	586	53%
Group/Convention	340	31%
Tourist/Transient	185	16%
	1,111	100%

EXHIBIT 2-3 Example of Projected Growth Rates by Market Segment

Market Segment	2111	2112	2113	2114	2115
Single/Commercial	3%	2%	2%	3%	3%
Group/Convention	1	2	2	2	3
Tourist/Transient	2	3	4	4	4

EXHIBIT 2-4 Example of Addition and Deletion of Rooms

Beginning Average Daily Room Supply	2111 1,803	2112 1,603	2113 1,758	2114 2,258
Holiday Inn	(200)			
Stratford Inn		150		
Mariott			250	
Hyatt			250	
End of Year				
Average Room Supply	1,603	1,758	2,258	2,258

The next logical step is to determine the proposed hotel's market penetration. Generally, a new hotel will take occupancy away from older properties. The property usually operates at a higher occupancy rate than the competition and thus captures a greater market share. This anticipated demand is reflected in the projected occupancy rate shown in Exhibit 2-5. Note that for the first year, the projected occupancy rate will be lower than those for surrounding properties. This is usual for properties just coming into the market as they establish themselves.

Once the demand has been reasonably determined, the consultant then will be able to determine the projected average room rate amounts for the various segments. These must be analyzed carefully, because increased room supply could raise the competition and thus reduce the average room rates. However, the consultant should present what he or she determines to be the most likely obtainable room rates under the facts. Exhibit 2-6 shows how the recommended room rates for a property might be presented to a developer.

EXHIBIT 2-5 Example of Projected Annual Occupancy of Proposed 200 Room Hotel

Year	Average Annual Room Occupancy
2111	60%
2112	65
2113	68
2114	72
2115	73

Based on the Above Average Occupancy
The Proposed Hotel's Room
Sales By Segment

Market Segment	Proposed Hotels Portion of Total
Single/Commercial	75%
Group/Convention	5
Tourist/Transient	20
	100%

EXHIBIT 2-6 Example of Average Daily Room Rates by Segment

Segment	Average Daily Rate
Single/Commercial	$48
Group/Convention	$46
Tourist/Transient	$54

Average Daily Rate in Proportion to Segment Sales

Segment	Average Daily Rate	Proposed Hotel's Portion of Total	Weighted Daily Room Rate (1)×(2)
Single/Commercial	$48	75%	$36.00
Group/Convention	$46	5	2.30
Tourist/Transient	$54	20	10.80
		100%	$48.10
		Round To	$48.00

The more logical the consultant's presentation of the data, the easier it will be for the developer to analyze it and the consultant's underlying assumptions. The developer should conclude whether the consultant's assumptions are reasonable. The project's risk is more easily analyzed when the consultant's assumptions are known.

As noted, usually the consultant projects the estimated annual growth rates for the different market segments studied for the next two to five years. Developers should realize that the further the estimates are made into the future, the less accurate they are likely to be. It is very important for the developer to realize that the estimates are based on assumptions that may not materialize in the future.

5. Recommended Facilities

Many times, the consultant is asked to recommend the type of hotel that would best fit the proposed location, given the feasibility study's overall analysis. Although this service is optional, such a recommendation might save a project in which the current concept proves to be inappropriate for the area. The starting point for such a recommendation is to critique the existing design plans for the proposed hotel. Unless it is absolutely necessary to recommend a totally different type of hotel, the feasibility report should recommend modifications to the existing plans based on market needs.

Often, the developer is franchising or building a chain-affiliated entity for which a certain design is required. The consultant should be informed of this so that he or she does not waste time or money redesigning a fixed plan.

Generally, the consultant will recommend an overall design concept to which he feels the planned hotel's market is most receptive. The recommended design should fit into the community, and the hotel's décor should be planned with the hotel's typical guest in mind.

It is very important that the consultant consider the ever changing guest preferences in design and amenities when reviewing a hotel's design. Such design considerations as room size, carpeting, air conditioning, layout and design, heating fixtures, and room supplies are all important when trying to please the increasingly sophisticated traveler.

This section of the report should also discuss guestrooms. The number of guestrooms supplied should closely match the number of rooms demanded. The developer should ensure that the projected occupancy levels are reasonable, not based solely on the consultant's most optimistic projections. Also, the mix of single- and multiple-occupancy rooms should match projected demand. Finally, the consultant should address any special room considerations such as suites, whirlpools, and wet bars.

Often in the past, a hotel paid less attention to food and beverage operations than to the room operations. However, with increased competition in the industry, hotels are beginning to see food and beverage operations as profit centers. The consultant should review the capacity and size of food and beverage facilities to ensure that the expected hotel demand will support these facilities. It is also important for the consultant to review the demand for the food and beverage facility from nonguests because they can represent a significant market.

6. Estimates of Operation Results

The Estimate of Operation results is the final section of a market study that includes operating projections. This section is based on the results of the demand analysis and presents estimated revenue and expenses and/or cash projections before debt service and return on investment. The consultant will generally use the Uniform System of Accounts for Hotels developed by the American Hotel and Motel Association in presenting the information. Exhibit 2-7 below shows a projected statement of cash flow before management fees, property taxes, debt service, and income taxes. Amortization and depreciation expense are not included because they are non-cash items.

The developer usually takes these numbers and applies to them the cost of building, financing costs, real estate taxes, management fees, and income tax to calculate the after-tax return on the project. However, many times the consultant is asked to complete the projected income and loss projections and to supply the relevant rate of return calculations for the developer. Since the information for such calculations is present in other sections of this book, this chapter will focus on the cash flow before the fixed expenses listed above.

The developer should begin with the estimated room occupancy and average room rate developed in the demand analysis section. It is very important for the developer to analyze the average room rate expected in relation to the demand analysis to ensure a reasonable number. This number is very important because all the variable cost factors will be related to the total revenue developed. Exhibit 2-8 shows the projected room revenue developed for the hypothetical hotel shown in Exhibit 2-7 below.

Many times, the consultant will base the data for future years on a projected inflation rate. This must be taken into account by the reader and adjusted if necessary; otherwise operations could appear to be better (or worse) than they actually are. A better method would be to show the forecasted revenue and expenses in current year constant dollar amounts or to show the constant dollar and inflated dollar amounts separately.

EXHIBIT 2-7 Example of Projected Cash Flow Before Management Fees, Property Taxes, Debt Service, and Income Taxes(000's omitted)

Revenues	**2111**	**2112**	**2113**	**2114**	**2115**
Guestrooms	$2,102	$2,277	$2,432	$2,575	$2,664
Telephone	38	45	49	51	53
Other	32	34	36	39	40
Total Revenue	$2,172	$2,356	$2,517	$2,665	$2,757
Department Expenses					
Rooms					
Payroll	$543	$565	$579	$560	$579
Other	239	259	252	267	276
Total Rooms Expense	$782	$824	$831	$827	$855
Telephone	40	46	47	46	46
Total Departmental Expense	$822	$870	$878	$873	$901
Gross Operating Income	$1,350	$1,486	$1,639	$1,792	$1,856

EXHIBIT 2-7 (continued)

Unallocated Operating Expenses	2111	2112	2113	2114	2115
Administrative and General	$174	$188	$176	$187	$165
Marketing	43	47	50	40	41
Advertising	42	47	48	42	42
Franchise Fee	87	94	101	107	110
Energy Costs	141	141	151	160	165
Property Operation and Maintenance	141	142	153	162	169
	$628	$659	$679	$698	$692
Income Before Management Fees, Fixed Charges, and Reserve	$722	$827	$960	$1,094	$1,164
Fixed Charges and reserves:					
Insurance	$9	$9	$10	$11	$11
Reserve for Replacement of Fixed Assets	87	89	76	77	72
	$96	$98	$86	$88	$83
Cash Flow Before Management Fees, Property Taxes, Debt Service, and Income Taxes	$626	$729	$874	$1,006	$1,081

EXHIBIT 2-8 Example of Projected Room revenue by Segment For Proposed 200 Room Hotel

Year	(1) Average Annual Room Occupancy	(2) Number of Rooms	(3) Average Daily Rate*	Room Revenue (1)×(2)×(3)×365 days
2111	60%	200	$48	$2,102,400
2112	65	200	48	2,277,600
2113	68	200	49	2,432,360
2114	72	200	49	2,575,440
2115	73	200	50	2,664,500

The food and beverage department is another revenue generator. The consultant determines the gross revenue from this department from the demand analysis. To do this, the consultant calculates the anticipated number of hotel guests who will be served breakfast, lunch, and dinner segments. In addition, the consultant estimates the number of non-guests who will choose to eat in the establishment. The hotel then calculates the total covers by meal period for each year. Total food revenue is then calculated by taking the total number of covers by meal period for each year. Total food revenue is then calculated by taking the total number of covers for the various meal segments and multiplying them by the average check for each meal. (See Exhibit 2-9 below for an example of projected food revenue.)

Other income sources include meeting room income, telephone calls, rental income, and vending machines income. These are based on the occupancy of the hotel and are stated as a percent of total room revenue.

It is just as important for the developer to analyze operating expenses as well. The consultant should state in the report the assumptions used in deriving the carious operating expenses of the project. Frequently, these expenses are obtained from industry statistics in studies conducted by Laventhol & Horwath or Pannell, Kerr, Foster for similar properties. The consultant then adjusts these statistics for local market conditions. These adjustments should be stated in the report. For example, marketing expenses should also have been computed on the basis of a fixed and a variable cost relationship. Also, the consultant should include a breakdown as to what marketing activities generated the expenses incurred.

The biggest category of expense for most hotels is "rooms expense." And the largest single component of rooms expense is salaries paid to maintain guestrooms, including housekeeping, bellmen, laundry, and front desk personnel. The consultant should be able to determine the hours worked from the property's anticipated work schedules. Some of the salaries paid in the rooms division vary as room occupancy varies, but a fixed portion is based on the minimum staff required to service guests.

EXHIBIT 2-9 Example of Projected Food Revenue

Outlet	(1) Average Check	(2) Average Daily Cover	Total Yearly Revenue (1)×(2)×(3)×365
Coffee Shop	$6.50	63	$149,468
Restaurant	9.00	79	259,515
Banquets	7.00	67	171,185
Room Service	7.50	27	73,913
		Total Food Revenue	$654,081

Other expenses for the rooms division include linens, uniforms, toiletries, reservations expenses, and complimentary services such as newspapers, continental breakfasts, and laundry supplies. Again, many of these expenses contain a fixed and variable portion, which varies from hotel to hotel. These expenses should decline as the property becomes more efficient.

The two biggest expenses associated with any food and beverage operation are sales and labor. The food and beverage costs are directly related to the amount of food and beverage sold. To obtain reasonable cost figures, the consultant projects sales and, comparing similar food and beverage operations, arrives at a percentage to total sales. Labor costs can be calculated from the work schedules developed for staffing the food and beverage operation.

Other expenses generally included in the food and beverage section include china, silverware, linens, cleaning, supplies, entertainment, licenses, laundry, and uniforms. Again, the consultant analyzes the expenses in light of what similar properties pay for these items.

The single biggest item associated with telephone usage is the cost of local and long-distance calls. Other costs include equipment and payroll. Generally, if a hotel breaks even for telephone service, it is considered to be doing well.

The next major expense category is unallocated operating expenses. Administrative and general expenses make up the largest dollar total for this category. The largest component in this category is the payroll expenses for all administrative personnel not directly connected with a department. This includes the general manager, accounting staff, and other support personnel.

Other expenses in the administrative and general category include commissions on credit cards, auditing and data processing, stationery, dues, publications, donations, postage, bad debts, security, and professional fees. The expenses in the administrative and general expense category tend to remain fixed.

If the company has hired an outside management firm to run the hotel, expense projections should include the fixed portion of the management fee (sometimes known as the basic management fee arrangement) under the undistributed operating expenses.

Because management will establish the annual budget for the marketing department, marketing expenses are usually the most discretionary aspect of the undistributed operating expenses. Since it takes some time before the results of any marketing efforts are realized, these expenditures are usually highest in relation to total sales during the first years. As time goes by, the ratio to total sales should decline. The consultant should be able to derive the marketing expenses for the proposed property from the operational marketing budget.

Franchise fees for franchised properties are usually stated as a percentage of gross room revenue. This is spelled out in the franchise agreement. The advertising assessments that many franchise agreements require may be shown as a separate expense category and is usually assessed on a percentage of gross room revenue also.

Energy costs for a hotel include electricity, heating fuel, water, and sewer service. Energy costs have received a great deal of attention in recent years as fuel costs have increased significantly. These are relatively fixed, although there is some variation in energy used by guests. The consultant must be particularly sensitive to possible changes in energy costs when making assumptions about overall future costs.

The property operation and maintenance expense section includes the salaries of the maintenance engineering staff. Other related expenses include supplies, painting, removal of waste material, landscaping, and electrical, building, furniture, and mechanical repairs. Except for repairs necessary to keep the property running, many maintenance expenses can be deferred for a number of years. Thus, they are variable to the extent to which management places a priority on maintenance. One expects fewer maintenance requirements for a new property than for an older property over the same time. The consultant should anticipate that maintenance expenses will increase as the property ages.

The last category is the fixed charges. Here, the consultant focuses on the facility's property taxes, property insurance, and reserve for replacement. Real property taxes are assessed by the local governing unit and are based on the fair market value of the hotel. The consultant analyzes the local tax rates and applies them to the anticipated fair market value of the property.

The consultant will need to forecast the insurance needs of the property. An insurance agent or broker can be most helpful in analyzing the property to determine adequate insurance requirements.

Because a hotel is used heavily by the public, there is considerable wear and tear on furniture, fixtures, and equipment. These items will have to be replaced regularly and the hotel must set aside a certain percent of annual income for this. A consultant normally designates the replacement reserve as a percentage of anticipated room sales. This is derived from the experience of similar properties in replacing their furniture, fixtures, and equipment.

As with other sections of the feasibility study, the consultant must make assumptions about the proposed operation of the project. Especially important are the expected occupancy and projected room rates. If projections are overly optimistic, the chances for a successful project dim significantly. The developer should examine the consultant's report for probable estimates rather than estimates that will hold up only if everything goes exactly as hoped for.

7. Summary

Financial institutions, developers, and investors all have used the feasibility study to help them determine whether a proposed hotel project has a chance to succeed. The feasibility study is even more important because the deductibility of tax shelter losses are limited for most investors in hotel projects.

The feasibility study should be realistic and major assumptions completely defined. The reader should not have to guess how the consultant arrived at his or her conclusions. There should be a frank discussion of the material factors that go into a successful hotel operation. The material factors include:

- Market area analysis
- Project site and area analysis

- Competition analysis
- Demand analysis
- Recommended facilities
- Estimates of operating results

The market area analysis is the macro view of the area where the proposed property will be located. Area characteristics such as demographic trends and economic development are critical to the future success of any hotel project. Retail sales are one of the best indicators of economic growth in the area.

The consultant relies on many resources for obtaining the most current and complete information possible for the area being studied. The local Chamber of Commerce is the best starting point, but other resources, such as the local library, local government units, and key individuals in the community, should also be consulted.

The project site and area analysis provide the micro view of the proposed hotel project. The consultant should show on a map the exact location of the project and its relationship to the main demand generators and competition. The map should also show the property in relation to main transportation arteries and transportation centers, such as airports.

The consultant analyzes the specific site and considers such factors as traffic flow, ingress/egress, visibility, neighborhood, land and improvements, parking, municipal regulations, and cost of the site. Specific examples should be provided for each factor.

One of the most important factors affecting the profitability of a hotel property is competition from both new existing and proposed properties. Not only should the other properties be reviewed and rated in comparison to the proposed hotel, but area food and beverage operations should also be analyzed for their impact (assuming food and beverage services will be provided at the proposed project).

To justify building a hotel project, there must be growth in the market. If the market is stagnant, the project can only be a justified if there is a reasonable expectation that it can take business away from the other hotels or restaurants in the area. The market is usually divided into three segments for a hotel: single/commercial, group/convention, and tourist/transient.

The consultant will determine the growth rate (if any) for these three segments and then compare them to the market the project is trying to attract. The consultant will also show the share of demand that the property should be able to obtain under the assumptions presented in the study. The developer must completely understand the consultant's assumptions to determine if they are reasonable.

The consultant is often asked to review and offer suggestions on the design of the proposed hotel project. Although many properties are franchised and thus limited in the number of changes that can be made to their design, the consultant can still comment on whether the facility can accomplish the developer's goals. After studying the area's market conditions, the consultant is in an excellent position to recommend how the project's overall design can maximize current market needs. The consultant should ensure that guestrooms are sufficient for the demand expected and that banquet and eating facilities will be adequate to service the anticipated number of guests.

The final section of the feasibility study is the estimate of operating results. The developer must analyze this part of the report carefully and make certain it is consistent with the financial data presented in precious sections of the study. Also, the assumptions used in developing the operating expenses must be examined carefully to ensure their reasonableness. Finally, the developer should remember that the study is based on major assumptions.

Chapter 03

Ownership and Operation

Chapter 03

Ownership and Operation

1. Choice of Business Entity

The form of business entity selected by the hospitality firm will have a major impact on economic as well as tax planning opportunities. The sole proprietorship is the simplest method of doing business and is appropriate for the small hospitality entrepreneur because of its simplicity and that income is taxed directly on individual tax returns. The disadvantages are that it is inadequate if there are any partners or if the owner wishes to take advantage of certain fringe benefits that are only offered to corporations. If the single hospitality owner wishes to expand operations to more than one operation, he or she will want to seriously consider forming separate corporations for each location.

The general partnership can be similar to the sole proprietorship, except when there is more than one owner. A general partnership can be structured very simply, without any written agreement (although this is never recommended). The main advantages of the general partnership are its flexibility in allocating income, losses, contributions, and deductions among the various partners. The partnership agreement can be structured so that the responsibility of the various partners is clearly spelled out to avoid confusion and disagreements. The big disadvantage of the general partnership is that individual partners have the authority to bind the other partners when acting on behalf of the partnership with firms that do business with the partnership.

The limited partnership derives its name from the fact that investors are not liable for debts of the partnership beyond their contributions if they agree not to be involved in the management of the hospitality business. This form of business entity has been one of the most popular methods of financing hospitality projects. The flexibility in how income and losses can be allocated to the individual partners is why this form of doing business is preferable to the corporate form of business, which also offers its shareholders limited liability.

The corporate business entity form is a separate legal entity. This makes the corporate entity separate from its owners (the shareholders). The corporate entity thus limits each shareholder's liability to the amount of equity invested. However, this is often more illusion than reality, especially since banks are likely to insist upon personal guarantees for any loans made to a start-up operation. Larger hospitality firms may be able to borrow money in the corporation's name, and thus the corporate form of business is more reasonable for this size of operation. Also, if the hospitality owner has more than one location, a separate corporation for each location may be a planning consideration until sufficient size is achieved to consolidate all the corporations into one company. The major disadvantage of the corporate form of doing business is that the corporation is treated as a separate business entity for tax purposes also. The corporation is taxed on the earnings, and then the shareholders are taxed on dividends distributed from the corporation. However, many closely held hospitality corporations can avoid the double taxation problem by paying out all earnings during the year as salary. The hospitality owners should be aware that any unreasonable compensation as defined by the regulations could result in excess salary being treated as a dividend.

The choice of business entity is a very important consideration for the hospitality owner. Careful planning maximizes both tax and legal aspects of operating a hospitality business in today's economy.

Table 3.1 Basic Factors in Selecting a Business Entity

	Sole Proprietor	Partnership	Limited Partnership	S Corporation	Corporate
Which tax rates apply	Individual	Individual	Individual	Individual	Corporate
Paperwork required	NO organizational	Partnership	Partnership	Incorporational papers;	Incorporationa l papers;
	documents; NO separate tax return	agreement desirable; separate tax return required	agreement required; separate tax return required	separate tax return	separate tax return
Allocation of income among owners	N/A	Possible	Possible	Must be in proportion to ownership share	Must be in proportion to ownership share
Character of losses in disposition of business	Ordinary or capital	Ordinary or capital	Ordinary or capital	Usually capital	Usually capital
Who may claim losses	Owner	Owners	Owners	Owners	Corporation
Character of gain at sale	Depends on assets sold	Depends on assets sold	Depends on assets sold	Usually Capital	Usually Capital

2. Ownership Structure

Whilst most family-run hotels are owned and operated on an individual basis many company hotels have an increasingly complex ownership structure (Table 3.2).

Separating hotel property ownership from the trading business enables a hotel company to expand at a faster rate and run more hotels than it could finance from its own resources. The acquisition of existing hotels may be funded in part by the purchase and simultaneous sale and lease-back of property or site. The method of releasing capital assets (property, land) is also used to reduce company borrowings and is particularly important in times of low growth in property values.

Table 3.2 Types of hotel ownership

Hotel ownership/ operating structures	Examples
Land owner - ground lessor	Development of leasehold sites Sale and leaseback of freehold Joint venture schemes with landowner
Hotel developer - sub-lessor	Development of property and sale to an institution, investment group or unit owner
Hotel lessee	Leasing of property by hotel company of hotel investment group
Franchisee	Investment in franchised hotel property by an individual or company. Master franchise rights may be obtained for a country or region
Hotel management-operator	Operation by hotel management company under contract agreement

1) Independent Hotels

Although family-owned and individual hotels run on and independent basis comprise the majority of units there is a continuing move towards company-affiliated hotels or conversion to self-catering. Small independent hotels are often under-capitalised, limited in scope for expansion and have difficulty in financing marketing and facility improvements.

However, the benefit from tourism incomes is often a valuable direct contribution to the local economy and governmental authorities are increasingly seeking ways of assisting this type of provision. Current approaches include:

- resort and regional promotion, collective advertising and syndication of purchasing
- development of national and regional reservation networks for touris information and reservation systems
- direct aid in grants and subsidized or guaranteed loans for imrovements in standards.

2) Company Hotels

Company - affiliated hotels include those:

- owned or leased and operated by a hotel company
- managed by a hotel company on a management contract with remuneration to the operator linked to revenue or profit
- operated by the owner but forming part of a marketing and reservation consortium
- operated by the owner or investor under a franchise agreement with a major hotel chain.

Company hotels, in general, have less difficulty in financing refurbishment and expansion and the professional standards of management enable performance to be monitored and operated with higher efficiency. Large international chains can develop central reservation systems either alone or linked with other international networks.

To identify with specific market segments and optimize the range of facilities and investment, hotel groups increasingly differentiate their properties into a number of tiered brands with specific characteristics and pricing levels (Table 3.3).

Table 3.3 Hotel description by market tier

Market tiers	Examples of descriptions
Luxury	Grand, Regency
Mid-tariff	Garden Court, Courtyard
Budget	Inn, Lodge
Resort	Resort, Club, Village

3. Standardization

The degree of standardization depends on company policy and the extent of brand conformity required. Some groups lay down precise specifications to achieve a uniform quality for their products; others adopt very broad guidelines to allow individual architectural and interior design diversity.

Most hotel chains have to detail requirements for their technical systems and operating equipment (front office and back-of-house) in order to achieve quality control, operating efficiency and compatibility throughout the chain.

As a broad division the degree of control over design depends largely on the need for cost control over construction and subsequent operation (Table 3.4).

Table 3.4 Degree of standardization

Types of hotels	Standardization
Luxury and high class hotels with emphasis on quality and sophistication	Individual designs within requirements laid down for space, range of facilities and quality control
Mid-scale hotels with branded identity for reliability of products	Detailed design brief with standard requirements for guest rooms and precise guidelines for planning of public and back of house areas. Operating equipment usually specified
The budget hotels with cost-efficient accommodation	Highly standardized design and repetitive construction techniques, often using prefabrication and systems building. Rationalized requirements for public facilities with detailed specifications including equipment suppliers

4. Company Strategies

In pursuing strategies leading to the sale or acquisition of other hotels, companies are influenced by several factors (Table 3.5).

In most disposals, sales have excluded particular areas of the company's operation such as profitable casinos and specialized hotel subgroups. Sales included company owned, franchised and managed hotels in the group.

In part, these projects reflect market positioning and expansion plans but also the development time delay in response to changing conditions.

Table 3.5 Factors influencing sale and acquisition of hotels

Strategy	Company objectives
Purchase	
Operation	Synergy of identity and advantages of enlarged group. Acquisition of balanced portfolio in one transaction with immediate prospects of increased cash flows, market representation, extension of reservation and referral systems and flexibility of staff movement
Overseas expansion	Entree into overseas markets following near saturation of home demand
Competitive costs	Costs per room advantage compared with new development
Sale	
Reduction of gearing	Lowering of borrowings at time of high interest on debt
Realization of high property values	Sale in anticipation of falling rates of return on property investment
Sectorization	Market repositioning and concentration on particular sectors of hotel and resort operation

The increasing value of prime city center locations has also led to higher investment in upgrading and refurbishment.

Chapter 04

Investment

Chapter 04

Investment

1. Commercial Feasibility

Hotel development involves a high investment intensity with a long-term commitment of the bulk of the capital in fixed assets. Revenues are invariably dictated by external conditions and profit margins affected by operating expenses (Table 4.1).

Table 4.1 Consideration involved in hotel investment

Hotel investment	Consideration
Costs	
High capital costs	Usually 2 to 4 times annual revenues[1]. Sensitive to opportunity costs of capital. High fixed costs limit operational flexibility
Fixed use	Trading orientated rather than property investment. Location and efficient design critical. Cannot be easily converted to other uses
High operating costs	Expends some 65-75% of revenues[1]. Difficult to reduce without affecting standards and prices
Revenues	
Price sensitivity	Prices set by competition and comparison. Tourism and budget markets tend to be discretionary and cost sensitive
Demand variation	Usage is affected by short term and cyclical fluctuations[2], economic and political influences[3] and changes in locality
Perishability of products	Revenues are highly dependent on maintaining occupancy levels. Involves costs in marketing and reservation systems as well as rack rate discounting

Notes: [1] Depending on sales mix.

[2] Particularly seasonal and weekday/weekend variations.
[3] Particularly risks to personal security.

2. Influences on Investment

Investment in hotels tends to follow cyclical changes in economic growth. Conditions influencing the direction and timing of capital expenditure include those listed in Table 4.2.

The conditions usually apply generally over the region or country rather than to individual projects. Thus hotel development tends to occur in cycles when investment is favored and this may lead to overbuilding with the resultant competition lowering occupancies and profitability.

Table 4.2 Conditions influencing capital expenditure

Changes	Conditions
Economic	Low rates of interest charges on loans and the availability of capital for investment
Business	Progressive increase in hotel prices and property values compared with other sectors (price and cost indices)
Demand	Expansion of demand arising from growth in tourism or/and investment in the attractions of the area
Incentives	Government-regulated incentives for new investments and conversion/ refurbishment schemes (see section 1.4.3)

3. Development Incentives

The overall climate for investment in a country, region or locality may be improved by government encouragement and assistance:

- *Government cooperation* includes measures such as enacting legislation which is conductive to investment and direct information for prospective investors, guarantees and fiscal concessions.
- *Planning and infrastructure provisions* through Development Plans and government-financed infrastructure services (utility services, roads, airports, etc.).
- *Reducing investment requirements* by provision of land at less than market value (often in return for equity participation), by awarding grants to offset specific project costs, through loans on favorable terms and duty concessions.
- *Fiscal and operational requirements* to improve the profitability of specific projects costs, through loans on favorable terms and duty concessions.

Development incentives are generally targeted at deprived areas such as neglected inner city districts, or redundant industrial wasteland.

In order to stimulate tourism, grants and other incentives are also provided on a selective regional basis, assisting those areas with relatively high unemployment and limited resources for alternative development.

Specific incentives may be available more generally in certain countries to encourage the provision and improvement of tourist accommodation, mainly to increase foreign tourism and currency exchange earnings. And also to extend opportunities for domestic and social tourism.

4. Risk limitation

A hotel investment may be separated into the land, building shell, interior assets and operating systems. The land and building shell may be:

- separately owned as a part of a mixed development of shops, offices etc., and leased to a hotel company

- sold to a property company or financial institution under a leaseback arrangement
- assessed on a rental basis as a part of company policy to provide financial control over its property assets
- operated through a management contract arrangement by a separate hotel company.

Various other financing arrangements may also be adopted to reduce initial investment outlays, defer capital repayments or raise additional cash:

- Rental or hire purchase of equipment and furnishing
- Loan negotiation and restructuring, including repayment of interim and short-term finance
- Increase in company equity through stock market flotation or cash calls on investors

5. Benefits of Development

- *The market value* of a hotel building which is well located and managed tends to appreciate compared with the book value represented by the original cost less depreciation. Revaluation of assets may be used to increase the level of borrowings and depreciation allowances.
- *Hotel tariffs* can respond rapidly to inflationary trends compared with properties which have long intervals between rent reviews.
- *Preference to hotel developments* (by earmarking sites or offering planning concessions) is often used as a means of stimulating and supporting other commercial investment in urban redevelopment schemes. Hotel use is also compatible with the restoration or

conservation of many redundant buildings.

- *Taxation benefits* in the form of capital and depreciation allowances also have a significant impact. These vary both in place (district region country) and time (government policies, specific concessions). Fixed assets may be depreciated over agreed periods using the straight line or diminishing balance methods. In exceptional circumstances (to encourage investment) accelerated depreciation may allow all or a large part of the plant to be written off for tax purposes in the initial years.

6. Sources of Finance

Methods of financing projects and sources of funding depend on the location and scale of development. For a large project capital finance is often in two or more phases:

- Interim finance: high risk or venture capital to cover the costs of investigation, site development and building works, hotel fitting out and pre-opening costs through company equity together with short-term loans. Interim costs may also be net by bank overdraft facilities and mezzanine financing of projects in anticipation of sale.
- Long-term development finance: repaid over a period of amortization secured by the collateral of land and/or property.

Sources of capital funding can be considered under three main categories: equity, loans and public funding.

1) Equity

Equity usually covers the initial funding and a significant part of the capital requirement. This may be provided out of retained profits, issue of share capital or sale and roll-over of finance from other assets. Typically, the equity amounts to 30-40% but this will depend on the level of other borrowings (gearing or leverage) and economic conditions.

Equity finance may be provided by:

- *Hotel companies* either directly or as part of a larger conglomerate.
- *Development or investment companies* in association with hotel groups or independently (prior to management contract).
- *Franchisees* (entrepreneurs or companies) investing in development as part of a licence or contract agreement with a hotel group. Financing of development of specific projects may also be assisted by simultaneous:
- *Sale and leaseback* of land or property to release capital asset values.
- *Forward sale* of property for development to investment groups (which may include hotel companies).

2) Loans

Loans from commercial banks, etc., are charged at a percentage above the base lending rate depending on the borrower and security provided. It is often necessary to organize a package of loans to cover the capital requirements and the terms and conditions may allow for initial suspension of interest or a moratorium on repayments:

- *Merchant Banks:* venture capital and funding packages. Higher interest rates charged for unsecured loans and the bank may seek a share of the equity.
- *Clearing banks:* similar short-term loans (up to 3 years). Usually require additional security.
- *Institutions:* (Insurance companies, Pension Fund Management, etc.): long-term loans secured by appreciating asset value of property or land.

- *Mortgages:* long-term loans (10-25 years) with repayments of debt at intervals and agreed scheduling of interest. The first mortgage is usually limited to percentage (e.g., 70%) of the agreed value of the project.

High gearing (leverage) of loan to equity is most advantageous at times of an upturn in property values. However, the higher fixed costs also make profitability highly sensitive to change both in performance and interest rates.

3) Public Funding

Public funding is generally limited to specified projects or areas and in time and amount. The contribution may be in loans or direct grants (generally, no more than 20-30%) and must be agreed prior to commencement. The range of public funding agencies is wide and changes with economic and political circumstances as represented by the following examples:

International agencies

- International Bank for Reconstruction and Development (IBRD) and its affiliates
- United Nations Development Fund (UNDF) - often working in association with the World Trade Organization (WTO)
- Organization for Economic Cooperation and Development (OECD) mutual aid programs
- European Union (EU) and other regional and national organizations as well as bilateral aid agreements between countries.

Regional agencies

- European Regional Development Fund (ERDF) and other EU coordinated programs
- European Development Bank

National funding

- Specific funding for infrastructure (roads, airports, technical services)
- Urban Development Grants, Derelict Land Grants
- Selective grants for small businesses, rural industries
- Building of historic or Architectural Interest
- Development Grants for Assisted Regions
- Grants and loans for specific projects approved by the Tourist Boards.

7. Valuations

Valuation of hotel properties is normally on a value per room basis broadly assessed from:

- earnings achievable: commercial return on capital invested
- comparative per room values for similar properties (sales indices)
- estimates of new building costs less depreciation (cost indices).

A standard approach is to use discounted cashflow methods to calculate expected receipts, payments and operating performance of a hotel together with expected capital expenditure over a period of time and any residual value.

Property surveys take into account the individual details in Table 4.3.

Table 4.3 Property survey considerations

Details	Considerations
Location	Benefits (prestige, convenience, prominence), surrounding, progressive changes in area (positive or detrimental)
Facilities	Numbers of rooms and extent of other facilities, recent expenditure incurred and assessment of improvements/refurbishments required
Markets	Analyses of trading patterns, operating revenues and costs, market trends and potential for changes
Investment	Capital requirements balanced against current borrowing costs. trends in property asset values (effect of adverse conditions)
Tenure	*Freehold* - asset value for gearing purposes *Leasehold* - more problematic: length of unexpired lease, current rental value, frequency of rent reviews, rental charges relative to the open value or property *Managed* - value highly dependent on operator's expertise and reputation

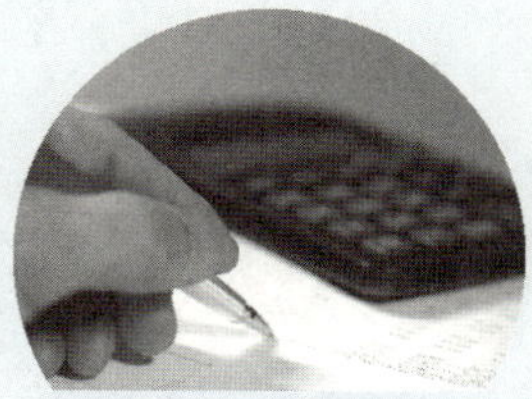

Chapter 05

Corporation and Management

Chapter 05 Corporation and Management

1. Corporation

In its simplest form, the corporation comprises three sets of distinct interests: the shareholders (the owners), the directors, and the corporation officers (the top management). Traditionally, the shareholders control the corporation's direction, policies, and activities. The shareholders elect board of directors, who in turn select top management. The top management serves as corporate officers and manages the operation of the corporation in the best interests of the shareholders.

The separation of ownership from management gives the corporation several advantages over proprietorships and partnerships:

A. Because ownership in a corporation is represented by shares of stock, ownership can be readily transferred to new owners.
B. The corporation has unlimited life. Because the corporation is separate from its owners, the death or withdrawal of an owner does not affect its existence.
C. The shareholders' liability is limited to the amount invested in the ownership shares.

Limited liability, easy of ownership transfer and perpetual succession are the major advantages of the corporation form of business organization. These give the corporation an enhanced ability to raise cash.

2. Managers and Shareholders

1) Managers

Managerial goals are different from those of shareholders. How will managers maximize if they are left to pursue their own goals rather than shareholders' goals?

Donalson (1984) conducted a series of interviews with the chief executives of several large companies. He concluded that managers are influenced by three underlying motivations in defining the corporate mission:

A. Survival. Organizational survival means that management must always command sufficient resources to support the firm's activities.

B. Independence. This is the freedom to make decisions and take action without encountering external parties or depending on outside financial markets

C. Self-Sufficiency. Managers do not want to depend on external parties.

When a conflict of interest exists between management and shareholders, who wins? Does management or do the shareholders control the firm? Several control devices are used by.

A. Shareholders determine the membership of the board of directors by voting. Thus, shareholders control the directors, who in turn select the management team.
B. Contracts with management and arrangements for compensation, such as stock option plans, can be made so that management has an incentive to pursue the goal of the shareholders. Another device is called performance shares. These are shares of stock given to managers on the basis of performance as measured by earnings per share and similar criteria.
C. If the price of a firm's stock drops too low because of poor management, the firm may be acquired by a group of shareholders, by another firm, or by individuals. This is called a takeover. In a takeover, the top management of the acquired firm may find itself out of job. This puts pressure on the management to make decisions in the stockholders' interests. Fear of a takeover gives managers an incentive to take actions that will maximize stock prices.
D. Competition in the managerial labor market may force managers to perform in the best interest of stockholders. Otherwise they will be replaced. Firms are willing to pay the most will lure good managers. These are likely to be the firms that compensate managers based on the value they create.

2) Common Stockholders

The common stockholders are the owners of a corporation, as such they have certain rights and privileges.

(1) Control of the Firm

The stockholders have the rights to elect the firm's directors, who in turn elect the officers who manage the business. In a small firm, the major stockholder typically assumes the positions of president and chairperson of the board of directors. In a large, publicly owned firm, the managers typically have some stock, but their personal holdings are insufficient to provide voting control. Thus, the management of most publicly owned firms can be removed by the stockholders if they decide a management team is not effective.

Various laws stipulate how stockholders' control is to be exercised. First, corporations must hold an election of directors periodically, usually once a year, with the voting taken at the annual meeting. Frequently, one-third of the directors are elected each year for a three-year term. Each share of stock has one vote; thus, the owner of 1,000 shares has 1,000 votes. Stockholders can appear at the annual meeting and vote in person, but typically they transfer their right to vote to a second party by means of an instrument known as 'proxy'. Management always solicits stockholders' proxies and usually gets them. However, if earnings are poor and stockholders are dissatisfied, an outside group may solicit the proxies in an effort to overthrow management and take control of the business. This is known as a 'proxy fight'.

The question of control has become a central issue in finance in recent years. The frequency of proxy fights has increased, as have attempts by one corporation to take over another by purchasing a majority of the outstanding stock. This is called "takeover"

Managers who do not have majority control (more than 50 percent of their firms' stock) are very much concerned about proxy fights and takeover, and many of them are attempting to get stockholder approval for changes in their corporate charters that would make takeovers more difficult. For example, a number of companies have gotten their stockholders to agree:

(1) to elect only one-third of the directors each year (rather than electing all directors each year)
(2) to require 75 percent of the stockholders (rather than 50 percent) to approve a merger
(3) to vote in a "poison pill" provision which would allow the stockholders of a firm that is taken over by another firm to buy shares in the second firm at a reduced price. The third provision makes the acquisition unattractive and, thus, wards off hostile takeover attempts. Management seeking such changes generally cite a fear that the firm will be picked up at a bargain price, but it often appears that managers' concerns about their own positions might be an even more important consideration

(2) The Preemptive Right

Common stockholders often have the right, called the preemptive right, to purchase any additional shares sold by the firm. The purpose of the preemptive right is twofold. First, it protects the power of control of current stockholders. If it were not for this safeguard, the management of a corporation under criticism from stockholders could prevent stockholders from removing it from office by issuing a large number of additional shares and purchasing these shares by, itself. Management could thereby secure control of the corporation and frustrate the will of the current stockholders. Second, and by far the most important, reason for the preemptive right is that it protects stockholders against a dilution of value. For example, suppose 1,000 shares of common stock, each with a price of $100, were outstanding, making the total market value of the firm $100,000, if an additional 1,000 shares were sold at $50 a share, or for $50,000, this would raise the total market value of the firm to $150,000.

When the total market value is divided by the new total shares outstanding, a value of $75 a share is obtained. The old stockholders thus lose $25 per share, and the new stockholders have an instant profit of $25 per share. Thus, selling common stock at a price below the market value would dilute its price and would transfer wealth from the present stockholders to those who were allowed to purchase the new shares. The preemptive right prevents something like occurrences.

3. The Goal of Financial Manager

- Management's primary challenge is to add value to the Hotel
- Value adding means increasing the overall market value of the Hotel
- Market value is generally assessed by share price valuation, a function of discounted cash flows
- The capital market community has significant influence on how your hotel is valued
- Global market forces are affecting the valuation process

Two dimensions:

1. Maximizing value of the firm
2. Maximization of shareholder's wealth

1. Firm Value maximization

$$V = \frac{CF_1}{(1+r)} + \frac{CF_2}{(1+r)^2} + \ldots + \frac{CF_t}{(1+r)^t} = \sum_{t=1}^{\infty} \frac{CF_t}{(1+r)^t} \qquad \text{[Eq.5-1]}$$

CF = Free cash flows to firm

r = WACC (Weighted Average Cost of Capital)

2. Shareholders value maximization

$$S = \frac{CF_1}{(1+r)} + \frac{CF_2}{(1+r)^2} + \ldots + \frac{CF_t}{(1+r)^t} = \sum_{t=1}^{\infty} \frac{CF_t}{(1+r)^t} \qquad \text{[Eq.5-2]}$$

CF = Free cash flows to equity

r = Ke (Cost of capital for equity)

These values are affected by:

1. Expected future earning (EPS : Earning Per Share)
2. Timing of future earning
3. Riskiness of future earning
4. Use of debt
5. Dividend policy
6. Economic condition
7. Interest rate
8. Legal constrained
9. Tax laws

Profit maximization is not a goal of financial management because it is not consistent with the maximization of stock price.

▶▶▶Check Point

Agency Costs

A firm is nothing more than a set of contracts. One of the contract claims is a residual claim (equity) on the firm's assets and cash flows. The equity contract can be defined as a principal-agent relationship. The members of the management teams are the agents, and the equity investors (shareholders) are the principals. It is assumed that the managers and the shareholders, left alone, will each attempt to act in their self-interest. The shareholders, however, can discourage the managers from diverging from the shareholders' interests by devising appropriate incentives for managers and then monitoring their behavior. Doing so, unfortunately, is complicated and costly. The costs of resolving the conflicts of interest between managers and shareholders are special types of costs called "agency costs". These costs are defined as the sum of monitoring costs of the shareholders and the incentive fee paid to the managers. It can be expected that a contract will be devised that will provide the managers with appropriate incentives to maximize the shareholders' wealth. Thus, agency problem does not mean that the corporate firms will not act in the best interests of shareholders, only that it is costly to make it do so. However, agency problems can never be perfectly solved, and the managers may not always act in the best interests of the shareholders.

▶▶▶Check Point

* What is Investment Decision & Finance Decision?

- The Investment Decision: What types of assets should the firm invest in and how much should be paid for them
- Finance Decision : How funds will be raised to acquire assets

Investment Decision must:

1. Return invested capital
2. Offset anticipated inflation
3. Compensate investors for the risk they're talking

Required return = return of capital + return on capital to offset inflation + return on capital to offset perceived risk

* Perceived risk = likelihood of achieving projected cash flows

* Factors to be considered for successful investment?

-Investment decision and risk
-Assessing risk
-Probability of occurrence
-Risk Premium
-Cost of capital
-The concept of expected return
-The required rate of return
-Security market line
-Capital market pricing model
-Wealth of common shareholders

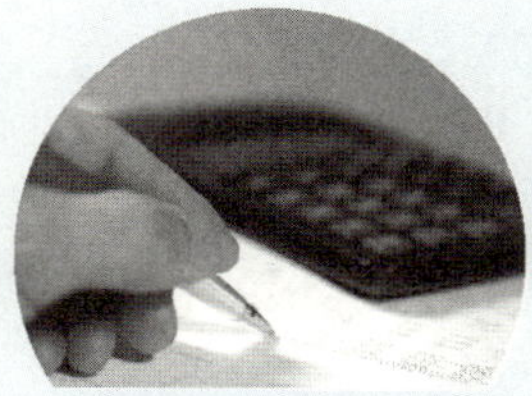

Chapter 06

Cash Flows and Measuring Their Values

Chapter

06 Cash Flows and Measuring Their Values

I. Introduction

1. Cash Flow and Cash Flow Statement

Cash flow is the amount of money generated by a hotel project after payments have been made (1) on all operating expenses (2) for replacement reserves, (3) for debt service (principal plus interest). Cash flow determines which of the various discounted measurements to use that will be discussed later in the chapter.

Cash flow statements differ significantly from income statements. The income statement is an accounting statement that matches income and expenses for a given period regardless of whether the cash is actually paid out at that time or not. Thus, a hotel operation can show large operating losses due to non-cash deductions, such as depreciation, and still generate positive cash flow. In another sense, cash flow can be defined as the difference between the inflows and outflows of cash during the year.

The biggest difference between the income statement and a cash flow statement is usually depreciation. Depreciation is a deductible and noncash expense allowable for income tax purposes. It does not affect cash and must be added back to net income in order to arrive at cash flow. Also, any accrued expenses, such as accounts payable must be added back to net income because they have not yet been paid out. Items that would be subtracted from net income are any accrued income items, such as accounts receivable.

The income statement also must be adjusted for cash items paid that do not appear on the income statement. The most common example is principal repayments of loans and dividends made during the year. (See Exhibit 6-1 below for a simplified income statement and cash flow statement comparison.)

EXHIBIT 6-1 Comparison of Income Statement to a Cash Flow Statement

Income Statement		Cash Flow Statement	
		Sources	
Gross Revenues	$3,168,200		
		Net Profit(Loss)	$(81,722
Less: Hotel Operating Expenses	1,900,900	Depreciation	317,500
Gross Operating Profit	1,267,300	Loan Proceeds	60,000
		Total Sources	295,778
Less: Fixed Charges			
Mortgage Interest	854,100		
Depreciation	317,500	Application	
Management Fee	177,422	Accounts Receivable	$126,000
	1,349,022	Principal Repayment on Mortgage Debt	28,600
		Distributions to Owners	100,000
		Total Application	254,600
Net Profit(Loss)	($81,722)	Net Cash Flow for the Year	$41,178

When the hotel operation's expenses exceed cash inflows, the operation is said to be operating in a "negative cash flow" position. This means that the hotel firm has to draw upon cash reserves, borrow additional funds, or raise more equity from investors in order to stay solvent. A hotel operation can show a profitable net income statement and still operate with a negative cash flow.

2. Cash Flow and Present Value Theory

Present Value Theory

Present value theory is the key for understanding any of the more complex rate of return methods. An investor in a hotel project is concerned not only with how much cash he or she receives from the project but also with the timing of those cash flows. In this light sooner is better and there are several reasons why a dollar received today is more valuable than a dollar received in the future. Inflation is the most obvious reason.

Unfortunately no matter how hopeful we are of receiving payment in the future there is always some risk that the payment will not be made. Obviously, the greater the risk perceived the more likely the investor is to demand a higher return on his or her investment to assume that risk. This is one reason why so many business people are willing to offer cash discounts from the sale of goods and services. The longer before payment is received, the greater is the possibility that the hotel firm will not receive its money.

<Key formula for measuring time value of money:>

$$Discounting: PV = \frac{FV_n}{(1+i)^n} = FV_n = (\frac{1}{i+i})^n = FV_n(PVIF_{i,n})$$

$$Compounding: (FV_n = PV(1+i)^n = PV(FVIF_{i,n})$$

$$Annuity(Future\ Value)$$

$$: FVA_n = PMT\sum_{t=1}^{n}(1+i)^{n-t} = PMT[\frac{(1+i)^n - 1}{i}] = PMT(FVIFA_{i,n})$$

$$Annuity(Present\ Value)$$

$$: PVA_n = PMT\sum_{t=1}^{n}[\frac{1}{1+i}]^t = PMT[\frac{1 - \frac{1}{(1+i)^n}}{i}] = PMT(PVIFA_{i,n})$$

$$FVIF_{i,n} = Future\ Value\ Interest\ Factor\ for\ i\ and\ n$$

$$PVIF_{i,n} = Present\ Value\ Interest\ Factor\ for\ i\ and\ n$$

3. Time Line

One of the most important tools in time value of money analysis is the time line, which is used to help us visualize what is going to happen in a particular situation and then to help us set up the solution for problem. To illustrate the time line concept, consider the following diagram:

Time:	0	1	2	3	4	5
	I	I	I	I	I	I
Cash flows:	-100					

Time 0 is today; Time 1 is one period from today, or the end of period 1; time 2 is two periods from today, or the end of period 2; and so on. Thus the values on top of the tick marks represent end-of-period values. Often the periods are years, but other time intervals such as semiannual periods, quarters, months, or even days are also used. Cash flows are placed directly below the tick marks, and interest rates are shown directly above the time line.

II. Time Value of Money Analysis

Does money have a time value?

Is a dollar in hand today worth more to a manager than a dollar to be received sometime in the future?

We say "yes" because of

1) alternative uses of money on the pure time value of money
2) an allowance or premium for risk on uncertainty
3) an allowance or premium for inflation

We live in an uncertain world, and frequently the more distance the future, the more uncertainty. Also, the world has the probability of continued inflationary tendencies.

1. Future Value

A dollar in your hand today is worth more than a dollar to be received in the future because, if you had it now, you could invest it, earn interest, and end up with more than one dollar in the future. The process of going from today's values, or present values (PV), to future values is called compounding.

⇒ Deriving Formula. Don't forget this!

[Future Value & Present Value]

$$FV_1 = PV_1 + INT(interest)$$
$$= PV_1 + PV(i)$$
$$= PV(1 + i)$$

$$FV_2 = FV_1 + (1 + i)$$
$$= PV(1 + i)(1 + i)$$
$$= PV(1 + i)^2$$

$$\therefore FV_n = PV(1 + i)^n$$

$$PV = \frac{PV_n}{(1+i)^n}$$

$$i = \frac{k}{m}$$

$$\boxed{FV = PV\left(1 + \frac{k}{m}\right)^{mxy}}$$

Note : FV : Future Value
PV : Present Value
i : Periodic rate
k : Annual %, rate(APR)(m×i)
m : Number of compounding per year
y : Number of year
n : Total number of compounding (m×y)

- Compounding: how a PV grows to a FV
- Discounting: how to derive the PV from FV

Understanding by cases

Suppose the expected annual return required making you rollover the $100 for the first year, in view of the expected risk, is 4.0%. If you leave the $100 in the investment and earn 4.0% during the first year, you will have $104.00.

$$FV_1 = CF_1 = CF_0 * (1 + r_1) \text{ ········ [Eq.6-1]}$$

where "r" is required rate of return for every year.

$$FV_1 = CF_1 = \$100 * (1 + 4\%)$$
$$FV_1 = CF_1 = \$104$$

Where FV = Future Value; CF = Cash Flow

FIGURE 6-1

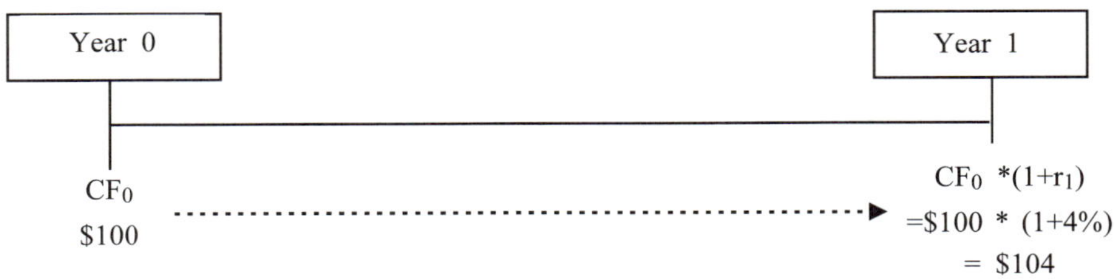

Suppose the expected annual return required making you rollover the $104 for the second year, in view of the expected risk, is 4.5%. If you leave the $104 in the investment and earn 4.5% during the second year, you will have $108.68. Note that the 2-year future value is higher due to the compound rate of return, as well as the fact that in this example. You felt a modestly higher annual return was required for you to remain in the investment for a second year.

Compounding means you are generating a return on the $4 interest earned in the first year from the principal of $100. Specifically, the $4 of interest from the first year generates 18 cents of interest in the second year ($4 * 4.5%).

Expanding Equation 6-1 to incorporate year 2, you can express the future value in year 2(FV_2) of $100 ($CF_0$) today as:

$FV_2 = CF_2 = CF_1 * (1 + r_2) = CF_0 * (1 + r_1) * (1 + r_2)$ ······· [Eq.6-2]
$FV_2 = CF_2 = \$104 * (1 + 4.5\%) = 100 * (1 + 4\%) * (1 + 4.5\%)$
$FV_2 = CF_2 = \$108.68$

Where r_2 is the expected annual return you need to receive to make it worth the risk of you investing for the second year. In Equation 6-2, the \$100 initial investment earn 4% interest in year 1 to generate the future value one year from today of \$104 at the end of year 1 becomes \$108.68 at the end of year 2. Figure 6-2 illustrates graphically the concept of compounding and future value for a 2-year investment.

FIGURE 6-2

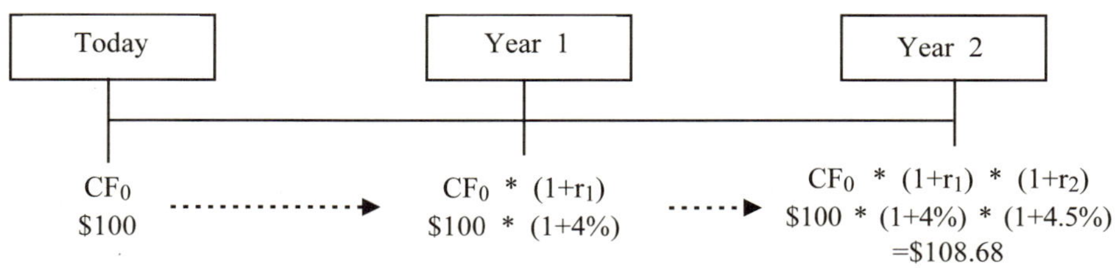

Expanding this example, assume that the required annual expected rate of return necessary to make you rollover the now \$108.68 for a third year is 3.9%. In this case, if you leave the \$108.68 invested for the third year, you will have \$112.92 at the end of the third year. Thus, the future value of \$100 today given this 3-year risk profile is \$112.92 in three years. Expanding Equation 6-2 to incorporate the third year, you can express the future value in three years (FV_3) of \$100 (CF_0) today as:

$FV3 = CF_3 = CF_2*(1 + r_3) = CF_0*(1 + r_1) * (1 + r_2) * (1 + r_3)$ ············ [Eq.6-3]
$FV_3 = CF_3 = \$108.68 * (1 + 3.9\%) = 100 * (1 + 4\%) * (1 + 4.5\%) * (1 + 3.9\%)$

$FV_3 = CF_3 = \$112.92$

Where r_3 is the expected annual return you need to receive to make it worth the risk of investing for the third year. Figure 6-3 graphically represents this third year of investing.

FIGURE 6-3

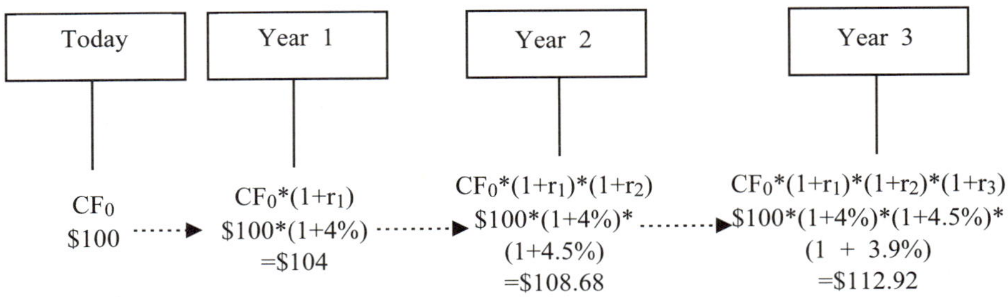

You can extend Equation 6-3 to calculate the future value for any year, where each year, you continue to reinvest at the expected annual return that compensates you for rolling over your investment. Expressed generally, the future value in year T is equal to the previous year's cash flow times the required expected annual rate of return in return in year T.

$$FV_T = CF_T = CF_{T-1}*(1+r_T) = CF_0*(1+r_1)*(1+r_2)*(1+r_3)*\cdots\cdots.*(1+r_T) \quad \cdots\cdots \text{[Eq.6-4]}$$

Assessing each year's specific required expected annual returns and utilizing this equation can become quite cumbersome. As a result, this general equation is usually simplified by assuming that the required expected annual return is the same in every future year. But this simplifying assumption may not be true. When this simplifying assumption is false, you must use the generalized equation 6-4. However, if this is a reasonable simplifying assumption, the future value of cash flow in time period T is expressed as:

$$\text{Future Value (in year T)} = CF_T = CF_0 * (1 + r)*T \quad \text{[Eq.6-5]}$$

Where "r" is, required rate of return for every year. Figure 6-4 illustrates the general formula for future value for a constant rate r.

FIGURE 6-4

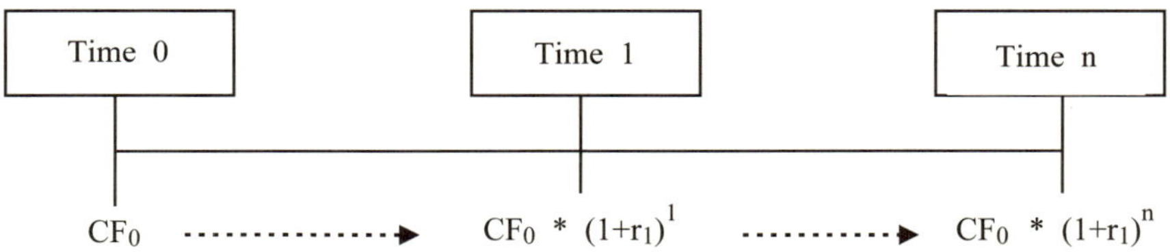

Although we have used years thus far, you can use quarters, months, days, or weeks as your time unit, as long as you are consistent in your application of the equation. For example, if you use months to represent time, you must apply a monthly required return to monthly cash flows.

***Finding FV of a cash stream**

To illustrate, suppose you deposited $100 in a bank account that paid 5% interest each year. How much would you have at the end of one year? In this example, n = 1, so FV can be calculated as follows:

$$\begin{aligned} FV &= PV + \text{interest} \\ &= PV + PV\ (i) \\ &= PV\ (1 + i.) \\ &= \$100\ (1 + 0.05) = \$100\ (1.05) = \$105 \end{aligned}$$

Thus, the future value at the end of one year equals the present value multiplied by 1.0 plus the interest rate, so you will have $105 after one year.

What would you end up with if you left your $100 in the account for five years? Here is a time line set up to show the amount at the end of each year:

	0	1	2	3	4	5
	I	I	I	I	I	I
Initial deposit:	-100	FV1=?	FV2 =?	FV3 =?	FV4 =?	FV5 =?
Interest earned:		5	5.25	5.51	5.79	6.08
Amount at the end of each period:		105	110.25	115.76	121.55	127.63

In general, the future value of an initial sum at the end of nth years can be found by applying following equation:

$$FV_n = PV\ (1 + i)^n$$

Three ways to solve time value of Money Problems

By numerically with a regular calculator

One can use a regular calculator and either (1) multiply (1+i) by itself n times or (2) use the exponential function to raise (1+i) to the nth power. With most calculators, you would enter 1+i = 1.05 and multiply it by itself four times, or else enter 1.05, then press the y* (exponential) function key, and then enter 5. In either case, your answer would be 1.2763, which you would multiply by $100 to get the final answer, $127.6282, which would be rounded to $127.63.

By Using Interest Tables(Appendix C)

The $FVIF_{i,n}$, for 5-year, 5 percent interest problem can be found in interest table by looking down the first column to period 5, and then looking across that row to the 5 percent column, where we see that FVIF(5%,5) = 1.2763. Then, the value of $100 after 5 years is found as follows:

$$FVN = PV\ (FVIF_{i,n}) = \$100\ (1.2763) = \$127.63$$

Financial Calculator Solution

A number of equations have been programmed directly into financial calculators. Note that calculators have five keys which correspond to the five most commonly used time value of money variables:

N **I** **PV** **PMT** **FV**

Here

- N represents the number of periods; some calculators use n rather than N.
- I represents interest rate per period; again, some calculators use i rather than I.
- PV stands for present value.
- PMT stands for payment. This key is used only if the cash flows involve a series of equal, or constant, payments (an annuity).
- FV stands for future value.

On some financial calculators, these keys are actually buttons on the face of the calculator, while on others they are shown on a screen after going into the time value of money (TVM) menu.

In this chapter, we will deal with equations which involve only four of the variables at any one time — three of the variables will be known, and the calculator will then solve for the fourth (unknown) variable. When we deal with bonds, we will use all five variables in the bond valuation equation.

To find the future value of $100 after 5 years at 5 percent interest using a financial calculator, note again that we are dealing with Equation.

$$FV_n = PV(1 + i)^n.$$

The equation has four variables, FV_n, PV, i, and n. If we know any three, we can solve for the fourth. In our example, we can enter PV = 100, I = 5, and N = 5. Then, when we press the FV key, we will get the answer, FV = 127.63 (rounded to two decimal places). [100PV, 5I, 5N, FV]

Many financial calculators require that all cash flows be designated as either inflows or outflows, and then outflows must be entered as negative numbers, In our illustration, you deposit, or put in, the initial amount (which is an outflow to you) and you take out, or receive, the ending amount (which is an inflow to you). If your calculator requires that you follow this sign convention, the PV would be entered as - 100. (If you entered 100, then the FV would appear as - 127.63.) Also, on some calculators you are required to press a "Compute" key before pressing the FV key.

We should also note that financial calculators permit you to specify the number of decimal places that are displayed. Twelve significant digits are actually used in the calculations, but we generally use two places for answers when working with dollars or percentages, and four places when working with decimals. The nature of the problem dictates how many decimal places should be displayed.

Technology has progressed to the point where it is far more efficient to solve most time value of money problems with a financial calculator. However, you must understand the concepts behind the calculations and know how to set up time lines in order to work complex problems. This is true for stock and bond valuation, capital budgeting, lease analysis, and many other important types of problems.

<Key Note> * Compounding periods and periodic rate

$$FV_y = PV\left(1 + \frac{k}{m}\right)^{m \times y} = PV(1 + i)^n$$

k = annual % rate → APR

y = # of years

m = # of compounding periods per year

Ex) daily → 365, monthly → 12

i = periodic rate $(\frac{k}{m})$

$$FV_y = PV(1 + i)^n$$

$$(1 + i)^n = \frac{FV}{PV}$$

$$1 + i = \sqrt[n]{\frac{FV}{PV}}$$

$$i = \sqrt[n]{\frac{FV}{PV}} - 1$$

sime $i = \frac{k}{m}$, $K = mi$

$$k = m \times \left(\sqrt[n]{\frac{FV}{PV}} - 1 \right)$$

Practice Question 6-1

A. What's the annual return if there's an investment which pays \$200 for \$100 invested after 5years?

$$k = m \text{ x } \left(\sqrt[n]{\frac{FV}{PV}} - 1 \right)$$

$$k = 1 \text{ x } \left(\sqrt[5]{\frac{200}{100}} - 1 \right)$$

$$k = \sqrt[5]{2} - 1$$

$$= 0.1487$$

∴ 14.87%

<Key Note> *Finding Y (number of years)

How many it takes for "x" PV to grow a certain amount of FV

$$FV_y = PV(1+\frac{k}{m})^{m \times y}$$

$$\frac{FV_y}{PV} = (1+\frac{k}{m})^{m \times y}$$

$$\log(\frac{FV_y}{PV}) = m \times y log(1+\frac{k}{m})$$

$$y = \frac{\log\frac{FV_y}{PV}}{m log(1+\frac{k}{m})}$$

Practice Question 6-2

A. How long does it take to double your $100 at 12% compounded annually?

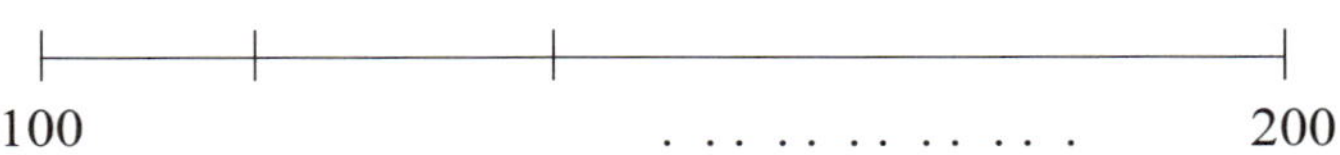

$$y = \frac{\log\frac{FV}{PV}}{m log(1+\frac{k}{m})}$$

In this case, PV=100, FV=200, m=1, k=12%

$$y = \frac{\log_n\frac{200}{100}}{1(\log_n(1+0.12))} = \frac{\log 2}{\log 1.12} = \frac{0.693}{0.113} = 6.115$$

y = 6.115 (∴ 6.12)

Practice Question 6-3

A. How much is $100 worth at the end of 2 years at an annual rate of 12% compounded annually?

$$FV = PV(1+i)^n$$
$$FV = 100(1+.12)^2 = 100(1.12)^2 = 125.44$$

B. How much is $100 in 2years worth today at an annual rate of 12%?

$$PV = \frac{FV}{(1+i)^n}$$

$$100 = PV(1+0.12)^2, PV = \frac{100}{(1.12)^2},\ PV = 79.719$$

C. How long does it take to double your money $100 at 12% compounded annually?

$FV=PV(1+i)^n$, $n=m\times Y$, $m=1$, so, $n=Y$.

$$n=Y=\frac{\log\frac{FV}{PV}}{m\log(1+\frac{k}{m})}$$

$$200 = 100(1.12)^n,\quad n = 6.12$$

(Note : refer practice Question 6-2)

2. Present Value

With this background, you can calculate how much a dollar today is expected to be worth at any future time for the required expected annual returns reflective of the risks of the investment (r_1, $r_2 \cdots r_T$). But how much is the present value of a future dollar? In our investment example, if you could receive either \$104 in one year or \$100 today, which would you pick? Since 4% is the return required to make you indifferent between receiving \$100 today and \$104 in the future, the options are equivalent. That is, receiving \$104 in one year is equal to \$100 today. Rearranging Equation 6-1, the present value of future cash flow received one year from today is expressed as:

$$\text{Present Value} = FV_1 \ / \ (1 + r_1) = CF_1 * (1 + r_1)^{-1} \quad \text{[Eq.6-6]}$$

Where the discount rate is r_1 and the discount factor is $(1+r_1)^{-1}$

Applying Equation 6-6 to our example, \$104 in one year is equal to \$100 today, that is, a present value of \$100:

$$\text{Present Value} = FV_1 \ / \ (1 + r_1) = CF_1 * (1 + r_1)^{-1}$$
$$\text{Present Value} = \$104 * (1 + 4\%)^{-1} = \$104 * 0.9615 = \$100$$

So in this example, \$100 is the present value, the discount factor is 0.9615, and the discount rate, i.e., the required expected annual return, is 4%. Figure 6-5 illustrates graphically the concept of present value, where the arrow indicates that the future cash flows are discounted back to the present, using the required rate of return (r_1).

FIGURE 6-5

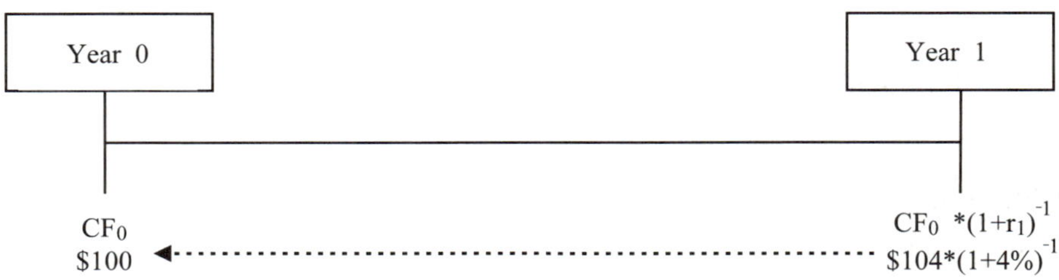

In our example, what is the present value of the future \$108.68 value in two years? Again, you are indifferent between receiving \$100 today and \$108.68 two years from today, if you deem that the required return is 4% in year 1 and 4.5% in year 2. Therefore, the present value of \$108.68 at this risk profile for two years is \$100. Rearranging Equation 6-2 and solving for the present value of cash flow received two years from today yields:

$$FV_2 = CF_2 = CF_0 * (1 + r_1) * (1 + r_2) \cdots\cdots \text{[Eq.6-2]}$$

$$FV_2 = CF_2 = \text{Present Value} * (1 + r_1) * (1 + r_2)$$

$$\text{Present Value} = FV_2*[(1+r_1)*(1+r_2)]^{-1} = CF_2/[(1+r_1)*(1+r_2)]^{-1} \cdots\cdots \text{[Eq.6-7]}$$

In this case, the discount factor is $[(1 + r_1) * (1 + r_2)]^{-1}$, and there are two discount rates (r_1 for year 1, and r_2 for year 2).

Applying Equation 6-6 to our example, \$108.68 in two years at these discount rates (i.e., required expected annual returns in view of the risk profile) is:

$$\text{Present Value} = FV_2*[(1+r_1)*(1+r_2)]^{-1} = CF_2*[(1 + r_1)*(1 + r_2)]^{-1}$$

$$\text{Present Value} = \$108.68 * [(1 + 4\%) * (1 + 4.5\%)]^{-1} = \$100$$

So the present value of \$108.68 in two years given these discount rates is \$100, and the discount factor is 0.92.

Figure 6-6 illustrates the concept of discounting cash flow in year 2 back to the present, using the required rate of return for each year.

FIGURE 6-6

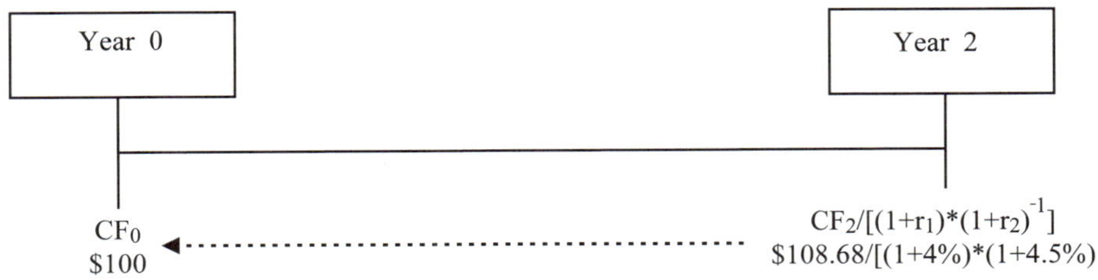

Expanding our example to the third year, if you receive $112.92 in year 3 at the previously discussed risk profile, you would be indifferent between $100 today otherwise $112.92 in three years.

Applying our formula to this example, $112.92 in three years equals $100 today, where the discount factor is $[(1 + r_1) * (1 + r_2) * (1 + r_3)]^{-1}$ and there are three specific discounts rates:

$$\text{Present Value} = FV_3/[(1+r_1)*(1+r_2)*(1+r_3)] = CF_3/[(1+r_1)*(1+r_2)*(1+r_3)^{-1}] \quad \text{[Eq. 6-8]}$$

$$\text{Present Value} = \$112.92/[(1+4\%)*(1+4.5\%)*(1+3.9\%)] = \$100$$

So the present value is $100, the discount rate profile is 4%, 4.5%, and 3.9% in years 1, 2, and 3 respectively, and the discount factor is 0.886.

Figure 6-7 graphically depicts the discounting process for cash flow received in year 3.

FIGURE 6-7

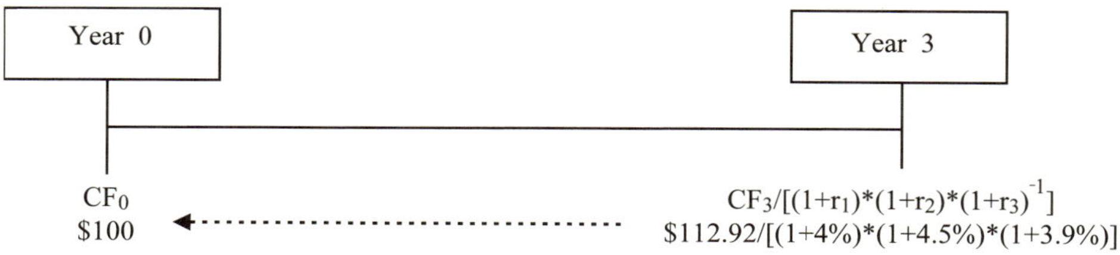

As with the future value equation, the present value equation can be expanded to express the present value of cash flow in the year T as:

$$\text{Present Value}=FV_T*[(1+r_1)*(1+r_2)*(1+r_3)*\cdots\cdots*(1+r_T)]^{-1} \quad \text{[Eq.6-9]}$$

If the required expected annual return, i.e., the discount rate, is approximately the same in each year, this formula simplifies to:

$$\text{Present Value}=\text{Future Value (in year T)}*(1+r)^{-T}=CF_T*(1+r)^{-T} \quad \text{[Eq.6-10]}$$

Where $(1+r)^{-T}$ is the discount factor, and r is the common discount rate for all years.

As with future value, the time unit can be quarterly, monthly, weekly, or daily, as long as you are consistent in application. Therefore, if you use months to represent time, you must also use a monthly discount rate and monthly cash flows. Figure 6-8 illustrates the general formula for future value at a constant discount rate.

FIGURE 6-8

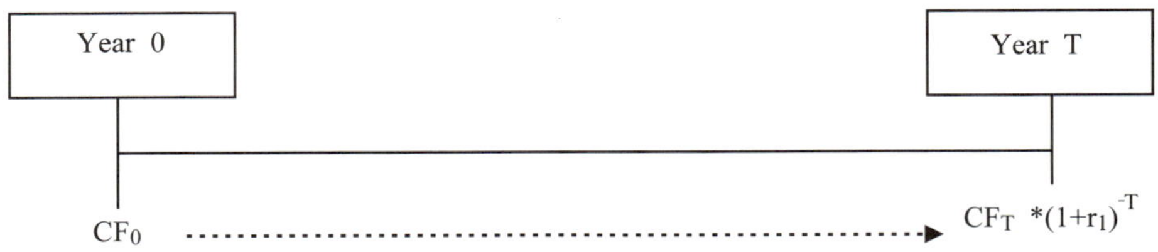

A constant discount rate is generally a productive simplification, but before using it, you must determine whether it is a good approximation of the risk profile of the investment. If so, use the simplified version; if not, use the full version.

Practice Question 6-4

Now, suppose you have some extra cash, and you have a chance to buy a low-risk security, which will pay $127.63 at the end of 5 years. Your local bank is currently offering 5 percent interest on 5-year certificates of deposit, and you regard the security as being as safe as a CD (Certified Deposit). The 5 percent rate is defined as being your opportunity cost rate, or rate of return you could earn on alternative investments of similar risk. How much should you be willing to pay for the security?

From the future value example presented in the previous section, we saw that an initial amount of $100 invested at 5 percent per year would be worth $127.63 at the end of 5 years. As we will see in a moment, you should be indifferent to the choice between $100 today and $127.63 at the end of 5 years and the $100 is defined as the present value, or PV, of $127.63 due in 5 years when the opportunity cost rate is 5 percent. If the price of the security is anything less than $100, you should definitely buy it. If the price is greater than $100, you should turn it down. If the price is exactly $100, then you could either buy it or turn it down, for \$100 is the security's fair value.

Finding present value is called discounting, and it is simply the reverse of compounding - if you know the PV, you can compound to find the FV, while if you know the FV, you can discount to find the PV.

Solutions

Numerical Solution

Divide \$127.63 by 1.05 five times, or by $(1.05)^5$

Tabular Solution:

Use $PVIF_{i,n}$ TABLE

Financial Calculator Solution:

Enter 5N, 5I, 127.63FV, and then press PV to get PV = -100.

<Key Note> ***Uneven Cashflow**

-Treat each CF as a lump sum problem

-Convert all CF to the same year before addition / subtraction

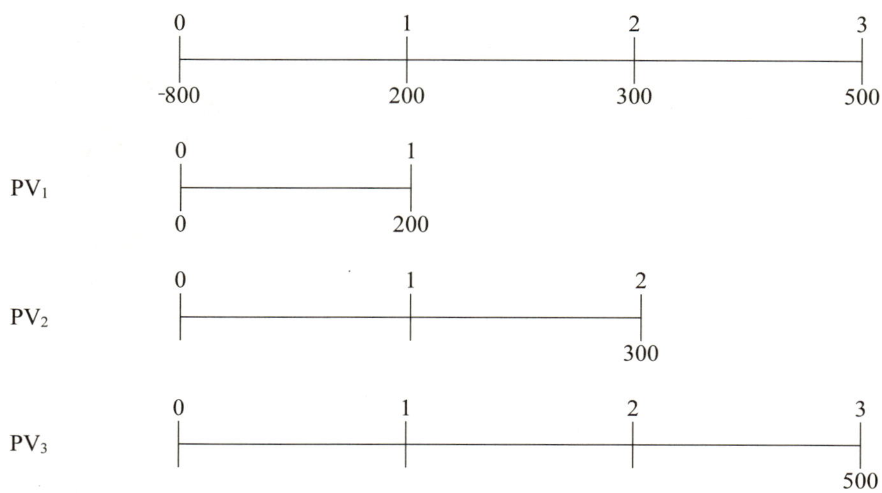

Let m = 1

k = 12%

$$PV_1 = 200 \times \frac{1}{1+0.12} = 178.57$$

$$PV_2 = 300 \times \left(\frac{1}{1+0.12}\right)^2 = 239.16$$

$$PV_3 = 500 \times \left(\frac{1}{1+0.12}\right)^3 = 355.89$$

$\Sigma 773.62$

$$PV_0 = \sum_{t=0}^{n} CF_t \times \left(\frac{1}{1+i}\right)^t$$

By calculator,

12 I

0 CF

200 CF

300 CF

500 CF

NPV → \$773.62

Practice Question 6-5

Time Line

0	1	2	3	4
0	100	100	x	200

If

PV of all CF = 438.46

m = 1

k = 12%

A. What is the value of x?

Solutions

$$\text{PV of all CF} = \sum_{t=0}^{4} CF_t \times \left(\frac{1}{1+i}\right)^t$$

$$PV_1 = 100 \times \left(\frac{1}{1+0.12}\right)^1 = 89.29$$

$$PV_2 = 100 \times \left(\frac{1}{1+0.12}\right)^2 = 79.72$$

$$PV_3 = x \times \left(\frac{1}{1+0.12}\right)^3 = \boxed{142.35} \leftarrow [438.46-(89.29+79.22+127.10)]$$

$$PV_4 = 200 \times \left(\frac{1}{1+0.12}\right)^4 = 127.10$$

$$\overline{\quad 438.46 \quad}$$

$$X \times \frac{1}{(1+0.12)^3} = 142.35$$

$$X = 142.35 \times (1.12)^3$$

$$= 199.99 \fallingdotseq 200$$

<Discount Rate:>

A key input into any DCF analysis is the discount rate. Discount rates are always determined by your best assessment of risk of the cash stream you are discounting. That is, how high does the annual expected return have to be to make you willing to invest in something with the risk of the cash stream being discounted? For real estate projects, risk reflects many things, including: liquidity and exit risk, operating risk, lease-up risk, tenant credit risk; market risk, etc.

Determining the appropriate discount rate requires judgment, and is a disciplined yet imprecise exercise. The discount rate will not only vary between investments, but you may need to apply different discount rates to the cash flows for different years. For instance, if you are considering a development project, you will apply a lower discount rate to the initial cash outflows than to the expected future cash inflows upon completion, as the development cash outflows are fairly certain to occur, while the operating cash inflows are relatively uncertain. If, on the other hand, it is a reasonable approximation that the risk of each year's cash flow is the same, utilize the simpler present valuation formula.

3. Annuity

An annuity is a series of equal payments made at fixed intervals for a specified number of periods. For example, $100 at the end of each of the next three years is a 3-year annuity. The payments are given the symbol PMT, and they can occur at either the beginning of the end of each period. If the payments occur at the end of each period, as they typically do, the annuity is called an ordinary, or deferred, annuity. If payments are made at the beginning of each period, the annuity is an annuity due.

Terminology:

*Annuity: A series of payments of an equal amount of fixed intervals.

*Ordinary annuity (Annuity in arrear): an annuity whose payments occur at the end of each period.

*Annuity due (Annuity in advance): An annuity whose payments occur at the beginning of each period.

1) Future Value of an Annuity

Since ordinary annuities are far more common in finance, when the term "annuity" is used in the book, you should assume that the payments occur at the end of each period unless otherwise noted.

Ordinary Annuities:

$$FV_y = PMT[\sum_{t=1}^{n}(1+i)^{n-t}]$$

Time Line:

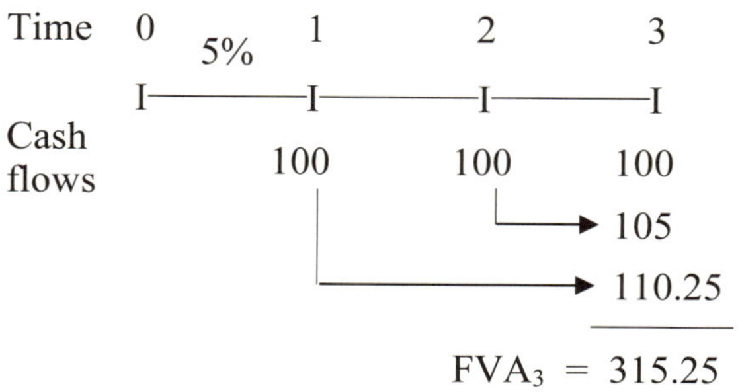

Solutions

Numerical Solution

The future value of each cash flow is calculated, and those FVs are summed to find the FV of the annuity. This is tedious process for long annuities.

Tabular Solution

Use the $FVIFA_{i,n}$ table.

Financial Calculator Solution

Input 3N, 5I, -100PMT, FV, then you would get 315.25

Annuity Due

$$FV_y = PMT[\sum_{t=1}^{n}(1+i)^t]$$

Time line and Numerical Solution

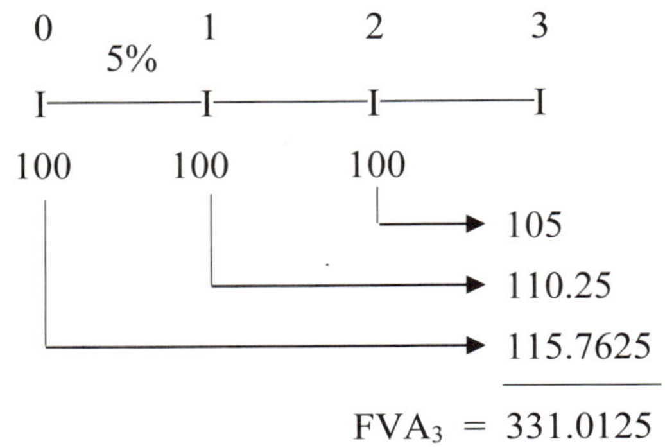

Solutions

Tabular Solution

In an annuity due, each payment is compounded for one additional period, so the future value of the entire annuity is equal to the future value of an ordinary annuity compounded for one additional period. Here is the tabular solution:

$$FVAn = PMT\ (FVIFA_{i,n})\ (1+i.)$$
$$= \$100\ (3.1525)\ (1.05) = \$331.0125$$

Financial Calculator Solution:

Input 3N, 5I, BEGIN −100 PMT, FV, then you would get 331.0125.

2) Present Value of Annuity

Suppose you were offered the following alternatives: (1) a 3-year annuity with payments of $100 at the end of each year or (2) a lump sum payment today. You have no need for the money during the next three years, so if you accept the annuity, you would simply deposit the payments in a savings account that pays 5 percent interest per year. Similarly, the lump sum payment would be deposited into the same account. How large must the lump sum payment today be to make it equivalent to the annuity?

[Ordinary Annuities]

$$PV = PMT[\sum_{t=1}^{n} \frac{1}{(1+i)^t}]$$

Time line and Numerical Solution

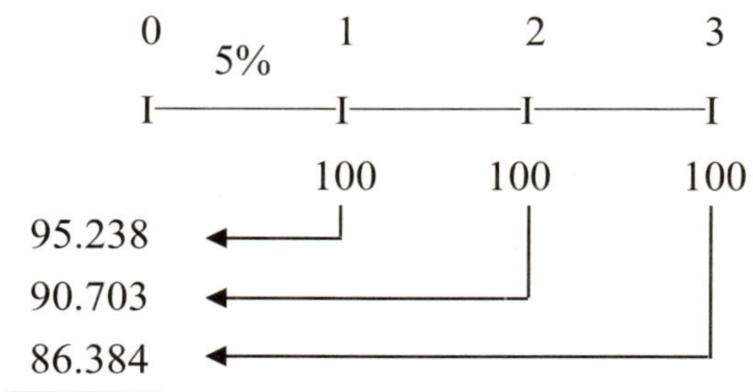

$PVA_3 = 272.325$

Solutions

Tabular Solution

Use $PVIFA_{i,n}$ table. Look down the 5% column to the third period. The PVIFA is 2.7232, so the present value of the \$100 annuity is \$272.32 (\$100×2.7232).

Financial Calculator Solution

Input 3N, 51, -100 PMT, PV, and then you would get 272.32.

[Annuity Due]

$$PV = PMT[\sum_{t=1}^{n} \frac{1}{(1+i)^{n-t}}]$$

Time line and Numerical Solution

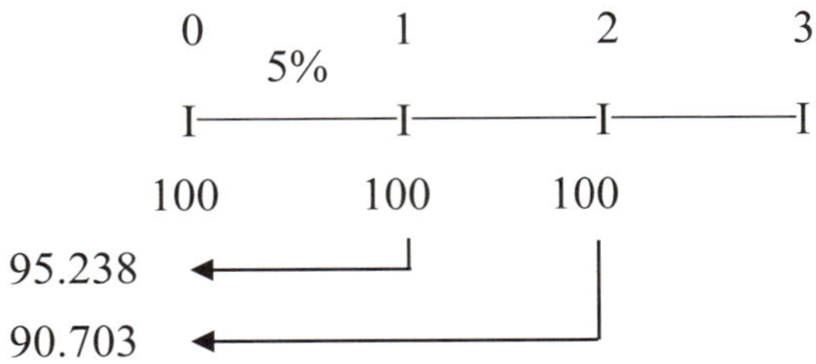

PVA_3 = 285.941

Solutions

Tabular Solution

Use PVIFAi,n table. Look down the 5% column to the third period. The PVIFA is 2.7232. An annuity due is more valuable than an ordinary annuity, and this higher value is found by multiplying the PV of an ordinary annuity by (1+i.), in this case, 1.05. So the present value of the $100 annuity is $285.94 ($100×2.7232×1.05).

Financial Calculator Solution

Input 3N, 5I, Begin -100 PMT, PV, then you would get 285.94.

Practice Question 6-6

∴ Combining annuities and Lump sum

1) Time Line

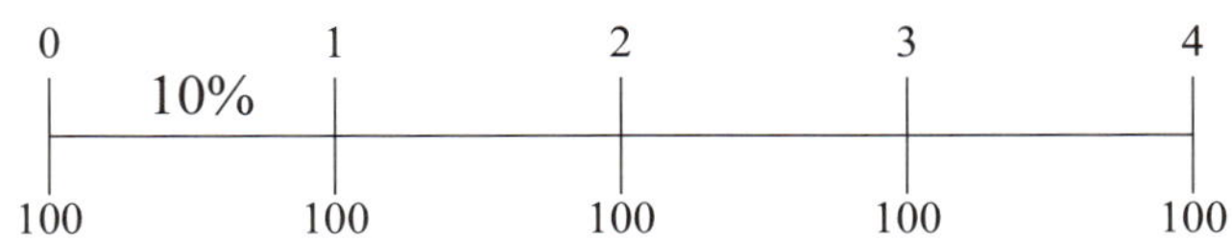

How much is this investment worth at the end of year four? (I=10%)

Solutions

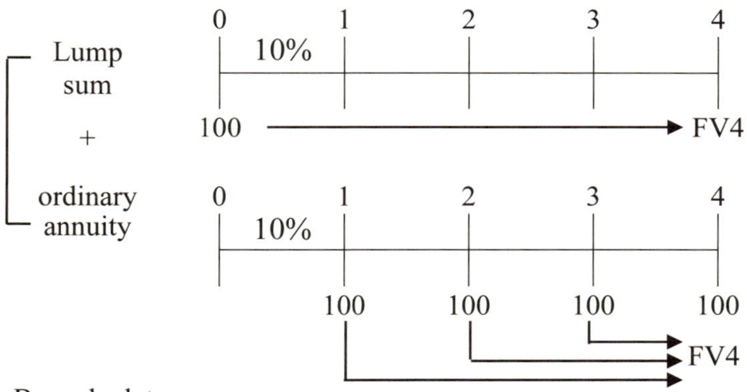

By calculator

	m = 1
lump sum	100 PV
annuity	100PMT
	10 I
	4 N
	FV → \$610.51

2) Time Line

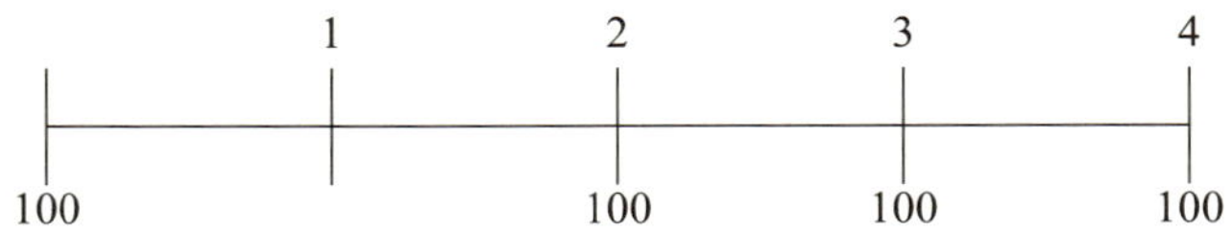

Find PV of this cash flows using K = 10%, m = 1

Solutions

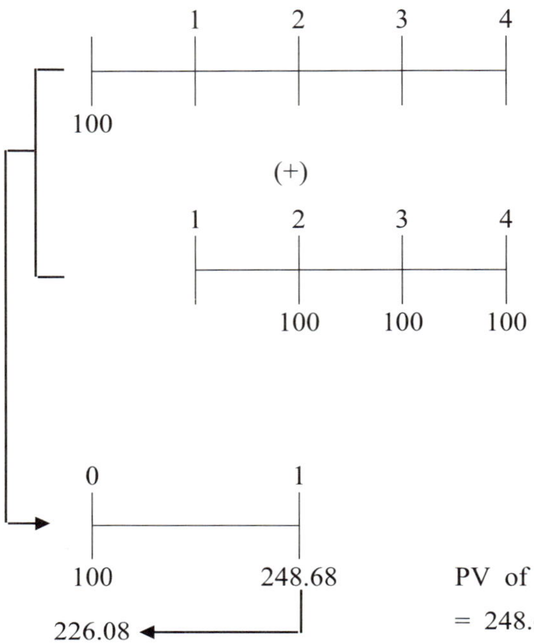

$\Rightarrow$ PV = 100

$\Rightarrow$ PV_1 = ordinary annuity

m = 1
100 PMT
3 N
10 I
PV $\rightarrow$ \$248.68

PV of \$248.68

$$= 248.68 \times \frac{1}{1.1}$$

$$= 226.08$$

So, PV of this cash flows is \$100+\$226.08 = \$326.08

4. Perpetuities

Perpetuity

Most annuities call for payments to be made over some finite period of time. However, some annuities go on indefinitely, or perpetually, and these annuities are called perpetuity. PV of a perpetuity is found by applying Equation

$$PV = \frac{payment}{interest\ rate} = \frac{PMT}{i}$$

-A stream of equal payments expected to continue forever.

-An annuity that lasts forever.

-Payment must be consistent.

For example, the PV of following perpetuity is :

Time Line

0	1	2	3	4	5	……
10%						
-1500	100	100	100	100	100	Forever

$$PV = \frac{100}{0.1} = 1{,}000 \qquad NPV = 1{,}000 - 1{,}500 = -500$$

Application

1. Valuation of perpetual bond
2. Valuation of stock (preferred stock)

5. Effective Annual Rate (EAR)

EAR - Effective Annual Rate : The annual rate of interest actually being earned as opposed to the quoted rate. In other words, it is the rate which would produce the same earning value if annual compounding were used.

$$\textbf{EAR} = (1+\frac{k}{m})^{m} - 1 \qquad APR(k) = [(1+EAR)^{\frac{1}{n}} - 1] \times m$$

k = annual % rate(APR) ∴ APR should less than EAR.

Practice Question 6-7

1) 12% compounded monthly. What's EAR?

$$EAR = \left(1 + \frac{0.12}{12}\right)^{12} - 1$$

$$= 12.68\%$$

2) Bank A- 10% compounded annually

Bank B- 9.5% compounded monthly

Which one is better?

A) m=1

$$EAR_A = \left(1 + \frac{0.10}{1}\right)^{1} - 1 \Rightarrow 10\%$$

B) m=12

$$EAR_B = \left(1 + \frac{0.095}{12}\right)^{12} - 1 \Rightarrow 9.925\%$$

6. Amortized Loan

Amortized Loan

One that is "killed off" over time

-Repay a loan in equal installment

-Each installment includes both interest and principle

Interest component is largest in the first year, and it declines as the outstanding balance of the loan goes down.

- Periodic interest (interest portion)
  ⇒ Periodic rate X Remaining balance
- Principle portion
  ⇒ Installment − Interest portion
- Remaining Balance
  ⇒ Beginning balance − Principle portion

Practice Questions 6-8

1. Borrowed $10,000 for 5 yrs at 12%

(A) What is monthly payment?

$m = 12 \quad i = \frac{k}{m} = \frac{0.12}{12} = 1\%$

$PV = 10,000 \quad n = m \times y = 12 \times 5 = 60$

By calculator
m = 12
10.000 PV
1 I
60 N
PMT →
⇒ $222.44

(B) What is the remaining balance after 12th payments?
This breakdown is given in the amortization schedule.

Payment	Beg. Balance	Int. port	Principle Port	Remaining Balance (Beg Balance-principle port)
#1	10,000	100 (10.000×0.01)	122.44 (222.44-100)	9877.56
#2	9,877.56	98.775	123.664	9753.89
#3	9,753.89	97.53	124.90	9628.98
⋮	⋮	⋮	⋮	⋮
#12	( )	( )	( )	( )

By calculator

m = 12

10.000 PV

1 I

60 N

1 [Input] 12

[AMOT] per 1-12

Push [=] button, then

→ [=] interest(1,116.43)

→ [=] principle(1,552.89)

→ [=] Balance(8,447.10)

7. Balloon Payment

Part of the loan is deferred to be repaid at maturity

Practice Question 6-9

Borrowed $10,000

k=12%, Y=5yrs, monthly payment

Balloon payment= $3,000

Time Line

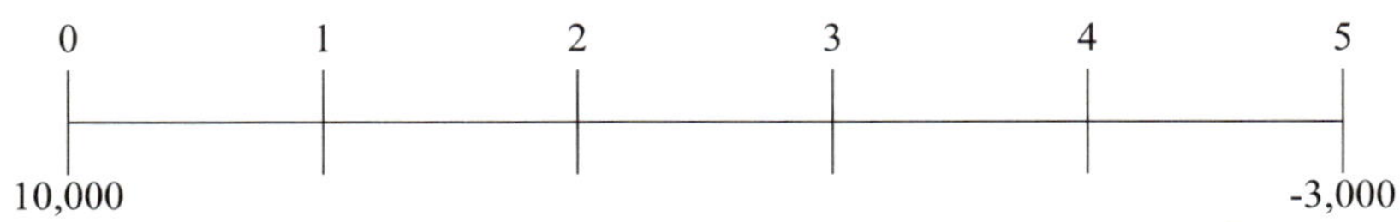

What is monthly payment?

① ordinary annuity

m = 12

PV = 10,000

$i = \frac{k}{m} = \frac{12\%}{12} = 1\%$

N = m × Y = 12 × 5 = 60

② lump sum

-3,000 FV5

By calculator,

m = 12

10,000 PV

1 I

60 N

-3,000 FV

PMT → $-185.71

8. <Advanced Learning> Continuous Compounding and Discounting

So far we dealt only with situations where interest is added at discrete intervals-annually, semiannually, monthly, and forth. In some instances, though, it is possible to have instantaneous, or *continuous*, growth. In this section, we discuss present value and future value calculations when the interest rate is compounded continuously.

1) Continuous Compounding

The relationship between discrete and continuous compounding is illustrated in Figure 8A-1. Panel a shows the annual compounding case, where interest is added once a year; Panel b shows the situation when compounding occurs twice a year; and Panel c shows interest being earned continuously. As the graphs show, the more frequent the compounding period, the larger the final compounded amount, because interest is earned on interest more often.

To illustrate, let PV=\$100, i=10%, and n=5. At various compounding periods per year, we obtain the following future values at the end of 5 years:

$$\text{Annual: } FV_5 = \$100(1+\frac{0.10}{1})^{1(5)} = 100(1.10)^5 = \$161.05$$

$$\text{Semiannual: } FV_5 = \$100(1+\frac{0.10}{2})^{2(5)} = 100(1.05)^{10} = \$162.89$$

$$\text{Monthly: } FV_5 = \$100(1+\frac{0.10}{12})^{12(5)} = 100(1.0083)^{60} = \$164.53$$

$$\text{Daily: } FV_5 = \$100(1+\frac{0.10}{365})^{365(5)} = \$164.86$$

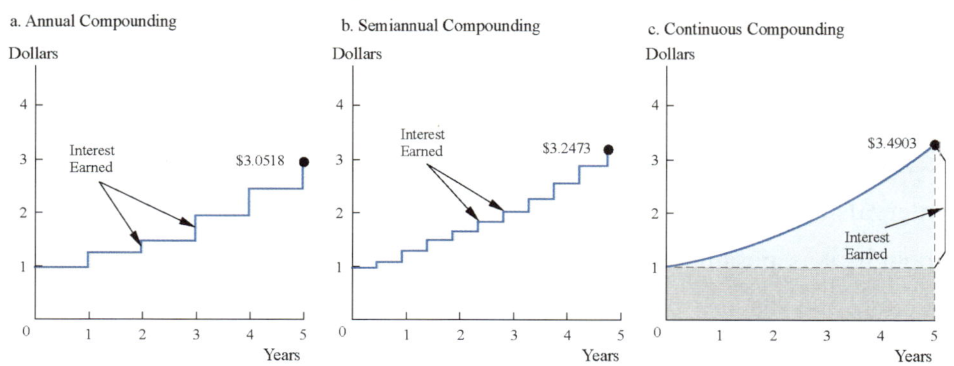

Figure 8A-1 Annual, Semiannual, and Continuous Compounding: Future Value with i=25%

We could keep going, compounding every hour, every minute, every second, and so on. At the limit, we could compound every instant, or *continuously*. The equation for continuous compounding is

$$FV_n = PV(e^{in}) \quad \text{(8A-1)}$$

Here e is the value 2.7183... .[2] If $100 is invested for 5 years at 10 percent compounded continuously, then FV_5 is computed as follows:

$$\text{Continuous: } FV_5 = \$100[e^{0.10(5)}] = \$100(2.7183...)^{0.5} = \$164.872$$

2) Continuous Discounting

Equation 8A-1 can be transformed into Equation 8A-2 and used to determine present values under continuous discounting:

$$PV = \frac{FV_n}{e^{in}} FV_n/e^{in} = FV_n(e^{-in}) \quad \text{(8A-2)}$$

Thus, if $1,649 is due in 10 years, and if the appropriate *continuous* discount rate, is 5 percent, then the present value of this future payment is

$$PV = \frac{\$1,649}{(2.7183...)^{0.5}} = \frac{\$1,649}{1.649} = \$1,000$$

Practice Question 6-10

1) Find FV of $100 in 2 years compounded continuously at 12%!

2) Calculators with exponential functions can be used to evaluate Equation 8A-1.

Solution:

<$FV = PV \times e^{k \times y}$>

$$FV_2 = 100 \times e^{.12 \times 2}$$
$$= 100 \times (2.7183)^{.24}$$
$$= 100 \times 1.27125$$
$$= 127.125$$

2) You receive \$100 at the end of 2 years using 12% compounded continuously.

How much is it worth today?

$$FV = PV \times e^{k \times y}$$
$$PV = \frac{FV}{e^{K \times Y}}$$
$$= \frac{100}{e^{.24}}$$
$$= \$78.66$$

<Note> EAR(Effective Annual Rate) of compounded continuously.

$EAR = e^{k-1}$ ($\therefore$ e = 2.7182)

(eg) 12% compounded continuously → EAR = by calculator

enter .12 $\boxed{e^x}$

→ 1.1275

So, EAR = 1.1275-1 = 0.1275

= 12.75%

$\therefore$ (K)APR = ln(1 + EAR)

(eg) EAR 12% compounded continuously

→ APR ⇒ ln(1+0.12) = ln(1.12)

= 11.33%

Practice Questions

True (T) or False (F)

01. The reference point on a time line indicates the point on the time line where we want to value the cash flows.

02. The financial markets account for the time value of money through the compounding process.

03. Future value refers to the worth today of some amount of money received in the future.

04. The greater the compounding rate, the lower the future value is.

05. The value additive principle allows us to add the present values of individual cash flows in order to find the present value of the entire cash flow stream.

06. A cash flow stream with equal payments for an infinite period of time is called an annuity.

07. In an ordinary annuity, payments are made at the beginning of each period.

08. One example of perpetuity is the dividends paid on preferred stock.

09. The concept of perpetuity is often applied to the valuation of a hotel or restaurant.

10. The table of future value factors for an annuity assumes that the first cash flow of the annuity occurs at the beginning of the first period.

11. The rate of return on an investment is also called internal rate of return.

12. The more often money is compounded during a year; the higher will be the effective annual return.

▣ Multiple Choices

13. All of the values are less than 1 on which of the following tables?

a. present value factors for a single cash flow
b. present value factors for an annuity
c. future value factors for a single cash flow
d. future value factors for an annuity

14. A cash flow stream with equal payments for a finite period of time is called:

a. an effective annual return.
b. an annuity
c. a perpetuity.
d. a present value factor.

15. An amortization table for a loan shows the loans':

a. leverage ratio
b. tax rate
c. principal payments
d. All of the above

16. The discount rate in discounted cash flow analysis represents

a. The present value of the cash flow stream
b. The time in the future that the cash flows will be received
c. The opportunity costs involved in receiving dollars in the future instead of the present
d. The interest earned on prior period's interest
e. The number of periods over which the cash flows is discounted

17. For a given cash flow stream

a. Increasing the discount rate will increase the present value of the stream.
b. The present value of the stream will always exceed the future value of the stream when using a specified rate of interest.
c. An increase in the compounding periods will decrease the future value.
d. Decreasing the discount rate will increase the present value of the stream.
e. More than one of the above.

18. An investment promises to pay $1800 at the end of seven years. If interest rate for this type of investment is expected to be 11% over the next seven years, how much would you be willing to pay for the investment?

a. \$652.28　　　b. \$742.93
c. \$866.99　　　d. \$907.13
e. \$988.99

19. An investor purchases a stock for \$40. He expects a \$2 dividend per year at the end of the next three years. At the end of the third year, he expects to sell the stock for \$56. What is the investor's expected rate of return?

a. 15.41%　　　b. 16.37%
c. 17.85%　　　d. 18.21%
e. 19.68%

20. After successfully completing the Hotel investment and Finance course, you land in a high paying job in a very prestigious company. You now become accustomed to a life of luxury. To assure this luxurious lifestyle after retirement, you begin making equal annual deposits, starting today and ending when you retire, into an account that earns 11%. You expect to retire at age 65 and will withdraw \$75,000 per year for the next twenty years. If you are currently 25, how much must the equal annual installments, (x), be in order to meet your goal?

25	26	27	…	64	65	66	67	…	84	85
X	X	X		X	X	\$75,000	\$75,000		\$75,000	\$75,000

a. \$923.35　　　b. \$1015.63
c. \$1215.17　　　d. \$1586.34
e. \$1621.41

Answers to the Practice Problems:

Answer Keys T, T, F, F, T, F, F, T, T, F, T, T, A, B, C, C, D, C, B, A

Chapter 07

Interest Rate : the Price of Money

Chapter 07 Interest Rate : the Price of Money

1. Interest Rate

Interest - Price of Money (Return)

(1) Real rate of interest (K^*) – determined by supply & demand

(2) Nominal risk-free rate ($K_{Rf} = K^* + I_P$(Inflation Premium))

(3) Nominal interest rate ($K = K^* + I_P + M_{RP} + D_{RP} + L_{RP}$)

Ex) $K^* = 2\%$ $I_P = 4\%$ $M_{RP} = 1\%$ $D_{RP} = 1\%$ $L_{RP} = 0.5\%$	$K_{TB} = K_{Rf} = K^* + I_P$ $= 2\% + 4\%$ $= 6\%$ $K_{CB} = 6\%+1\%+1\%+0.5\%$ $= 8.5\%$	M - Maturity RP - Risk Premium D - Default L - Liquidity TB - Treasury Bond (Risk Free) CB - Corporate Bond (=Nominal interest rate)

1) The Factors Affecting Interest Rate.

(1) Production opportunities

(2) Time preference for consumption

(3) Risk

(4) Inflation

2) The Components of Market Interest Rate

(1) The Real Risk-free Rate

This is defined as the interest rate that would exist on a riskless security if no inflation was expected.

(2) Nominal Risk Free Rate

This is the real risk free rate plus a premium for expected inflation.

(3) Maturity Risk

M_{RP} = maturity.

Longer term bond are exposed to a significant risk of price declines, and a maturity risk premium is charged by lenders to reflect this risk.

(4) Default Risk (=credit risk)

D_{RP} = default risk premium.

= This premium reflects the possibility that the issuer will not pay interest or principle on a security at the stated time and in the stated amount. It is rises as the riskiness of issuers increase.

① The risk that a borrower will default on a loan interest or principle

② The greater the default risk, the higher the interest rate

③ The difference between the interest rate on a Treasury bond and a corporate bond of equal maturity and marketability.

(5) Liquidity Risk: The risk that an asset cannot be sold on notice for its fair market value.

L_{RP} = liquidity; or marketability premium.

= This premium charged by lenders to reflect the fact that some securities cannot be converted to cash on short notice at a "reasonable" price. It is relatively high on securities issued by very small firms.

① Risk level

Real assets > Financial assets

Private markets > Public markets

Securities of small company > Securities of government

(6) Interest Rate Risk

① The risk that the value of an asset fluctuates due to changes in interest rate

A. Price risk: the value of assets declines when interest rates increase.

B. Reinvestment risk: The investment return declines when interest rates decrease.

② The longer the maturity, the higher the interest rate risk

(7) Country Risk

The risk that is arise from investing or doing business in a particular country. This risk depends on the country's economic, political and social environment.

(8) Exchange Rate Risk

The risk that a foreign currency transaction will be negatively exposed to fluctuations in exchange rates.

2. The Term Structure of Interest Rates

Bonds

- Par value (assume $1,000)
- Annual coupon payment
- Coupon payment periods
- Maturity date

- Annual coupon payment = coupon rate X par value
- YTM (Yield To Maturity) = Market interest rate for bonds with similar maturity coupon payment (Risk class)
- Yield Curve = Relationship between YTM & years to maturity for bonds in the same Risk class

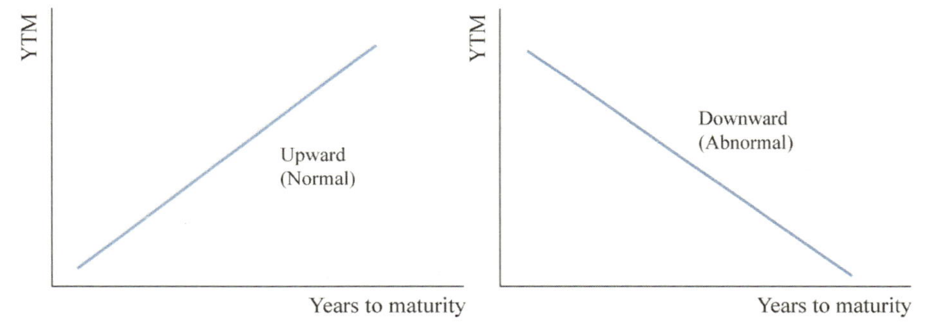

Investors expect increased inflation in the future

Yield Curve when the inflation rate is expected to decline

Expectation theory

Interest rates represent investor's expectation on future inflation

$$K = \underbrace{K^* + IP}_{K_{rf}} + \underbrace{M_{RP} + D_{RP} + L_{RP}}_{\text{Risk premium}}$$

$K_{rf} = K^* + IP_t$

IP - average expected inflation rate

For example, we have following situation.

- Annual yield on 2-year T/B : 11.5%
- Annual yield on 1-year T/B : 10%
- $K^* = 3\%$
- $M_{RP} = 0$

A. Forecast "K" on 1-year Bond during the 2nd year?

(the yield on a 2-year Bond= average yield on 1-year bond in year 1 and year 2)

11.5%= (10+x)/2

X= 13% <yield on 1 year bond during 2nd year>

B. Expect inflation rate in year 1 and year 2?

At first, Find $K_{rf(2)}$

$K_{rf(2)} = k^* + IP_2$

Year 1: $10\% = 3\% + X_1 \quad \therefore X_1 = 7\%$

Year 2: $13\% = 3\% + X_2 \quad \therefore X_2 = 10\%$

Year	During	K* + IP	
2××3	1year	10% = 3% + 7%	
	2year	11.5% = 3% + 8.5%	← (Inflation 2003 + Inflation 2004)/2
2××4	1year	13% = 3% + 10%	

Normal yield curve is upward because investors expect increased inflation in the future. Following case shows this.

Year	Expected Inflation	Duration	Avg. expected inflation
2111	2%	1yr	2%
2112	3%	2 yrs	(2+3)/2= 2.5%
2113	4%	3 yrs	(2+3+4)/3= 3%
2114	5%	4 yrs	(2+3+4+5)/4= 3.5%
2115	3%	5 yrs	(2+3+4+5+3)/5= 3.4%

1 year Bond

$$K_{rf} = K^* + IP$$

K_{rf} (1) = 2% + 2% = 4%

K_{rf} (2) = 2% + 2.5% = 4.5%

K_{rf} (3) = 2% + 3% = 5%

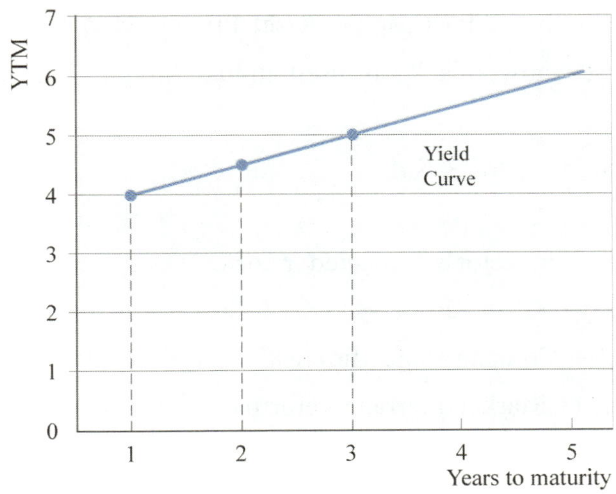

Practice Question 7-1

Incase of :

3yrs Government Bond 8% (K_{rf})

$K^* = 2\%$

Expected inflation in 2114 = 4%

in 2116 = 6%

Then, what about expected inflation in 2115?

$K_{rf} = K^* + IP$

$8\% = 2\% + IP. \therefore IP = 6\%$

$\therefore IP = \text{Inflation}(2114 + 2115 + 2116)/3$

$6\% = \text{Inf}(4\% + 2115 + 6\%)\ /3$

$18\% = 10\% + 2115\ \text{Inf}$

So, Inflation in 2115 is

8%(18% - 10%)

Note : We study CAPM(Capital Asset Pricing Model) in the following chapter, and see how this k_{rf} is used in the Model. The formula is:

$$K_i = K_{rf} + \beta_i(K_m - K_{rf})$$

Where : K_i = invector's expected return.

$K_{rf} = K^* + IP$

β_i = Company specific risk

K_m = Market arerrage returrn

Chapter 08

Risk & Return

Chapter 08

Risk & Return

1. Risk and Probability Distribution

1) A Coin Gamble

Let's think about a Coin Gamble!

* You are offered the following gamble

1) You can receive $60 for certain
2) You can accept following gamble

⇒ A fair coin is tossed
If heads come up, you win $400
If tails come up, you lose $200

Would you choose the safe $60 or accept the gamble, the coin toss?

Here is your solution!!

<Probability & Expected value Table>

	Prob.		Ki	E(k)
Heads	0.5	X	400	200
Tails	0.5	X	200	-100

Σ = $100

Since : $100 > $60

Choose the gamble!!

<Key Note> ***Procedure of assessing risk**

1) Identify variables likely to have impact in each risk category
2) Identify various scenarios surrounding each variable
3) Estimate the probability of occurrence regarding each scenario
4) Determine expected value, impact of each scenario

2) Risk: refers to the chance that some unfavorable event will occur.

If you engage in skydiving, you are taking a chance with your life-skydiving is risky. If you bet on the horses, you are risking you money. If you invest in speculative stocks, you are taking a risk in the hope of making an appreciable return.

To illustrate the riskness of financial asset, suppose we buy $100,000 of short-term government bonds with an expected return of 10 percent. In this case, the rate of return on the investment, 10percent, can be estimated quite precisely, and the investment is defined as being risk free.

However if the $100,000 were invested in the stock of a company just being organized, then the investment's return could not be estimated precisely. We might analyze the "expected" rate of return in a statistical sense, but the "actual" rate of return could range frans +100% -100%. Because there is a signifiant danger of actually earning considerably less than the expected return, the stock would be described as being relatively risky.

Investment risk, then, is related to the probability of actual earing less than the expected return.

3) Probability Distribution

Probability Distribution is a listing of all possible outcomes, or events, with a probability (chance of occurlance) assigned to each outcome.

For example, a weather forecaster might state, "There is a 40% chance of rain today and a 60% chance that it will not rain."

We could set up the following probability distribution.

outcome (1)	prob. (2)			
Rain	0.4	=	40%	
No rain	0.6	=	60%	
	1.0	=	100%	← expressed as %
	↑			

expressed as decimals

Note that the probabilities must sum to 1.0 or 100%

Probabilities can also be assigned to the possible outcomes (or returns) from an investment. If you buy a bond, you expect to receive interest on the bond, and those interest payments will provide you with a rate of return on your investment.

The possible outcomes from this investment are :

1) that the issuer will make the interest payments.

or

2) that the issuer will fail to make the interest payments.

The higher th probability of failure to make the interest payments, the riskier the bonds, and the higher the risk, the higher your required rate of return on the bond.

If instead of buying a bond, you invest in a stock, the return will come from dividends plus capital gains.

Again, the riskier the stock - which means the higher the probability that the firm will fail to pay expected dividends on that stock price will not increase as much as you expected - the higher the expected return must be to induce you to invest in it.

2. Risk vs. Uncertainty

A number of economists have attempted to distinguish between risk and uncertainty, as originally proposed by Frank H. Knight (1921, pp. 226)[3].

(1) "Risk," Knight said, refers to situations where an individual is able to calculate probabilities on the basis of an objective classification of instances. For example, in tossing a fair die the chance of any single one of the six faces showing is exactly one-sixth.

(2) "Uncertainty" he contended, refers to situations where no objective classification is possible, for example in estimating whether or not a cure for cancer will be discovered in the next decade.

Risk is often defined as the variation in returns (probable outcomes) over the life of an investment project.[4] Uncertainty refers to a state of knowledge about the variable inputs to an economic analysis. If the analyst is unsure of the value of the information used as a basis for the study, there is uncertainty. The uncertainty of the market and other factors in hotel and resort development creates risks to investment capital. Analysis of investment potential is usually based on a "best estimate" financial

3) Knight, Frank H. « Risk, Uncertainty and Profit » , New York: Houghton Mifflin, 1921

4) D.J. Johnson, M.D. Olsen, and T.L.VanDyke, « Risk analysis in the Lodging Industry ». « The Practice of Hotel Managment II », AVI Publishing Co, pp. 393-406.

evaluation. The chances of the forecasts which are based on this evaluation vary directly with the quality of the background information which is incorporated into the study.

The investor will wish to compare returns on the proposed investment with returns from alternative opportunities. Usually, comparisons are made among the opportunity costs of several investments. It is important, therefore, to evaluate the degree of risk inherent in each project. Probability distributions take into account the exposure to risk in the calculation, and provide the investor or developer with a range of values on which to base decisions.[5)]

1) Risk Factors

The investor or the owner will have a wide range of investment opportunities to select from at varying risk levels when determining which projects will provide the greatest return. For instance, it may make very little sense to invest in a hotel project where the total return over the next 30 years may be calculated at 9 percent when treasury securities yield 9 percent with very little risk. Therefore, the hotel owners or investors must determine how much risk they are willing to assume on a project and what is a fair return on the risk assumed.

Although there are numerous types of risk to be considered by hotel investors or owners. The most important considerations are risk of future inflation, risk of failure, financial risk, and liquidity risk.

5) Harold E. Marshall, « Techniques for treating Uncertainty and Risk in the Economic Evaluation of Buildings », U.S. Department of Commerce, National Institute of Standards and Technology; NIST Special Publication 757, 1988.

2) Risk of Future Inflation.

It is very difficult to predict what the future inflation rate will be. Ever since the Great Depression, the United States has experienced various levels of inflation. However, during the past 10 years, the inflation rate has fluctuated to the greatest, making it increasingly difficult to predict future rates.

The risk to the investor or owner is to underestimate the inflation rate and its effect on the ability of the hotel operation to raise room rates or menu prices fast enough to keep pace with inflation. Failure to do so could result in a decline in cash flow. Although inflation itself does not cause a hotel property to increase in value, real estate values have tended to keep pace with inflation. Also because they can change their room rates and meal prices quickly, hotel properties are in a better position to pass along rising prices to guests than other forms of real estate investment.

In recent years, high inflation accompanied by an economic recession has been another problem. This has resulted in not only higher prices for financing, building materials, and supplies, but also in lower room occupancies and restaurant sales.

3) Risk of Failure.

Risk of failure is the hotel property's inability to perform as expected. Hotel businesses rely on good management; therefore, they are more susceptible to losses due to poor management than other types of real estate investments. Thus, it is generally true that a well-known project will lower the risk of failure as opposed to an independent management company.

Another business risk common to the hotel industry is that if in the future competitors build in the vicinity of the property there is a risk that the projected cash flow for the property will not be sufficient to generate the projected rate of return. Other factors that increase business risk in the hotel industry are changing customer tastes, demographic changes in the area where a property is located, local or regional economic disruptions, and changes in transportation routes.

4) Financial Risk.

Financial risk is only the inability of the hotel project to generate enough cash to support the debt service. Again, due to the riskiness of certain hotel projects many syndications may guarantee payment of debt service for a number of years to make a hotel project more attractive to investors.

5) Liquidity Risk.

Many investors and owners have experienced liquidity risk when they have had to sell their interest in a hotel project quickly and could find no buyers or only buyers who were willing to pay a small fraction of the real worth of the project's value.

Hotel projects generally are not liquid assets such as money market accounts or bank lines of credit to see him or her through cash shortages. Many hotel investors and owners have lost valuable property because they have been forced to sell their properties at below market value to meet loan obligations.

3. Assessing Risk and Return

1) 3 Statistics for Measuring Risk

1) Expected value (mean)
2) Variance
3) Standard deviation

(1) Expected Value

A. Identify variables likely to have impact in each risk category
B. Identify various scenarios surrounding each variable
C. Estimate the probability of occurrence regarding each scenario
D. Determine expected value, impact of each scenario

(John M. Tarras, a Practical Guide to Hotel Finance, Van Nostrand Reinhold, New York, p99-100.)

Expected returns

$$E(k) = \sum_{i=1}^{n} P_i k_i$$

Where :

E(k) = Expected return
P_i = the probability of obtaining the *i*th outcome k_i
k_i = the *i*th possible outcome - return
n = number of possible outcomes

* Expected Return can be affected by many different variables in both environmental category and functional category.

P_i	K_i	
Environmental Category	**Functional Category**	
Remote Task Functional	Finance Human Resources Operating	Marketing Research & Development Administration

Key issues to be addressed

1. Local market vs. national market- supply / demand
2. Current production technology- core technology
3. Local environment
4. Future variance vs. past performance
5. Project life or concept life

(2) Variance

Variance is the most common measure of variability or dispersion

Variance

$$\sigma^2 = \sum_{i=1}^{n} P_i (K_i - E(k))^2$$

Where :

σ^2 = Variance

P_i = the probability of obtaining the *i*th outcome k_i

K_i = the *i*th possible outcome - return

E(k) = expected return

Step 1) Take the *i* individual return (K_1, K_2, K_3 …)

Step 2) Subtract the average return (E(k))

Step 3) Square the result, multiply with each probability

Step 4) Add them up

Step 5) We get δ^2(variance)

$$\sigma^2 = \sum_{i=1}^{n} P_i(K_i - E(k))^2$$

(3) Standard Deviation

The large enough sample drawn from a normal distribution looks like the bell shaped curve

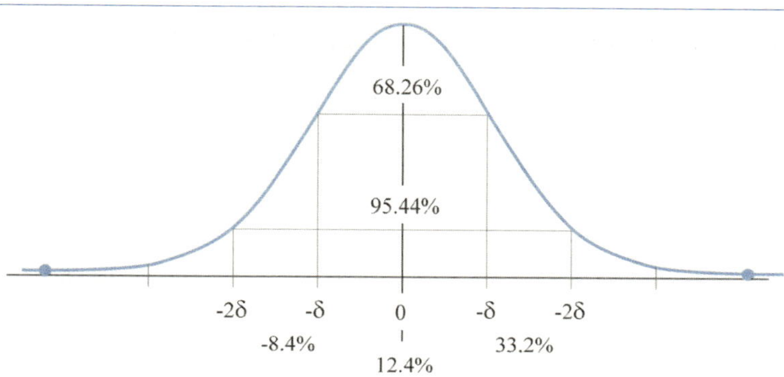

In the case of normal distribution, there is a 68.26% probability that a return will be one S.D of the mean. There is 68.26% probability that a yearly return will be between -8.4% and 33.2%

Standard Deviation

$$SD = \sqrt{\sigma^2}$$

Where :

$$\sigma^2 = \sum_{i=1}^{n} P_i(K_i - E(k))^2$$

P_i = the probability of obtaining the *i*th outcome k_i

K_i = the *i*th possible outcome - return

E(k) = expected return

The standard deviation is always just the square root of the variance

$$\sqrt{\sigma^2} = \sigma$$

This S.D is equal to "Total Risk"

The tighter, or more peaked, the probability distribution, the more likely it is that the actual outcome will be close to the expected value, and consequently, the less likely it is that the actual return will end up far below the expected return. Thus, the tighter the probability distribution, the lower the risk assigned to a stock.

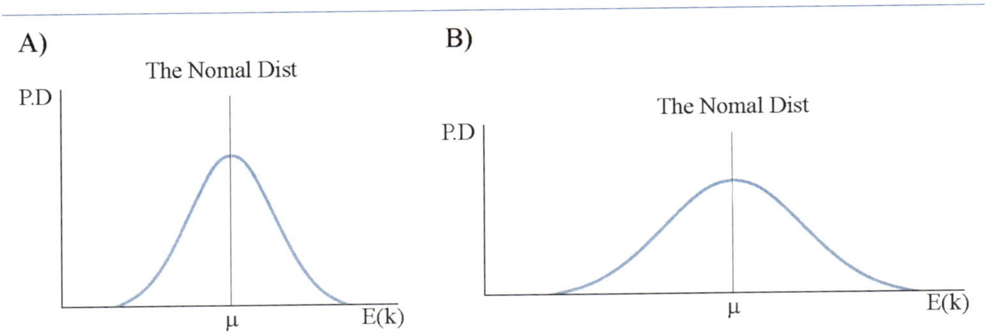

Example:

For following events and probability distribution of possible outcome, the total risk for a certain project or business is calculated as follows:

Event	P_i	K_i	P_i K_i	K_i-E(k)	$(K_i\text{-}E(k))^2$	$P_i(K_i\text{-}E(k))^2$
Loss	20%	-5%	-1%	-8.5%	0.72%	0.14
Settle	70%	5%	3.5%	1.5%	0.02%	0.02
Win	10%	10%	1%	6.5%	0.42%	0.04

$E_{(k)}$ = 3.5% Variance→ 0.2

$\therefore \sqrt{0.2} = 4.5\ \% \rightarrow$ S.D (Total Risk)

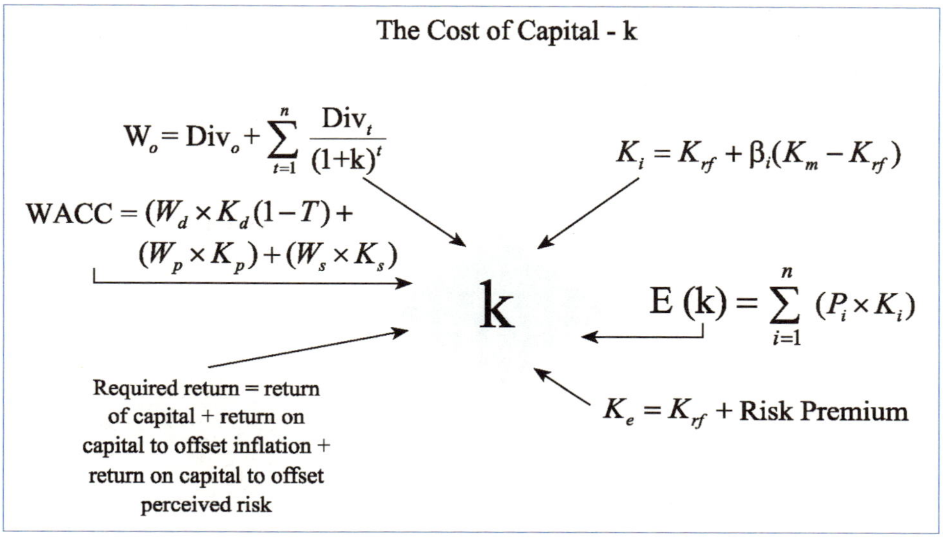

4. Portfolio's Return and Risk

1) Company Specific Risk vs. Market Risk

Most stocks tend to do well when the national economy is strong and badly when it is weak. Thus, even very large portfolios end up with a substantial amount of risk, but not as much risk as if all the money were invested in only one stock.

To see more precisely how portfolio size affects portfolio risk, consider the following Figure 8-1, which shows how portfolio risk is affected by forming larger and larger portfolios of randomly selected KOSPI stock. Standard deviations are plotted for an average one-stock portfolio, a two-stock portfolio, and so on, up to a portfolio consisting of all 1,500-plus common stocks that were listed on the KOSPI at the time the data were graphed. The graph illustrated that, in general, the riskiness of a portfolio consisting of average KOSPI stocks tends to decline and to asymptotically approach a limit as the size of the portfolio increases. In general, the standard deviation of a one-stock portfolio is approximately 28 percent. A portfolio that consisting of all stocks, which is called the market portfolio, would have a standard deviation of about 15.1 percent, which is shown as the horizontal dashed line in the figure 8-1.

FIGURE 8-1

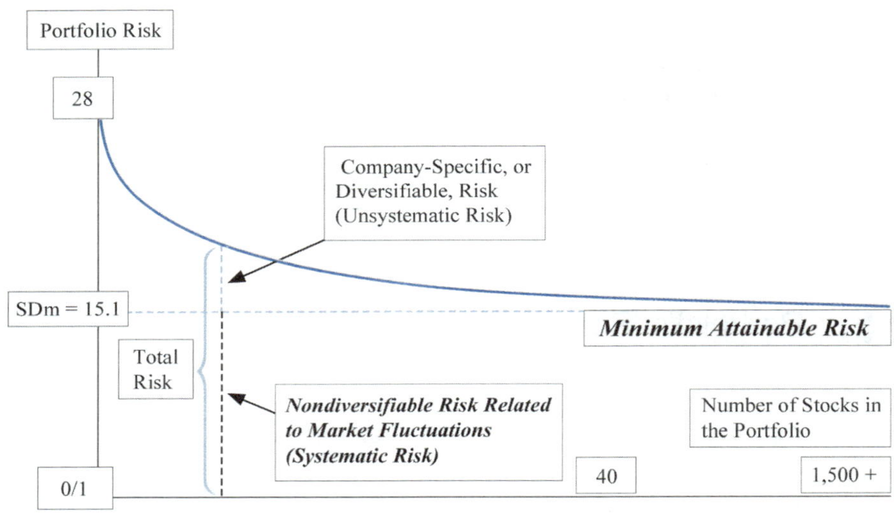

Thus, almost half of the riskiness inherent in an average individual stock can be eliminated if the stock is held in a reasonably well-diversified portfolio, which is one, containing 40 or more stocks. Some risk always remains, however, so it is virtually impossible to diversify away the effects of broad stock market movements that affect almost all stocks.

That part of the risk of a stock which can be eliminated is called diversifiable, or company-specific, or unsystematic risk; that part which cannot be eliminated is called non diversifiable, or systematic risk. That name is not especially important, but the fact that a large part of the riskiness of any individual stock can be eliminated is vitally important.

Company-Specific risk is caused by such things as lawsuits, strikes, successful and unsuccessful marketing programs, the winning and losing of major contracts, and other events that are unique to a particular firm. Since these events are essentially random, their effects on a portfolio can be eliminated by diversification-bad events in one firm will be offset by good events in another.

Market risk, on the other hand, stems from factors which systematically affect most firms, such as war, inflation, recessions, and high interest rates. As such most stocks will tend to be negatively affected by these factors; systematic risk cannot be eliminated by diversification.

We know that investors demand a premium for bearing risk; that is, the higher the riskiness of a security, the higher the expected return required to induce investors to buy (or to hold) it. However, if investors are primarily concerned with portfolio risk rather than the risk of the individual securities in the portfolio, how should the riskiness of an individual stock be measured?

The answer is, as provided by the Capital Asset Pricing Model (CAPM), is this: The relevant riskiness of an individual stock is its contribution to the riskiness of a well-diversified portfolio. In other words, the riskiness of Hilton's stock to a doctor who has a portfolio of 40 stocks, or to a trust officer managing a 150-stock portfolio, is the contribution that the Hilton stock makes to the portfolio's riskiness. The stock might be quite risky if held it by itself, but if most of its risk can be eliminated by diversification, then its relevant risk, which is its contribution to the portfolio's risk, may be small.

A simple example will help make this point clear. Suppose we are offered the chance to flip a coin once; if a head comes up, you win $20,000, but if it comes up tails, you lose $16,000. This is a good bet-the expected return is 0.5($20,000) + 0.5(-$16,000) = $2,000. However, it is a highly risky proposition, because we have a 50 percent chance of losing $16,000. Thus, we might well refuse to make the bet. Alternatively, suppose we were offered the chance to flip a coin 100 times and we would win $200 for each head but lose $160 for each tail. It is possible that we would actually flip about 50 heads and about 50 tails, winning a net of about $2,000. Although each individual flip is a risky bet, collectively we have a low-risk proposition, because most of the risk has been diversified away. This is the idea behind holding portfolios of stocks rather than just one stock, except that with stocks all of the risk cannot be eliminated by diversification- those risks related to broad, systematic changes in the stock market will remain.

Are all stocks equally risky in the sense that adding them to a well-diversified portfolio would have the same effect on the portfolio differently, so different securities have different degrees of relevant risk? How can the relevant risk of an individual stock be measured? The risk that remains after diversifying is market risk, or risk that is inherent in the market and it can be measured by the degree to which a given stock tends to move up and down with the market.

5. CAPM

1) CAPM (Capital Asset Pricing Model)

Investors require a higher return for taking on additional risk. While certain risks associated with individual projects or companies can be eliminated through **diversification** (i.e., the certain of a broad portfolio of different projects or companies), there is an underlying **market risk** that cannot be diversified away. In the context of securities, the risk of a diversified portfolio is determined by the market risk of the securities in the portfolio.

The **Capital Asset Pricing Model (CAPM)** (Professors *Harry Markowitz and William F. Sharpe)* is a commonly used model that relates a security's expected rate of return, and hence its associated cost of capital, to its contribution to the risk of a portfolio comprising the market as a whole - the theoretical **market portfolio**-using its **beta**(β_i), the risk-free rate, and the expected return of the overall market.

$$K_e = K_{rf} + \beta_i(K_m - K_{rf})$$

Where :

K_i = Required rate of return on equity

K_{rf} = Risk free rate (K^* + IP) $\therefore$ K^* : real rato of interest.

β_i = Beta Coefficient

Note : As Beta = 0, then $K_i = K_{rf}$

Beta = 1, then $K_i = K_m$

Note : (K_m - K_{rf}) represents market risk premium.

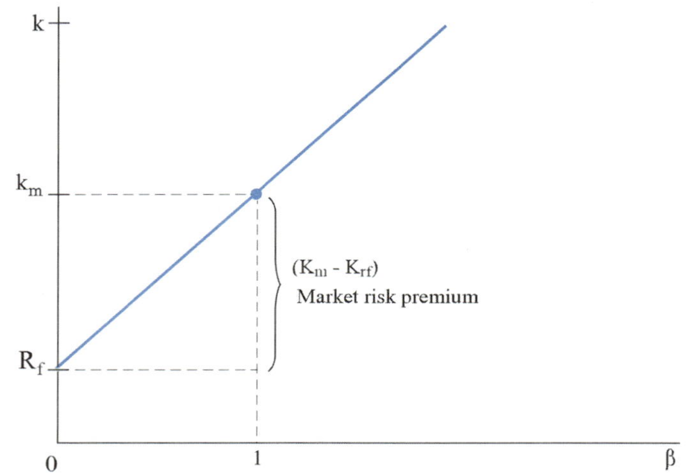

Note : IP ↑, SML Shift up.

$$\therefore K_i = K_{rf} + \beta_i(K_m - K_{rf})$$

↑ $K^* + IP$ (under K_{rf}) ↑ $K^* + IP$ (under K_{rf} in $(K_m - K_{rf})$)

- **Beta** is a statistical concept that measures the sensitivity of a security's return to the return of the market as a whole.
- The interest rate on long-term Treasury bonds (e.g., the 10-year Treasury) is typically used for the risk-free rate.

$$K_m - K_{rf}$$

- The difference is known as the market risk premium. While there is no precise way to measure this value, the market has returned approximately 7~8% above the 10-year Treasury bond on average over the past 70 years.

It should be noted that although CAPM approach appears to yield accurate, precise estimates of "K", there are actually several problems with it. First, if a firm's stockholders are not well diversified, they may be concerned with total risk rather than with market risk only; in this case the firm's true investment risk will not be measured by its beta, and the CAPM procedure will understate the correct value of "K". Further, even if the CAPM method is valid, it is hard to obtain correct estimates the inputs required to make it operational:

(1) There is controversy about whether to use long-term or short-term Treasury yields for K_{rf}.
(2) It is hard to estimate the beta that investors expect the company to have in the future.
(3) It is especially difficult to estimate the market risk premium. (Eugene F. Brigham, pp 305)

2) Beta

The Concept of BETA

The tendency of a stock to move with the market is reflected in its beta coefficient β, which is a measure of the stock's volatility relative to that of an average stock. Beta is a key element of the CAPM.

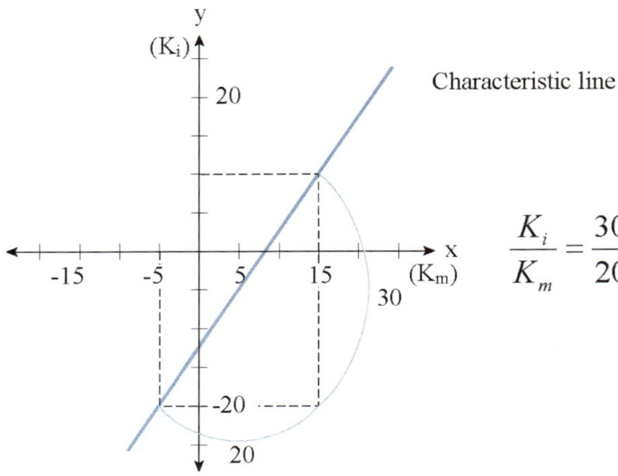

$$\frac{K_i}{K_m} = \frac{30}{20} = 1.5(\beta_i)$$

The best measure of risk of a security in a large portfolio is the beta(β) of the security.

$$\beta_i = \frac{COV(K_i, K_m)}{\sigma^2(K_m)} = \frac{Corr(K_i, K_m)\sigma_i, \sigma_m}{\sigma^2(K_m)}$$

$$\therefore \ COV(K_i, \ K_m) = \sum P_i[(K_i - \overline{E}(k)(K_m - \overline{E}(k)]$$

$\therefore \ \sigma^2(K_m)$ = the variance of the market

$$Since \quad COV(K_i, K_m) = Corr(K_i, K_m)\sigma_i \cdot \ \sigma_m$$

$$Corr(K_i, K_m) = \frac{COV(K_i, K_m)}{\sigma_i \cdot \ \sigma_m}$$

$$\rho_{i,m} = \frac{COV(K_i, K_m)}{\sigma_i \cdot \ \sigma_m}$$

$\rho_{i,m}$: correlation coefficient between each individual security and market average.

The lower ρ , the greater risk reduction as ρ = -1, maximum risk reduction.

$-1 < \rho < +1$

$0 < \rho < 1 \rightarrow$ risk reduction

$-1 < \rho < 0 \rightarrow$ risk reduction

$\rho = +1 \rightarrow$ No risk reduction

$\rho = -1 \rightarrow$ Max risk reduction

<Diversification>

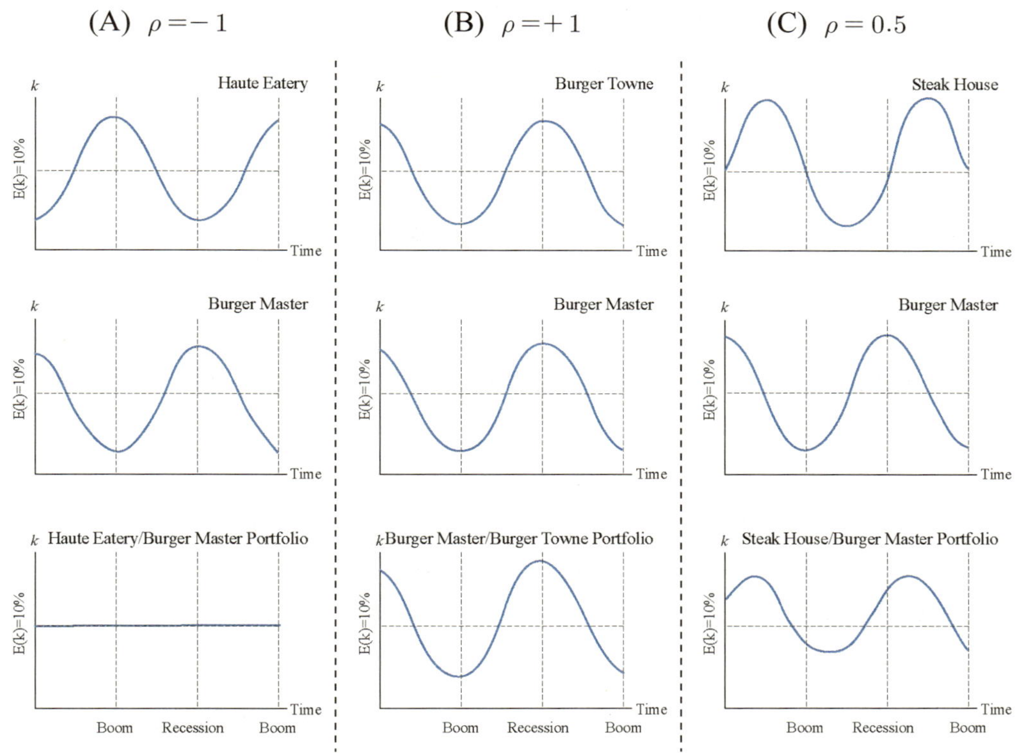

cov(Ki, Km) = $\rho_{K_i, K_m} \times \sigma_{K_i} \times \sigma_{K_m}$

since $\beta_i = \dfrac{COV(K_i,\ K_m)}{\sigma^2(K_m)}$

$$\beta_i = \frac{\rho_{K_i, K_m} \times \sigma_{K_i} \times \sigma_{K_m}}{\sigma^2_{K_m}}$$

So, $$\beta_i = \frac{\rho_{K_i, K_m} \times \sigma_{K_i}}{\sigma_{K_m}}$$

$$\boxed{\beta_i = \frac{\rho_{K_i, K_m} \cdot \sigma_{K_i}}{\sigma(K_m)}}$$

The basic intuition of beta is that it measure the sensitivity of a change in the return of an individual security to the change in return of the market portfolio.

One useful property is that the average beta acrosses all security, when weighted by the proportion of each security's market value to that of the market portfolios, is 1.

An average-risk stock is defined as one that tends to move up and down in step with the general market as measured by some index, such as the Dow Jones Industrials, the S&P 500, or the KOSPI. Such a stock will, by definition, have a beta, β, of 1.0, which indicates that, in general, if the market moves up by 10 percent, the stock will also move up by 10 percent, while if the market falls by 10 percent, the stock will likewise fall by 10 percent.

A portfolio of such β = 1.0 stocks will move up and down with the broad market average, and it will be just as risky as the averages. If β = 0.5, the stock is only half as volatile as the market- it will rise and fall only half as much- and a portfolio of such stocks will be half as risky as a portfolio of β = 1.0 stocks. On the other hand, if β = 2.0, the stock is twice as volatile as an average portfolio. The value of such a portfolio, you could quickly become a millionaire ‑or a pauper.

The following Figure 8-2 graphs the relative volatility of three stocks. This is so-called "characteristic lines". The data below the graph assumes that in 2116, the "market," defined as a portfolio consisting of all stocks, had a total return (dividend yield plus capital gains yield) of K_m = 10%, and stocks H, A, and L (for high, average, and low risk) also had returns of 10 percent. In 2117, the market went up sharply, and the return on the market portfolio was K_m = 20%. Returns on the three stocks also went up: H soared to 30%; A went up to 20%, the same as the market; and L only went up 15%. Now suppose that the market dropped in 2118, and the market return was K_m = -10%. The three stocks' returns also fell, H plunging to −30%, A falling to −10%, and L going down only to 0%. Thus, the three stocks all moved in the same direction as the market, but H was by far the most volatile; A was just as volatile as the market; and L was less volatile.

Its beta measures a stock's volatility relative to an average stock, which has β = 1.0 and stocks' betas can be calculated by plotting lines like those in Figure 8-2. The slopes of the lines show how each stock moves in response to a movement in the general market -indeed, the slope coefficient of such a "regression line" is defined as a beta coefficient. Beta for literally thousands of companies are calculated and published by Merrill Lynch, Value Line, and other organizations. If a higher-beta-than-average stock (one whose beta is greater than 1.0) is added to an average-beta portfolio, then the beta, and consequently the riskiness, of the portfolio will increase. Conversely, if a lower than average-beta is added to an average-risk portfolio, the portfolio's beta and risk will decline. Thus, since a stock's beta measures its contribution to the riskiness of a portfolio, beta is theoretically correct measure of the stock's riskiness.

Figure 8-2 Relative Volatility of Stocks H, A, and L. (Characteristic Line)

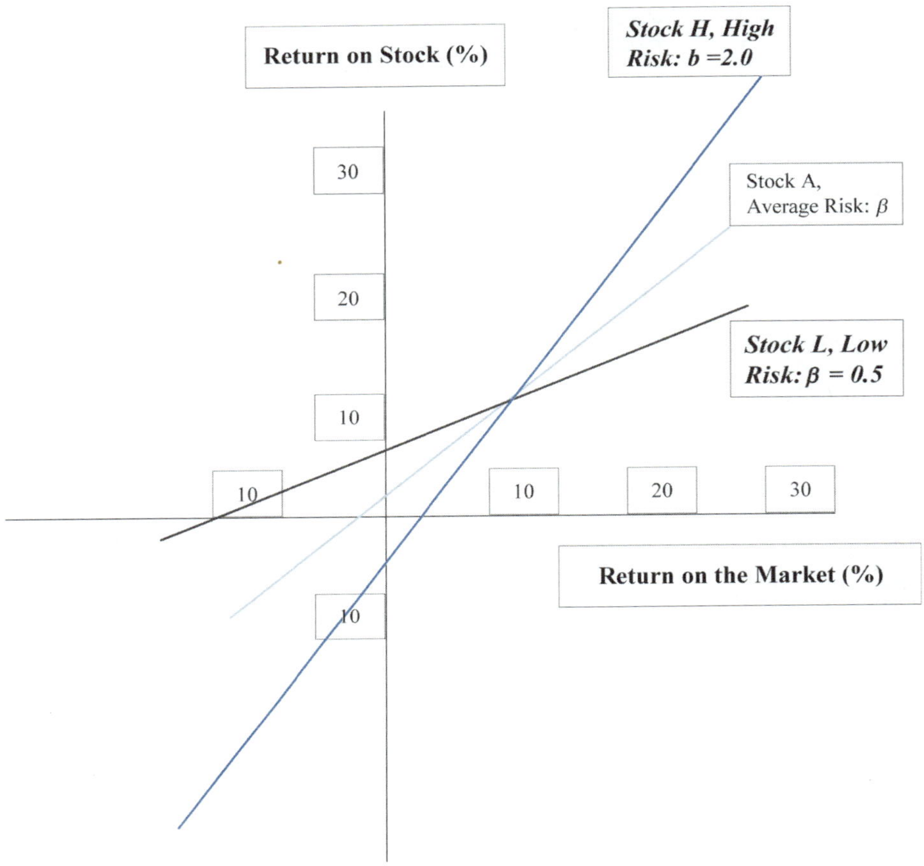

Return	H	A	L	Market
2116	10%	10%	10%	10%
2117	30%	20%	15%	20%
2118	-30%	-10%	0%	-10%

3) Relationship Between Risk and Return

It is common to argue that the expected return on a security should be positively related to its risk. That is, individuals will hold a risky security only if its expected return compensates for its risk. Now consider our world where all individuals:

(1) have homogeneous expectations and .

(2) all individuals can borrow and lend at the risk-free rate. All individuals hold the market portfolio of risky securities here. We have seen that the beta of a security is the appropriate measure of risk in this context. Hence, the expected return on a security should be positively related to its beta. This is illustrated in the above Figure 8-2. The upward-sloping line in the figure is called the Security Market Line (SML).

A. Beta of Zero. The expected return on a security with a beta of zero is the risk-free rate, R_f because a security with zero betas has no relevant risk, its expected return should equal the risk-free rate.

B. Beta of One. The equation ($K_e = K_{rf} + \beta_i(K_m - K_{rf})$) points out that the average beta across all securities, when weighted by the proportion of each security's market value to that of the market portfolio, is 1. Because the market portfolio is formed by weighting each security by its market value, the beta of the market portfolio is 1. Because all securities with the same beta have the same expected return, its expected return for any security with a beta of 1 is K_m, the expected return on the market portfolio.

C. Linearity. The intuition behind an upwardly-sloping curve is clear. Because beta is the appropriate measure of risk, high-beta securities should have an expected return above that of low-beta securities. The relationship between expected return and beta corresponds to a straight line.

Practice Question 8-1

We have following situation

Economic Situation	Probability(P_i)	Rate of Return(K_i)	P_i K_i	K_i-E(k)	$P_i(K_i\text{-}E(k))^2$
Recession	0.3	-10%	-3%	-20%	0.012
Recovery	0.4	10%	4%	0%	0
Boom	0.3	30%	9%	20%	0.012
			10%		$\sigma^2 = 0.024$

(1) What is $E_{(k)}$ of this project?

Expected value(mean)

(0.3 × -10%) + (0.4 × 10%) + (0.3 × 30%) = 10%

(2) What is $\sigma_{(k)}$ of this project?

$$\sigma^2 = \sum_{i=1}^{n} P_i (K_i - E(k))^2$$

$\sigma^2 = 0.024$

$\sigma = \sqrt{0.024} = 0.1549$

∴ 15.49

(3) If β is 0.6, K_m = 16%, R_f = 8%, K_i?

$K_i = K_{rf} + \beta_i (K_m - K_{rf})$

= 8% + 0.6 (16% - 8%)

= 0.128

∴ 12.8%

(4) Should we invest to this project?

Why? Or why not?

Answer is “No”

ROE = E(k) = 10% < Ke = 12.8%
Not a value creating investment!!

6. SML (Security Market Line)

Now, the figure 8-3 also shows a borrowing/lending line drawn from the risk-free rate through the market portfolio. This borrowing/lending line is another special line. It represents the risk and return combinations (where risk is measured by non-diversifiable risk) that any individual can achieve by investing in the market portfolio and borrowing or lending at K_{rf} as necessary. This special line is called the security market line or the market line for short.

The SML represents a no-effort risk/return benchmark or standard for individual projects or assets added to a diversified (market) portfolio. It is “no effort” because anybody can achieve any combination along it by investing in the market portfolio and borrowing or lending as necessary. It is a risk/return standard because it represents the borrowing/lending line through the best diversified portfolio (the market portfolio). It applies to individual projects or assets added to a diversified portfolio because we measure risk along it by non-diversifiable risk or beta.

The SML has very important implications for the evaluation of hotel projects. Since our hotel firm owners can achieve returns along the SML effortlessly on their own, any project that a hotel manager undertakes must earn a return (Return On Equity : ROE) for a given amount of risk (as measured by beta) at least as great as the return that the firm’s owners could earn for themselves by investing along the SML. Thus, the return along the SML represents the owner's opportunity cost or Ke for a particular level of risk (as measured by beta). We now have a way of determining what Ke is for a specific project. Since we also know how to estimate a project's expected return of E(k) (which is equivalent to the ROE for the owners investment in the project), we now have a model for helping us determine whether a project will create value (that is, whether it will generate an ROE > Ke).

FIGURE 8-3 Security Market Line (graph and equation)

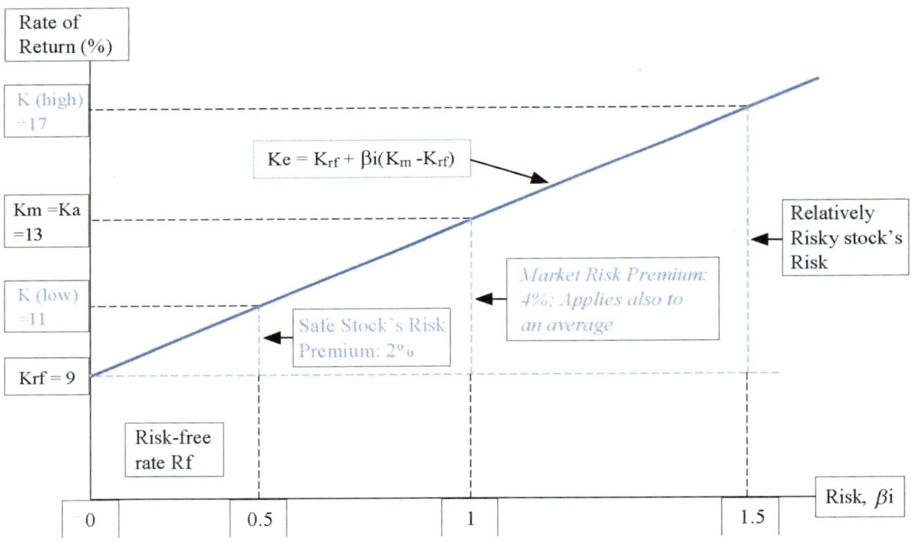

Evaluation of Investment Projects

The following figure 8-4 illustrates how the SML can be used to evaluate the desirability or value-creation potential of two hotel investment projects. Hotel A has an ROE/Beta combination which lies below the SML. This implies that the firm's owners could achieve a higher level of return for risk equal to beta A simply by investing along the SML. Thus, for hotel A, ROE a < Ke of a, and the hotel investment would be value destroying for the owners. Another way of saying this is that Hotel A would have an NPV <0.

FIGURE 8-4: USING SML

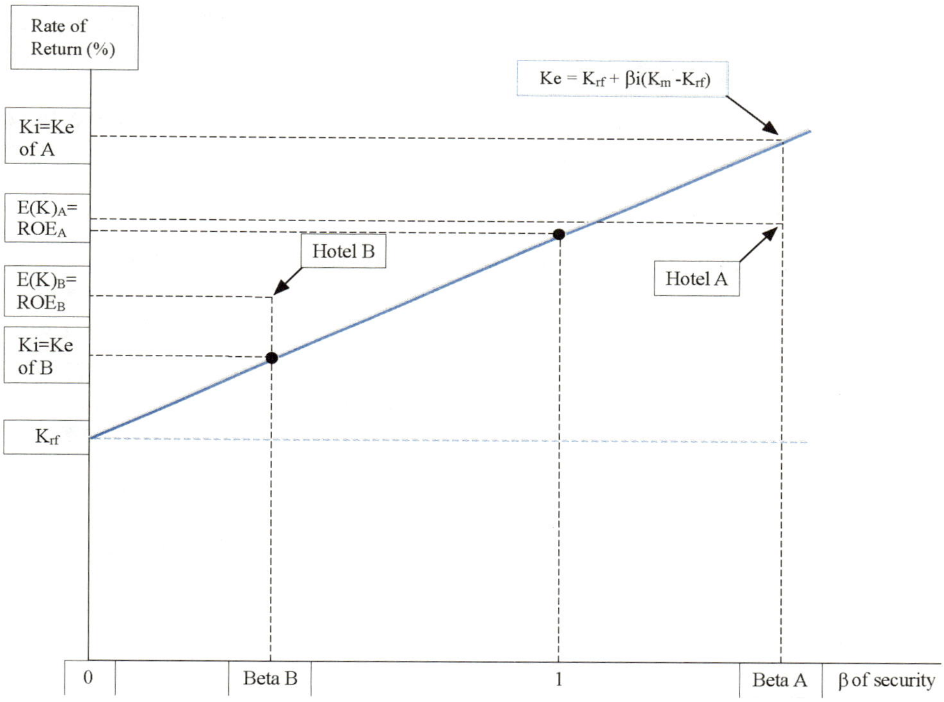

Hotel B, on the other hand, is expected to generate an ROE/beta combination that lies above the SML. Thus, the hotel B project offers the owners a higher rate of return for a given amount of risk (beta β) than the owners could achieve for themselves by investing along the SML. This project would do something for the owners that they could not easily do for themselves. Hotel B would generate an ROE (B) > Ke of (B) and thus would be value creating. Its NPV would be greater than zero.

From this example, it should be clear that any project or investment whose ROE/beta combination lies above the SML will be value creating (and have an NPV > O). Any project or investment whose ROE/beta combination lies below the SML will be value destroying (and have a NPV < 0). A project that lies on the SML will neither be value creating nor value destroying. It will have an ROE equal to Ke (NPV = 0) and the owners would be indifferent toward it.

Thus the SML represents a very important relationship, on that we need to quantify so that we can actually calculate Ke for a hotel project. Let's see the application of the model. As an example, suppose we are considering expanding a hotel by adding a new wing and we have estimated following information:

K_{rf} = 8%, K_m = 16%, Beta of the project (new wing) = 1.2

We could then estimate out owners' required rate of return, Ke, associated with the investment of their money in the new wing project:

$$\begin{aligned} Ke &= K_{rf} + (K_m - K_{rf})\ \beta\ (\text{new wing}) \\ &= .08 + [.16 - .08]\ 1.2 \\ &= 17.6\% \end{aligned}$$

This value indicates that our owners could effortlessly earn an expected return of 17.6% by investing in the financial markets at a risk equivalent to a beta of 1.2. Thus, for a project of the degree of risk of the new wing, the owner's opportunity cost is 17.6%. In order for the owners not to be adversely affected (that is, not have value destroyed), the project must earn a return of at least 17.6%. It must earn more than 17.6% if value is actually to be created.

7. B/L Line (Borrowing and Lending Line)

Concept: An investor could easily combine a risky investment with an investment in a riskless or risk-free security such as investment in government Treasury bill.

FIGURE 8-5: Borrowing and Lending Line

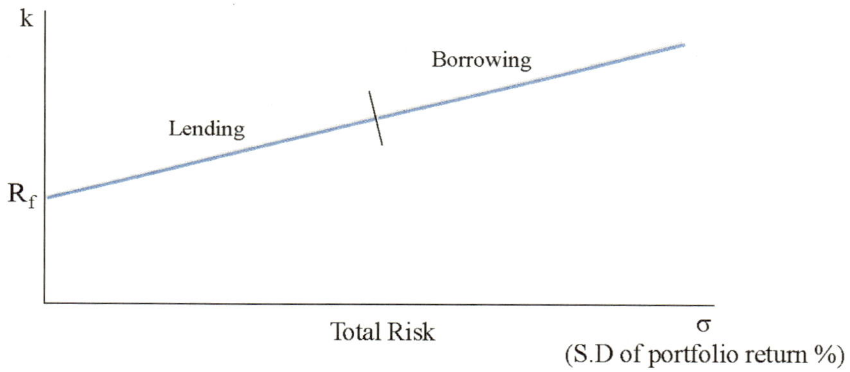

Practice Question 8-2

Michael is considering investing in the common stock of Sheraton. In addition, Michael will either borrow or lend at the risk free rate. The relevant parameters are

	E(K) on common stock of Sheraton	Guaranteed return on RF asset
Return	14%	10%
S.D	0.20	0

Suppose Michael chooses to invest a total of \$1,000, \$350 of which is to be invested in Sheraton and \$650 placed in the risk free rate.

The expected return on this total investment is simply a weighted average of two returns.

→ $(0.35 \times 0.14) + (0.65 \times 0.10) = 0.114 = 11.4\%$

Now, suppose that alternatively, Michael borrows \$200 at the risk-free rate "combining this with this original sum of \$1,000 he invests a total of \$1,200 in the Sheraton. Now his expected return would be

→ $(1.2 \times 0.14) + (-0.2 \times 0.10) = 0.148 = 14.8\%$

New S.D. is $(1.2 \times 0.2) = 0.24 = 24\%$

The S.D of 0.24 is greater than 0.20, the S.D of the Sheraton Hotel, because borrowing increases the variability of the investment.

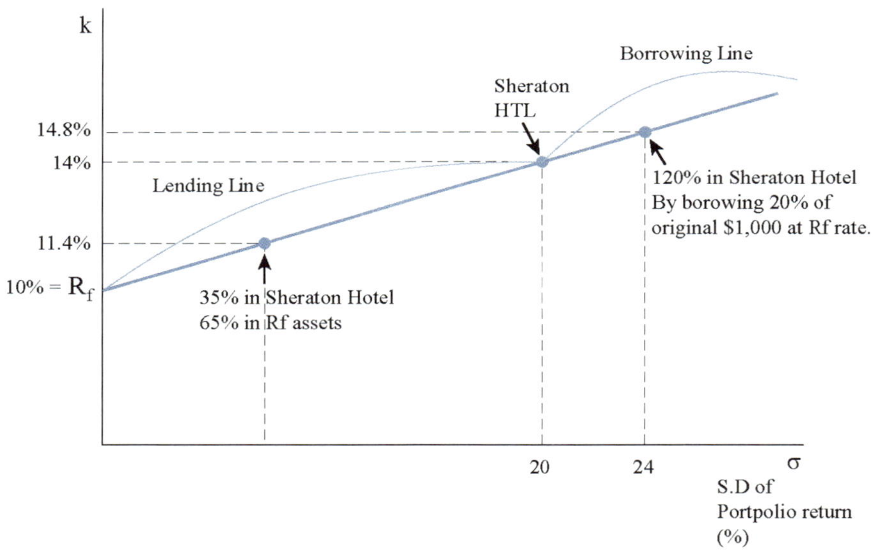

<Problem Solving>

* **Choosing among projects on the basis of expected return and total risk**

(1) Select project creating higher return and lower risk

(2) Domination

(3) Apply R_F

(4) Use B/L Line

* **Select higher B/L Line because it create higher return**

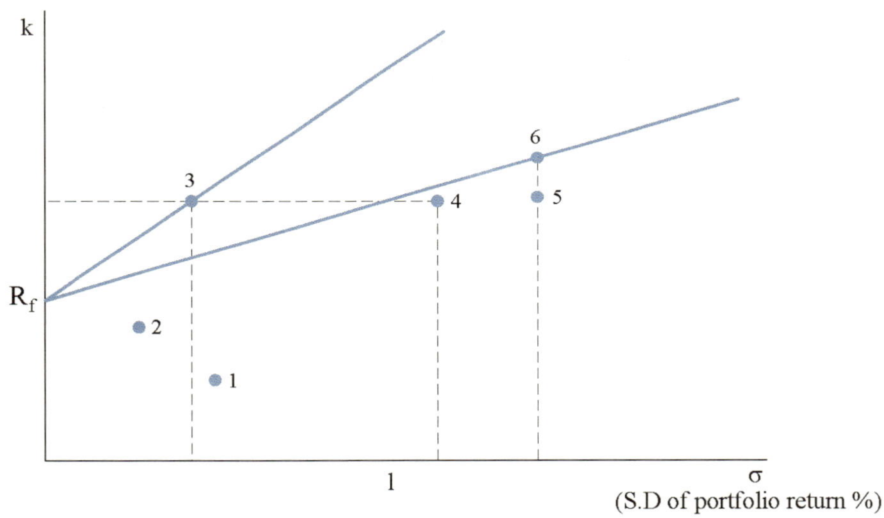

In this case, project 3 dominate all other project.

No mather what level of risk it takes, project 3 gets higher return than others.

Project 3 is selected.

▶▶▶Check Point

1. Risk simply means that the outcome or return that an investment will yield is uncertain.

2. If there is no risk involved, K_E will be equal to R_f.

3. The expected value measures the central tendency of a probability distribution.

4. The standard deviation is a measure of how much variability is possible in a set of outcomes.

5. Everything else being the same, to get a person to bear more risk, he or she must be offered a great expected return.

6. Regardless of their degree of aversion, investors choosing among potential investments will prefer the investment with the highest ballooning/lending line.

7. The risk of the market portfolio is non-diversifiable.

8. We say that beta is a relative measure of risk because it measures the risk of a project or investment relative to the risk of the market portfolio.

9. The sum of the probabilities in a probability distribution must be equal to one.

Practice Questions

Question 1

Use the security market line (graph and equation) to explain how a change in interest rates alters the equilibrium price of common shares. You may use any example you desire, but you must be precise. Be sure to carefully draw a graph and fully explain what you are attempting to display in your graph and equations.

Question 2

Briefly discuss how the *characteristic line* for any specific stock is determined. Specifically, explain the relationship between the line and the firm's market risk. Draw a graph representing the characteristic line. Carefully display both diversifiable and no diversifiable risk in your graph.

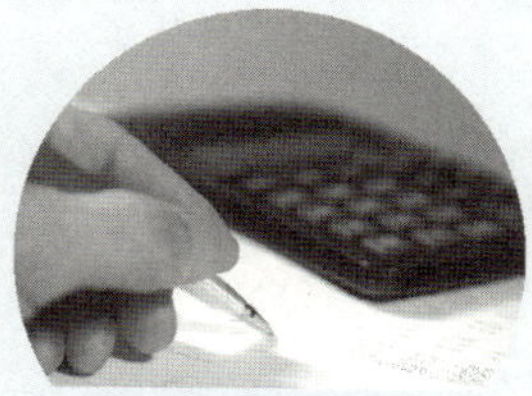

Chapter 09

Valuation of Investment

Chapter 09

Valuation of Investment

1. Characteristics of 3 Major Securities

Bond

- Par value or face value
- Less risky
- Coupon payment is fixed and predetermined
- Bond holder doesn't have voting rights
- Non payment of coupon can result in bankruptcy
- Requires refunding at maturity

Preferred Stock

- Preferred dividends are fixed and predetermined
- Non payment doesn't lead to bankruptcy
- No maturity date
- Preferred dividend is not tax deductible

Common Stock

- No fixed payment
- No maturity
- Possible dilution voting rights and control
- Expensive, risky
- Dividends are tax deductible

- Preemptive right : give existing common stockholders the opportunity to purchase new offfering to maintain their percentage of ownership.

Corporations raise capital in two primary forms-debt and common equity. We examine the valuation process for bonds, the principal type of long-term debt.

2. Security Valuation : Bond

A bond is a long-term promissory note issued by a business or governmental unit.

- Financial securities
- Factors determining security prices are;
  ① Amount of CF's
  ② Timing of CF's
  ③ Riskiness of CF's
- The discount rate (interest rate) takes into account to riskiness
- Price of security = PV of expected future CF's

1) Bond Valuation

(1) Bond

<Key Terminology>

Bonds:
- Coupon payment : The specified number of dollars of interest paid each period, generally each six months, on a bond.
- Coupon interest rate : The stated annual interest rate of interest on a bond.
- Par value : The stated face value of the bond ; it is usually set at $1,000.
- Maturity date : A specified date on which the par value of a bond must be repaid.
- Yield to maturity(YTM) : The rate of return earned on a bond if it is held to maturity.
- Yield to call(YTC) : The rate of return earned on a bond if it is called before its maturity.
- Call provision : A provision in a bond contract that gives the issuer the right to pay off the bonds under specified terms prior to the stated maturity date.

Coupon payment per Year = Coupon rate × Par value

$$\text{Current Yield} = \frac{Coupon\ payment\ per\ year}{Curent\ price}$$

Price = PV = PV of coupon payment + PV of par value

$$= \sum_{t=1}^{p} \text{coupon payment per period} \times \frac{1}{(1+\frac{ytm}{m})^t} + \text{per value} \times \left(\frac{1}{1+\frac{ytm}{m}}\right)^n$$

Where n = m × years to maturity

(m = # of payment per years)

Practice Question 9-1

20 year bond with 10% coupon rate paid semi-annually YTM for similar bonds are 8%

Assume par value = 1,000

What is the price of the bond?

$\Rightarrow$ Annual coupon payment = coupon rate × par value

= 0.1 × 1,000

= 100

m = 2

Coupon payment per period = $\frac{100}{2}$ = 50

YTM = 8%

V_y = Price of bond at t=0

$$PV_0 = \text{coupon per period} \times \sum_{t=1}^{n} \frac{1}{(1+\frac{ytm}{m})^t} + \text{par value} \times \frac{1}{(1+\frac{ytm}{m})^t}$$

When n = m × TTM (Time to maturity)

= # of coupon payment total

<Solution>

By Calculator,

$m = 2, \qquad i = \frac{k}{m} = \frac{8\%}{2} = 4\%$

press;

50	PMT
1,000	FV
8	i
40	n
Comp	PV

=1197.927

(1) Call provision

- Allow the company to pay off the bond before maturity 0
- Call premium = the price the company must pay if prior to maturity
  = usually higher than the per value
  the difference is the call premium
- Call protection premium
  = a bond cannot be called during the protection period

(2) Bond returns

1. YTM - Return if bond is held until maturity

$$V_B = \text{coupon pymt} + \text{per period} \times \sum_{t=1}^{n} \frac{1}{(1+\frac{ytm}{m})^t} + \text{par value} \times \frac{1}{(1+\frac{ytm}{m})^t} n = m \times TTM$$

2. YTC - Return if bond is called when it became callable

$$V_B = \text{coupon pymt} + \text{per period} \times \sum_{t=1}^{n} \frac{1}{(1+\frac{ytc}{m})^t} + \text{call price} \times \frac{1}{(1+\frac{ytc}{m})^n} n = m \times TTC$$

3\. HPR -Holding Period Return

- Return if bond is held to another investor prior to maturity

$$V_B = \text{coupon pymt + per period} \times \sum_{t=1}^{n} \frac{1}{(1+\frac{hpr}{m})^t} + \text{selling price} \times \frac{1}{(1+\frac{hpr}{m})^n} \quad n = m \times HP$$

Practice Question 9-1 **(continue-)**

20 TTM

n =2 (semi annual)

coupon rate = 10% ⇒ coupon pymt / period = 50

par value = 1,000

YTM = 8% ⇒ V_y = -1197.93

If the bond is callable after 5 yrs, what is the YTC with call price 1,100?

If you sell the bond for $300 after 10 yrs, what is your HPR?

m = 2, n = m× HP(Holding Period) = 2 ×10 = 20

m = 2, TTC = 5 n = 2 × 5 = 10

50	PMT
1,100	FV
10	n
-1197.93	PV
Comp	*i* =3.48%

YTC : I × m = 3.48% × 2 = 6.95%

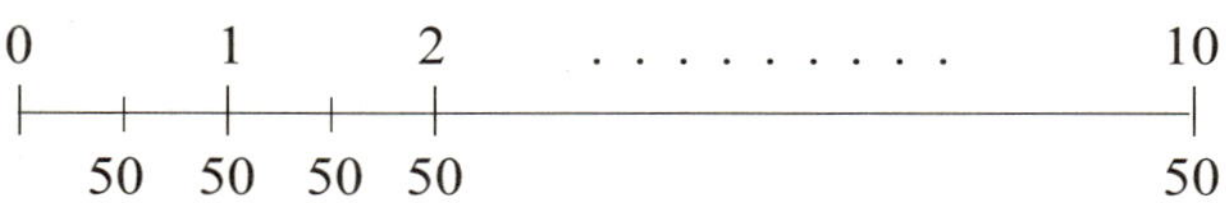

50	PMT	
900	FV	
-1197.93	PV	
20	n	
Comp	i	=3.27%

HPR = $i \times m \Rightarrow 3.27\% \times 2 = 6.54\%$

<Key Note> * **Bond price is a PV**

- Inverse relationship PV and interest rate

PV ↑ ⟶ i ↓

i ↑ ⟶ PV ↓

1. If YTM = coupon rate,
   the price = par value (at par)

2. If YTM > coupon rate,
   the price < par value (at discount)

3. If YTM < coupon rate,
   the price > par value (at premium)

∗Interest rate risk : Bond with long maturity.

⇒ Bond prices for bonds with long maturity have both a higher absolute (dollar)
change and higher relative (%) change when interest rate changed

∗Bonds with short maturity are subject to reinvestment risk

High coupon bond will have higher absolute price change when interest rate changes.

High coupon bond will have a higher relative price change when interest rate changes.

Practice Question 9-2

A	B
m = 2	m = 2
TTM = 20	TTM = 20
coupon rate 5%	coupon rate 10%
coupon per period $= \dfrac{0.05 \times 1{,}000}{2} = 25$	coupon per period $= \dfrac{0.1 \times 1{,}000}{2} = 50$
YTM 8%	YTM 8%

$m = 2,\qquad n = m \times TTM = 2 \times 40 = 40$

25 PMT

1,000 FV

40 n

8 i

PV = 703.11

Price A = ? B= 1197.93

If YTM goes up to 12%, what happens to bond price?

$$i = \frac{12\%}{2} = 6\%$$

Case of A	Case of B
25 PMT	50 PMT
1,000 FV	1,000 FV
40 n	40 n
.12	.12
New price for A = 473.38	New price for b= 849.54

Ⓐ Absolute price change

473.38 - 703.11 = -229.73

Ⓑ Absolute price change

849.54 -1197.93 = -348.39

$$\Rightarrow \% \text{ change} = \frac{\text{new - old}}{\text{old}}$$

Ⓐ $\frac{473.38 - 703.11}{703.11} = -32.67\%$

Ⓑ $\frac{849.54 - 1197.93}{1197.93} = -29.06\%$

3. Security Valuation: Common Stock & Preferred Stock

1) Common Stock Valuation

CS_s provides an expected future cash flow stream, and a stock's value is found in the same manner as the values of other financial assets-namely, as the PV of the expected future cash flow stream.

The expected CF_s consist of two elements.

(1) the dividends expected in each year.

(2) the price investors expect to receive when they sell the stock.

- the return of the original investment plus.
- a capital gain.

D_t = Dividend the stockholder expect to receive at the end of year t.

D_o : is the most recent dividend, which has already been paid.

P_0 = actual market price of the stock today.

P_t = expected price of the stock at the end of each year t.

g = expected growth rate in dividends as predicted by the marginal investor.

K_s = minimum, or required rate of return on the stock.

$\widehat{K_s}$ = expected rate of return which an investor who buys the stock actually expects to receive.

$\frac{D_1}{P_0}$ = expected dividend yield an the stock during the coming year.

$\frac{\widehat{P_1} - P_0}{P_0}$ = -expected capital gains yield.

$\widehat{K_s}$ = Expected total return.

= expected dividend yield $(\frac{D_1}{P_0})$ +

expected capital gain yield $(\frac{\widehat{P_1} - P_0}{P_0})$

Value of stock = $\widehat{P_0}$ = PV of expected future dividends

$$= \frac{D_1}{(1+K_s)^1} + \frac{D_2}{(1+K_s)^2} + \cdots\cdots \frac{D_\infty}{(1+K_s)^\infty}$$

$$= \sum_{t=1}^{\infty} \frac{D_t}{(1+K_s)^t}$$

(1) Stock Value with Zero Growth

= Dividends expected in future years are equal to some constant amount - that is, $D_1 = D_2 = D_3$ and so on.

Therefore, we can *drop the subscripts on D* and rewrite Equation as fallows.

$$\widehat{P}_0 = \frac{D}{(1+K_s)^1} + \frac{D}{(1+K_s)^2} + \cdots\cdots \frac{D}{(1+K_s)^\infty}$$

Therefore, a zero growth stock is a "perpetuity"

→ The value of the perpetuity is simply the payment divided by the discount rate

So. $\widehat{P}_0 = \dfrac{D}{K_s}$ if D = $1.15

K_s = 13.4%

them, $\widehat{P}_0 = \dfrac{1.15}{0.134}$ = $8.58

We could transpose the $\widehat{P}_0$ and the K_s in the above equation and solve for K_s to produce Equation.

$$K_s = \frac{D}{\widehat{P}_0}$$

(2) Normal Growth or Constant Growth.

$$D_t = D_o(1+g)^t$$

If allied food just paid a dividend of $1.15 (that is D_o = $1.15) and investor expects an 8%. growth rate,

the estimated dividend 1 year hence will be

$D_1 = \$1.15(1.08) = \$1.242$

$D_2 = \$1.242(1.08) = \$1.34 = 1.15(1.08)^2$

$D_t = D_o(1+g)^t$

If g is constant,

$$\hat{P}_0 = \frac{D_0(1+g)}{K_s - g} = \frac{D_1}{K_s - g}$$

(Gordon Model)

after Myron J. Gordon

Necessary condition for the derivation of Equation is that K_s is greater than g.

If not, the results will be meaningless.

→ inserting values into Equation, we find the value of the stock to be $23.00

$$\hat{P}_0 = \frac{\$1.15(1.08)}{0.134 - 0.08} = \frac{\$1.242}{0.054} = \underline{\$23.00}$$

2) Preferred Stock

- Pay a fixed dividend and does not have a maturity date
- Expected future CF's = dividend
- Evaluated on perpetuity

$$V_{Ps} = PV_t = \frac{PD_{TH}}{K_{PS}}$$

Ex) GM preferred stock

Dividend = Dividend rate × par value

Dividend = Dividend yield × price

Dividend = \$20 per year

Kps = 10%

Price today = $PV_0 = \frac{20}{0.1} = 200$

<Key Note>

⇒ Everybody wants to buy the stock, then

Price ↑, expected return ↓

⇒ Nobody wants to buy the stock, then

Price ↓, expected return ↑

(3) Factors affecting equilibrium stock price

- Inflation rate
- Risk aversion
- Stock's systematic risk (Beta)
- Stock's growth rate

Practice Questions

01 4 years remaining to maturity / interest annually

1,000 par value / 1 coupon interest rate 9%

a. What is YTM at current market price of 829

price = -829

par value = 1,000

coupon payment per period = coupon rate × par value

= 0.09 × 1000 = 90

TTM = 4 years

⇒ -829 PV

90 PMT

1000 FV

4 n

Comp i = 14.988 ≒ 15%

02 Issue of bond with ten year maturity, 1,000 par value, 10% coupon rate, semi-annual payment

a. Two years after the bond issued, rate of interest fell to 6%. What price would the bond sell?

Coupon payment per period: 1,000×0.1 → 100/2 = $50

TTM = 8 year left , n = 16

YTM_2 = 6%, 6/2 = 3%

1000 FV

50 PMT

16 n

3 i

Comp PV = 1,251.226

03 Common stock that paid a dividend of $2 last year.

Expect the dividend to grow 5% for the next 3 years.

Plus, buy the stock, hold it for 3 years. Then sell it.

a. Find expected dividend for each of next 3 years

That is calculate, D_1 D_2 D_3

Note the D_0 = $2

constant "g"

$D_t=D_0\times(1+g)^t$ (D_0 =2)

$D_1=2\times(1+0.05)^1=2.1$

$D_2=2\times(1+0.05)^2=2.205$

$D_3=2\times(1+0.05)^3=2.3153$

b. Discount rate 12% / first payment will occur 1 year from today D_1 D_2 D_3. Find PV of dividend stream / calculate PV of

① Using calculator,

∅	CFj
2.1	CFj
2.205	CFj
2.3153	CFj
12	*i*
	NPV ⇒ 5.2808

c. You expect the price of stock 3 years from now to be $34.73

That is, you expect P_3 to equal $ 34.73.

Discount 12% / what is PV of this expected future stock price?

(PV of $ 34.73)

34.73 FV

3 n

12 i

Comp PV = 24.72

d. If you plan to buy the stock, hold it for 3 years, and then sell it for $34.73

What is the most you should pay for it?

0	1	2	3
0	0.1	2.205	2.3153
			+ 34.73
			37.0453

∅ CFj

2.1 CFj

2.205 CFj

37.0453 CFj

12 I

Comp PV = 30.0009 × 30.01

04 If Ks = .15 $D_0 = \$2$, Expected g = -5%

a. What will be the stock value?

$D_1 = D_0 \times (1+g)^1$

$2 \times (1 - 0.05)) = 1.9$

$$P_0 = \frac{D_0(1+g)}{Ks - g} = \frac{D_1}{Ks - g} = \frac{1.9}{.15 - (0.05)} = \frac{1.9}{0.2} = 9.5$$

b. If g = 0%, $D_1 = 2$ Then what is the stock value?

$$P_0 = \frac{2}{0.15} = 13.33$$

Practice Questions

01 Harland Co's last dividend was \$3.50. If earnings and dividends are expected to grow at a constant 7%, and investor's required rate of return is 15%, what is the price of Harland's common stock?

a. \$17.02
b. \$25.81
c. \$31.26
d. \$37.75
e. \$46.81

02 The beta (b) of Sigma Corp.'s common stock is 1.25. If the market risk premium is 3% and the return on the market is 11%, what is the required rate of return on Sigma Corp.'s common stock?

a. 11.75%
b. 12.50%
c. 13%
d. 14.5%
e. not enough information given

03 The beta (*B*) of a stock

a. Measures the movement of the stock with respect to the market.
b. Represents no diversifiable risk of the stock
c. Is the best measure for the risk of a stock held in isolation?
d. Two of the above
e. All of the above

04 Using the following data, what is the price of Marriott's common stock?

> Beta = 2.0 Market return = 10% D1 =0.55
> 3 months T-Bill (rf) = 5% g (growth) -6%

a. $1.25
b. $2.62
c. $4.31
d. $6.25
e. not enough information given

Answers to the Practice Problems:

Answer Keys E, A, D(AC), B

[Advanced Issue]

Now, let's take another advanced question. "*Changes In Interest Rates Alter The Equilibrium Price Of Common Shares.*"

We have been hearing that the government is increasing interest rates and that this increase is leading to the price changes we have seen in the stock market. As a specific example, what will an increase in the rate on Treasury Bills from 9% to 11% do to the price of a stock that sells for $30.00? The stock has a growth rate predicted to be 7%, a $2.40 dividend expected this year, and a beta of 1.5 (there is no change in the market risk premium).

NOTE:

$Po = D1 \;/\; (Ks - g)$

$Ks = (D1 \;/\; Po) + g$

$Ks = K_{rf} + \beta(Km - K_{rf})$

$Km - Rf$ is market risk premium (RP_M)

So, $Ks = (2.4/\$30) + .07 = .15$

$.15 = .09 + (1.5)\,(RP_M)$, so $RP_M = .04$

Now, interest rate has been changed to 11%.

$Ks = .11 + (1.5)\,(.04)$

$\quad = .17$

$Po = 2.4 \;/\; (.17 - .07) = \$24.00$

As we have seen above formula, for each point investors expect a greater return which drives the price of our stock down, shift the SML up!

Chapter 10

Capital Structure

Chapter 10 Capital Structure

1. Capital Structure

THE ASSETS of the firm are on the left-hand side of the balance sheet. These assets can be thought of as current and fixed. Fixed assets are those that will last for a long time, such as a building. Some fixed assets are tangible, such as machinery and equipment. Other fixed assets are intangibles, such as patents, trademarks, and the quality of management. The other category of assets, current assets, comprises those that have short lives, such as inventory. The meats that your hotel has purchased but has not yet sold is are part of its inventory. Unless we have over-purchasing, it will be served in our hotel or restaurant shortly.

Before a company can invest in an asset, it must obtain financing, which means that it must raise the money to pay for the investment. The forms of financing are represented on the right hand side of the balance sheet. A firm will issue (sell) pieces of paper called debt (loan agreements) or equity shares (stock certificates). Just as assets are classified as long-lived or short-lived, so too are liabilities. A short-term debt is called a current liability. Short-term debt represents loans and other obligations that must be repaid within one year. Long-term debt is a debt that does not have to be repaid within one year. Shareholders' equity represents the difference between the value of the assets and the debt of the firm. In this sense, it is a residual claim on the firm's assets.

1) Managing Capital Structure

Financial arrangement determines how the value of the firm is sliced up. The persons or institutions that buy debt from the firm are called creditors. The holders of equity shares are called shareholders.

Sometimes it is useful to think of the firm as a pie. Initially, the size of the pie will depend on how well the firm has made its investment decisions. After a firm has made its investment decisions, it determines the value of its assets (e.g., its building, land, and inventories). The firm then determines its capital structure. The firm might initially have raised the cash to invest in its assets by issuing more debt than equity; now it can consider changing that mix by issuing more equity and using the proceeds to buy back some of its debt. Financing decisions like this can be made independently of the original investment decisions. The decisions to issue debt and equity affect how the pie is sliced.

The size of the pie is the value of the firm in the financial market. We can write the value of the firm, V as V = B + S where B is the value of the debt and S is the value of the equity. If so, the goal of the financial manager will be to choose the ratio of debt to equity that makes the value of the pie-that is, the value of the firm. How do financial managers create value?

A. The firm should try to buy assets that generate more cash than they cost.

B. The firm should sell bonds and stocks and other financial instruments that raise more cash than they cost.

Thus, the firm must create more cash flow than it uses. The cash flow paid to bondholders and stockholders of the firm should be higher than the cash flows put into the firm by the bondholders and stockholders. To see how this is done, we trace the cash flow the firm to the financial markets and back again.

Suppose we begin with the firm's investment activities. These include generating the working capital necessary to produce and sell goods and services, and the purchase of fixed assets. To finance its investment the firm sells debt and equity shares to participants in the financial markets. This results in cash flows from the financial markets to the firm. This cash is invested in the investment activities of the firm by the firm's management. The cash generated by the firm is paid to shareholders and bondholders. The shareholders receive cash in the form of dividends; the bondholders who lend funds to the firm receive interest and the initial loan is repaid, principal. Not all of the firm's cash is paid out. Some is retained, and some is paid to the government as taxes.

Over time, if the cash paid to shareholders and bondholders is greater than the cash raised in the financial market, value will be created.

2. Leverage

Most hotel projects are built with borrowed funds. It is extremely important to understand how leverage can work for a hotel project (positive leverage) and against a hotel project (negative leverage). Generally, the more debt there is in a hotel project the greater the leverage but also the greater the need for reliable cash flow to service the debt. Thus most hotel firms in which the seasonality of business can cause wide swings in cash flow from year to year may wish to consider leveraging the property to a lesser degree.

Positive financial leverage operates when the hotel investor or owner can borrow funds at a lower rate in interest than the rate of return the project earns. Under positive leverage the more the investor or owner can borrow, the more the return on the investment increases.

The following example shows how leverage works in the hotel industry. A group of investors have $300,000 to invest in a hotel project. They can purchase a small hotel for the $300,000 cash or use the money to make a 30 percent down payment on a $1 million hotel borrowing the remaining $700,000 at 12 percent for 20 years. Assuming that each project can generate a 15 percent return before debt service and income taxes the hotel property leveraged with 12 percent debt would generate the higher return to the investors or owners. The result is that in the first year, the all-cash deal would return $45,000 at a 15 percent return on the investors' investment, and the leveraged project would return $57,509 at a 19.17 percent return on the investors' investment. (See Exhibit 10-1 for the detailed calculation of these rates of return.)

As this simplified example demonstrates, by borrowing to help finance the project, the investor or owner increases the return on the equity actually invested. What happens if the estimate on earnings was overly optimistic? For example instead of a 15 percent return on the total investment, the project returns only 10 percent. Then, the return on total investment on the borrowed funds decreases significantly when compared to the all-cash investment hotel project. The total return on the all-cash deal will be $30,000, or 10 percent, on the investors' investment while the total return on the leveraged hotel project would be $7,509, or 2.51 percent, on the investment. This is an example of how negative leverage operates. (See Exhibit 10-1 for calculations and assumptions.)

On the other hand, an incremental increase in the rate of return above what is expected will significantly increase the return on investment for the leveraged investor of owner. For example, if earnings on the hotel investment increased to 20 percent of the total investment, the all-cash project return would be $60,000, or 20 percent, on the investors' investment, while the return on the leveraged project would be $107,509, or 35.84 percent on the investment. (See Exhibit 10-2)

The above examples show how leverage would operate for one year. The same concept would apply over a number of years and would include consideration of any appreciation in value of the hotel property over time. Thus understanding how leverage operates in the hotel development. This knowledge also explains why so many investors and owners have lost fortunes in hotel development when the financial leverage operates in a negative fashion.

Appreciation and Equity Build-Up

Predicting the future appreciation of a hotel property is one of the most difficult financial forecasts. Appreciation is simply the value of the property increasing over time. A real increase in the value of a hotel property can be due to the improvement of the surrounding area, thus increasing demand for the hotel property. This is different from property values increasing solely because of inflation.

One main reason why appreciation is so speculative in planning a hotel project is that so much of a hotel firm's value depends on providing satisfactory service. Because the quality of this service is important to persuading a guest to return to property, the property's management can influence the value of the underlying real estate either positively or negatively to a much greater extent than other real estate ventures that merely provide just space for rent.

EXHIBIT 10-1 Examples of Financial Leverage

Investor Return at 15%	
All Cash	**Leverage**
$300,000 Purchase Price	$300,000 Down Payment
	700,000 Mortgage
	$1,000,000 Purchase Price
$300,000	$1,000,000
× 15% (Rate of Return)	× 15% (Rate of Return)
$45,000 Profit Before Taxes	$150,000
	92,491* Less Debt Service
	57,509 (Profit Before Taxes)

Rate of Return in the Above Example	
All cash	**Leverage**
$45,000 ÷ 300,000 = 15%	57,509 ÷ 300,000 = 19.17%

Investor Return at 10%	
All Cash	**Leverage**
$300,000	$300,000 Downpayment
× 10% (Rate of Return)	700,000 Mortgage
$30,000 Profit Before Taxes	$1,000,000
	1,000,000
	× 10%
	100,000
	92,491* Less: Debt Service
	$7,509 (Profit Before Taxes)

Rate of Return in the Above Example	
All Cash	**Leverage**
$30,000 ÷ 300,000 = 10%	7,509 ÷ 300,000 =2.51%

Investor Return at 20%	
All Cash	**Leverage**
$30,000	$1,000,000
× 20% (Rate of Return)	× 20% (Rate of Return)
$60,000 Profit Before Taxes	$200,000
	92,491* Less: Debt Service
	$107,509 Profit Before Taxes

Rate of Return in the Above Example	
All Cash	**Leverage**
$60,000 ÷ 300,000 = 20%	$107,509 ÷ 300,000 = 35.84%

Contrary to what many people believe, inflation alone does not cause the underlying value of hotel properties to increase. As demand increases for hotel properties, so do the prices for the properties, regardless of the inflationary influences (although there is no question that inflation can influence the acceleration of values). For instance in Texas during the past few years, hotels have not increased in value, but have actually decreased as the market remains depressed from the collapse of oil prices and previous overbuilding of hotel properties. Therefore, the underlying value of a hotel property will either increase or decrease based on the supply and demand for that property, which are influenced by many factors, both local and national.

Historically, the underlying value of hotel firms has exceeded the inflation rate. Certainly, an owner or investor desires that the value of the hotel project exceeds the inflation rate. Many investors accept a smaller cash flow return from a hotel firm if they expect the future demand for the property to increase significantly over time.

Therefore, when projecting a total return from an investment in a hotel project, it is important to analyze not only the return from operations but also the projected return the investor will receive from the sale of the property. In fact, many hotel projects have been syndicated to investors where the entire rate of return was based on the projected sale of the property influenced by the increase in value of the land and building.

"Equity buildup" is another indirect form of appreciation. Because a hotel property is typically financed by some type of mortgage the loan is reduced over the years from the cash flow generated by the property's operations.

Therefore, even if the property is eventually sold for its original cost and the cash flow from operations was just sufficient to service the property, the investors would receive cash payments exceeding their original investment from the sale of the property based on the mortgage loan having been paid down.

But what happens if the hotel property cannot be sold at its original price but instead can only be sold for the balance remaining on the mortgage? In this case, taxable gain may result because the depreciation taken on the hotel property will cause the basis to the investor to be less than the redeeming value of the mortgage. This creates a taxable gain without generating any cash to pay the taxes owed.

<Key Note>

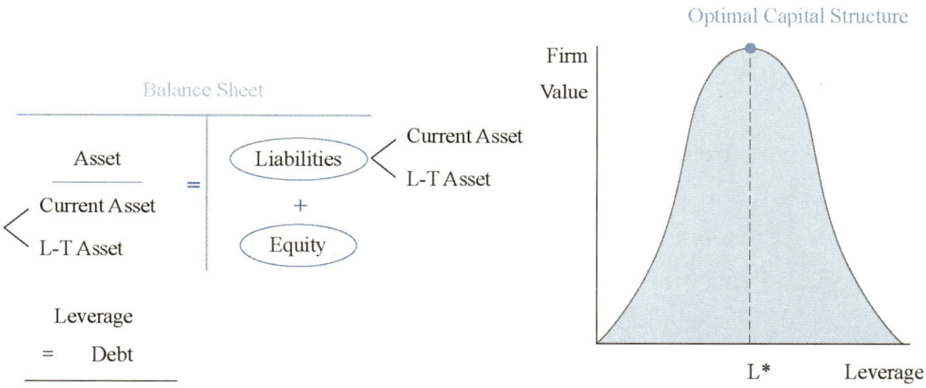

$$\text{Leverage} = \frac{\text{Debt}}{\text{Debt} + \text{Equity}}$$

"Leverage" occurs when the use of capital secured from creditors produces a greater return than that needed to cover the cost of the liability.

★ Under these condition, the exceeded return occurs to the stockholders.

Ex) Let's think about following 3cases!

The values of Return and Equity$\left(\frac{NI}{Eq}\right)$ for three cases are different because of different amount of debt and bond rates.

① Without Debt

All capital of Ⓐ company has been obtained by issuing stock.

B/S

Assets · · · · · $3,000,000 Equity · · · · · $3,000,000

I/S

Income from operation · · · · $1,000,000
(less) income tax(0.34) · · ·($3,40,000)
Net income $660,000

$$ROE = \frac{NI}{Eq} = \frac{660,000}{3,000,000} = 22\%$$

② W/$500,000 debt (15% bonds)

B/S

Assets · · · · · $3,000,000 Debt · · · · · $500,000
Equity · · · · · $2,500,000

I/S

Income from operation · · · $1,000,000
(Less) L-T debt interest · · · ($75,000) -15% of 500,000
income before tax $925,000
(Less) income tax (0.34) ($314,500)
NI $610,500

$$ROE = \frac{610,500}{2,500,000} = 24.4\%$$ Maximum of ROE, choose "ⓑ"

③ W/$500,000 debt (40% bonds)

B/S

Assets · · · · · $3,000,000 Debt · · · · · $500,000
Equity · · · · · $2,500,000

I/S

Income from operation · · · · $1,000,000
(Less) L-T debt interest · · · ($200,000) -40% of 500,000
income before tax $800,000
(Less) income tax (0.34) ($272,000)
NI $610,500

$$ROE = \frac{528,500}{2,500,000} = 21.1\%$$

Practice Question 10-1

Finding Interest rate, Net Income to meet required ROE (Return On Equity)

B/S

Assets	\$3,000,000	Liability	\$500,000
		Equity	\$2,500,000

I/S

Income from operation	\$1,000,000
(Less) L-T Debt interest	(166,666)
IBT(Income Before Tax)	(B)
Tax(0.34)	(C)
NI	(A)

Question:

To make ROE (Return On Equity) to 22%, find interest rate, Income Before tax, and Net income to complete the above Income Statement.

Solution:

1) Interest rate → 500,000 x X =166,666 X = 33.3%

2) A) $ROE = \frac{NI}{Eq} = 0.22 = \frac{NI}{2,500,000}$

NI = 550,000

B) IBT x (1 - 0.34) = NI (550,000)

IBT = 833,333

C) SO, Tax is 283,333 (833,333 × .34 or 833,333 - 550,000)

3. WACC (Weighted Average Cost of Capital)

A popular method of deriving the discount rate to use in a hotel project is the weighted cost of capital approach. This method combines the debt service factor along with the investor's desired rate of return in proportion to the total project cost. This method is most effective when dealing with hotel projects where equity contributions are from limited partners.

***Weighted Average Cost of Capital (WACC)**

$$WACC = Wd \times Kd \times (1 - T) + (Wp \times Kp) + (Ws \times Ks)$$

Wd = weighted of debt
Wp = weighted of preferred stock
Ws = weighted of common stock
Kd = cost of new debt
Ks = cost of retained earning
Kc = cost of common stock
Wd = cost of preferred stock
T = marginal tax rate

- Cost of external debt = market internal rate (YTM)
- Cost of new debt(Kd) = takes into account flotation costs
- Net proceed to firm = selling price - flotation cost

⇒ (1) To compute the Kd

1. Similar to computing UITM
   → PV = price of Bond − flotation cost
   = net proceed to the firm

⇒ (2) To compute the Kp

$$Kp = \frac{Dp}{\text{Net proceed(price - flotation cost)}}$$

⇒ (3) To compute Ks

1. SML: $Ks = K_{rf} + \beta_i(K_m - K_{rf})$
2. Dividend yield x capital gain yield

   If "g" is constant, capital gain yield is "g"

   (g= growth rate)

$$Ks = \frac{D_1}{P_0} + g$$

$$Ks - g = \frac{D_1}{p_0}$$

$$P_o = \frac{D_1}{K_s - q}$$

$D_1 = D_0 \times (1+g)$

Practice Questions 10-2

1. X Corporation:

Assets	Claims
Bonds	$200,000
Preferred (10%)	50,000
Equity	150,000
	$400,000

Where this firm pays a 15 % rate of interest on new debt and has a beta of 1.41. The corporate tax rate is 34 % and the risk premium on the market is 8.5%, and the current Treasury bill rate is 11 %. What is WACC?

Solution:

Bond:	\$200,000
P.D(10%) (Preferred stock Dividend)	\$50,000
Equity	\$150,000
	\$400,000
Interest rate on debt	= 0.15 .
Tax rate	= 0.34 .
Rf	= 0.11 .
Risk premium on the market	= 0.085 .
β	= 1.41 .

$$\begin{aligned} WACC &= \{Wd \text{ X } Kd\ (1\text{-}T)\} + (Wp \text{ X } Kp) + (Ws \text{ X } Ks) \\ &= \{0.50 \text{ X } 0.15\ (1\text{-}0.34)\} + (0.123 \text{ X } 0.10) + (0.375 \text{ X } Ks) \end{aligned}$$

$$\begin{aligned} Ks &= K_{RF} + \beta_i\ (K_m - K_{RF}) \rightarrow K_m - K_{RF}\text{: Risk premium on the market} \\ &= 0.11 + 1.41 \text{ X } 0.085 \\ &= 0.23 \end{aligned}$$

$$\begin{aligned} WACC &= \{0.50 \text{ X } 0.15\ (1\text{-}0.34)\} + (0.123 \text{ X } 0.10) + (0.375 \text{ X } 0.23) \\ &= 14.9\% \end{aligned}$$

4. Optimal Capital Structure

- The particular mix of debt and equity that a hotel firm uses to finance its asset structure also has a potential effect on owner's value.
- Because interest payments on debt are tax deductible and dividend payment are not, debt financing has the built-in advantage that some of the costs of borrowing are shared by the government in the form of reduced taxes.

- This interest tax shield represents a contribution to cash flow that the owners would not gain if the firm did not issue debt.
- Thus, the use of debt can make a direct contribution in increasing the present value of all future risky dividends since increasing cash flow means increasing ability to pay future dividends.

Problem? Yes.

- The larger the debt is used the more variable or risky the cash flows to the owners become.
- This increased risk is accomplished by a greater expected Return on Equity to the owner; increase the chances of the firm's suffering financial distress. In addition, as the probability of bankruptcy is perceived, creditors begin taking actions (including legal action) to protect their claims to the firm cash flows.
- If these costs are greater enough, it will offset the benefit of the interest tax shield.
- Theoretically, there is a certain point that makes a firm to maximize its value (by using debt and equity financing). We called the situation "Optimal Capital Structure".
- However, there is not much "competitive advantage" although hotel manager wants to operate his/her firm at this optimal level of debt and equity. This is simply because there are no entry barriers to prevent other hotel firms from operating at their optimal level. On the other hand, if you do not operate your firm at this point, you will get competitive disadvantage!

What do we need to do?

Therefore, we, strategic hotel managers, should focus on operation and also should hold the optimal capital structure to get "competitive advantage" in our competitive business environment.

1) Target Capital Structure

Optimal Capital structure = ideal structure
(Minimize WACC & Maximize stock price)
- Trade off of risk and return
  Higher debt ratio: benefit from the tax deduction of interest expense
  Higher debt ratio: the firm becomes more risky.

⇒ capital structure decision is to determine this trade off

Target Capital structure
= determined by management

2) Factors to be Considered

1. Risk: risk of a firm without debt
2. Tax position
3. Financing flexibility: ability to raise capital in average condition
4. Management conservativeness & aggressiveness

Business risk

1. Business climate
   - Variability in sales
2. Operating structure
   - The use of fixed cost
   - Variability of cost (operating structure)

Financial Risk

- additional risk due to use of debt

Goal is to maximize price or minimize WACC is NOT to maximize EPS.

5. Capital Structure Theories

1. It exist an optimal capital structure.
   -↗ debt ratio, ↗ tax benefit form debt
   -↗ debt ratio, ↗ cost of financial distress

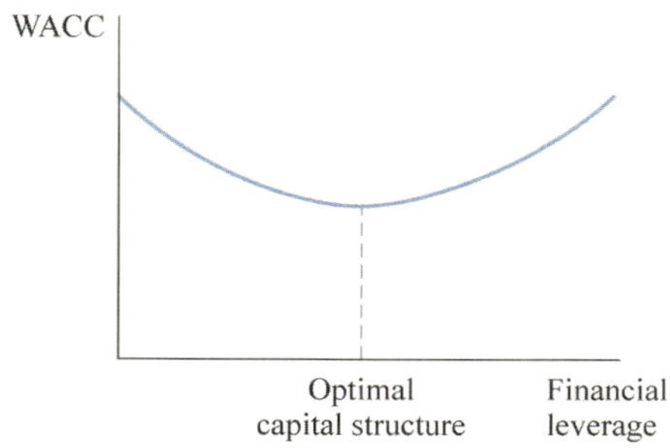

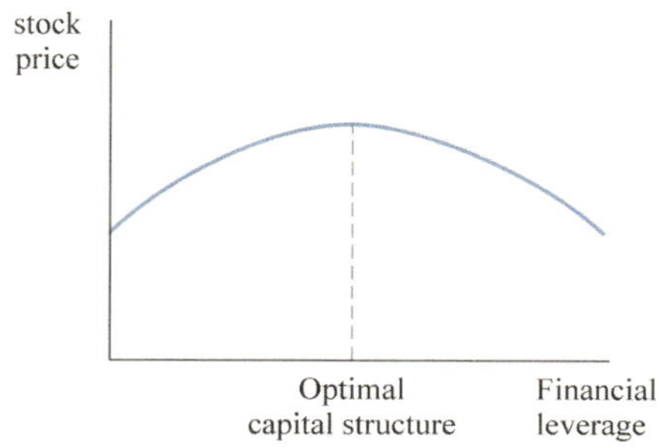

2. Trade off between tax benefits of interest expense and the cost of financial stock.
   - Modigliani & miller
   - Ideal world: No tax,

Cost of capital interest offered by the use of debt

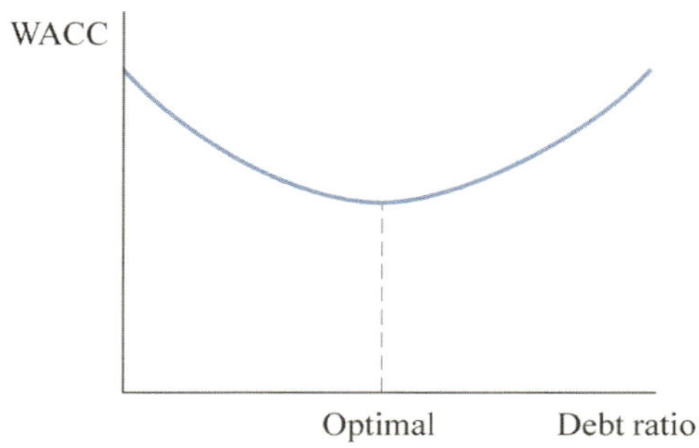

3. Agency cost theory
   - creditor and stockholders
   - monitoring costs
   - affect investment opportunity

4. Information asymmetry / signaling
   - Investor infer from management's action
   - The information possessed by management
   - Signal: use of debt is a signal of a "good" firm

6. Decision on the Capital Structures

- Target capital structure
  Trade-off tax benefit vs riskiness (fixed income obligations)
- Goal: minimize WACC
  Maximize stock price
- Tool: analysis the variability of EPS under difficult capital structure.

Revenue
\- TVC
Gross profit
\- FC
EBIT

(Revenue through EBIT) → Business risk
-Variability of EBIT

EBIT
\- T
EBT
\- T
EAT
\- PD
\- EAC

(EBIT through EAC) → Financial risk

Business risk + Financial risk = Total risk
-variability of EAC

OR

Variability of EPS

1) Break Even Analysis

- Break even sales = (EBIT = 0)

  EBIT = Revenue - TVC - FC

  Break even units⇒0=break even units×price-(VC×B.E unit)-(FC)

  Break even units = $\dfrac{PC}{\text{Price} - VC}$

- EBIT covers interest, taxes, and preferred dividend.
- EAC = (EBIT - I) × (1 - T) - PD

  $B \cdot E_{EBIT}$ ⇒ (EAC = 0) = ($B \cdot E_{EBIT}$ - I) × (1 - T) - PD

$$B.E_{EBIT} = \frac{PD}{1-T} + I$$

2) Indifference Analysis

- Indifferent sales

⇒ Revenues level at which the EBIT under both alternative are same.

$$REV_i - TVC_1 - FC_1 = EBIT_1$$
$$REV - TVC_2 - FC_2 = EBIT_2$$

$$REV_{IN} \Rightarrow EBIT_1 = EBIT_2$$
$$Unit_{IN} \times price - Unit_{IN} \times VC_1 - FC_1$$
$$= Unit_{IN} \times \text{Price} - Unit_{IN} \times VC_2 - PC_2$$

$$UNIT_{IN} = \frac{FC_1 - FC_2}{VC_2 - VC_1}$$

(Indifference - EBIT)

- EBIT level at which EPS_1 = EPS_2

$$EPS = \frac{EAC}{of\ CS\ shares} = \frac{(EBIT - I) \times (1-T) - PD}{of\ CS\ shares}$$

$$EBIT_{IN} \Rightarrow EPS_1 = EPS_2$$

$$\Rightarrow \frac{(EBIT_{IN} - I_1 \times (1-T) - PD_1}{SH_1}$$

$$= \frac{(EBIT_{IN} - I_2) \times (1-T) - PD_2}{SH_2}$$

$$\Rightarrow EBIT_{IN} = \frac{\left[SH_2 \times \left\{I_1 + \frac{PD_1}{1-T_1}\right\}\right] - \left[SH_1 \times \left\{I_2 + \frac{PD_2}{1-T_2}\right\}\right]}{SH_2 - SH_1}$$

3) Sensitivity Analysis

① Degree of Operating Leverage (DOL)

- Sensitivity of EBIT to revenue

$$\text{DOL} = \frac{Unit \times (\text{P}rice - VC)}{Unit \times (\text{P}rice - VC) - FC}$$

$$\frac{Revenue - TVC}{Revenue - TVC - FC}$$

$$\frac{EBIT + FC}{EBIT}$$

$$\frac{\%\triangle EBIT}{\%\triangle Revenue} \qquad \%\triangle = \%change$$

② Degree of financial leverage (DFL)

- Sensitivity of EPS to EBIT

$$DFL = \frac{EBIT}{EBIT - I - (\frac{PD}{1-T})}$$

$$= \frac{\%\triangle EPS}{\%\triangle EBIT}$$

③ Degree of combined leverage (DCL)

- sensitivity of EPS to Revenue

DCL = DOL × DFC

$$= \frac{\%\triangle EPS}{\%\triangle Revenue}$$

$$= \frac{EBIT - FC}{EBIT - I - (\frac{PD}{1-T})}$$

4) Liquidity Analysis

* Debt ratio that maximizes EPS

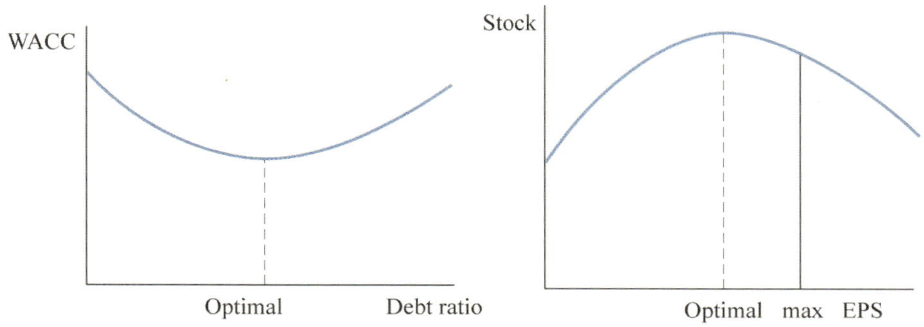

Ex) Current structure 6,000,000 Debt

5,000,000 CS

6,000,000 debts: 10% annual coupon bond, par 1,000

5,000,000 CS: par value 10,000,000

Need \$ 10,000,000 in capital budgeting dollars

Option 1) Use 100 % preferred stock (par value = \$ 45)

With 12% dividend.

Option 2) 50% CS (par value = \$ 50)

50% debt with 12% annual coupon

Shares of CS outstanding = 500,000

Tax 40%

Expected EBIT = 10,000,000

Option #1

Break even EBIT (i.e. EPS = 0)

Current interest: 6,000,000 × 0.10 = 600,000

New interest = 0

Current PD (preferred dividend) = 0

New PD = 100% × 10,000,000 × 12% = 1,200,000

Current CS share = 500,000

New CS share = 0

- Break even EBIT

$$= (600{,}000+0) + \frac{0+1{,}200{,}000}{1-0.4} = 2{,}600{,}000$$

- EPS $= \dfrac{(2{,}600{,}000-600{,}000)\times(1-0.4)-1{,}200{,}000}{600{,}000}$

$= 0$ (Correct)

$\therefore$ Expected EPS $= \dfrac{(10{,}000{,}000-600{,}000)\times(1-0.4)-1{,}200{,}000}{600{,}000}$

$= \$8.88$

Option #2

Current interest = 600,000

New interest = 50% × 10,000,000 × 12% = 600,000

Current PD = 0

New PD = 0

Current CS share = 500,000

New CS share $= \dfrac{60\% \times 10{,}000{,}000}{60} = 100{,}000$

- Break even EBIT $= (600{,}000+600{,}000) + \dfrac{0+0}{1-0.4} = 1{,}200{,}000$

- Expected EPS(Given expected EBIT = 10,000,000)

$$\frac{(10,000,000-600,000-600,000)\times(1-0.4)-0}{600,000+100,000}=\$8.88$$

- Indifference EBIT (i.e. $EPS_1 = EPS_2$)

$$\frac{(EBIT_{IND}-600,000)\times(1-0.4)-1,200,000}{600,000}$$

$$=\frac{(EBIT_{IND}-600,000-600,000)\times(1-0.4)-0}{600,000+100,000}$$

$EBIT_{IND}$ = 9,600,000

$$EPS_1=\frac{(9,600,000-600,000)\times(1-0.4)-1,200,000}{600,000}=8.4$$

$$EPS_1=\frac{(9,600,000-600,000-600,000)\times(1-0.4)}{600,000}=8.4$$

If fixed cost = 4,800,000

What is DOL?

$$\text{DOL}=\frac{EBIT+FC}{EBIT}$$

$$\frac{10,000,000+4,800,000}{10,000,000}$$

= 1.48

DCL = DOL × DFC

= 1.48 × 1.35

= 2

$$*\ DFL_1=\frac{\%\triangle EPS}{\%\triangle EBIT}$$

$$\Rightarrow \%\triangle EBIT\times DFL_1=\%\triangle EPS$$

1% × 1 = 1

1% × 2 = 2

$EPIT=10,000,000\Rightarrow EPS_1=8.88$

$\%\triangle EBIT=10\%\Rightarrow EPS_1=?$

$DFL_1=1.35$

$$13.5 = \frac{\% \triangle EPS}{10\%}$$

$$\% \triangle EBIT = 13.5\$$$

$$\frac{NewEPS - OldEPS(8.88)}{OldEPS} = 13.5$$

$\therefore$ New EPS = 10.08

Option 1

$$DFL_1 = \frac{EBIT}{EBIT - I_1 - (\frac{PD_1}{1-T})}$$

$$= \frac{10{,}000{,}000}{10{,}000{,}000 - 600{,}000 - \frac{1{,}200{,}000}{1-0.4}}$$

$= 1.35$

Ex) at be EBIT of 2,600,000

$$EFL_1 = \frac{2{,}600{,}000}{2{,}600{,}000 - 600{,}000 - \frac{1{,}200{,}000}{1-0.4}}$$

$$= \frac{2{,}600{,}000}{0} = Undefined\infty$$

Practice Questions

True (T) or False (F)

01 Liquidating value is the value assets have if they are sold apart from the business in which they are used.

02 The going-concern value of assets is usually lower than their liquidating value.

03 An owner's value today is equal to the value today of all future risky dividends to which the owner has a claim.

04 The market establishes V0 [DIVt] by determining the present value of a future dividend stream.

05 The dividend valuation model can be applied to a company's stocks as well as to individual projects.

06 A decrease in a current dividend will be matched by an equal decrease in retained earnings.

07 To use the retained earnings, equity, and debt/equity approaches to NPV, a manager must know the amount of each interest payment on the debt used to finance the project.

08 The depreciation tax shield is the dollar amount of taxes not paid because depreciation is a tax-deductible expense.

Answers to the Practice Problems:

Answer Keys T, F, F, T, T, F, T, T

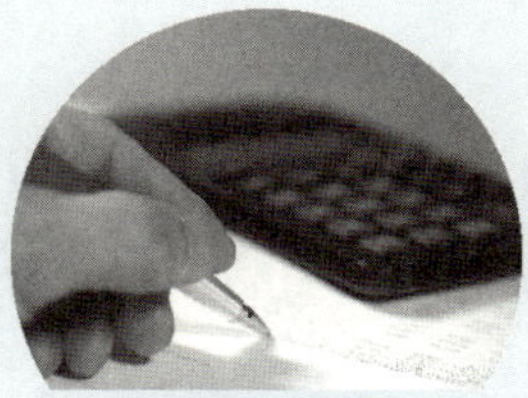

Chapter 11

Capital Budgeting

Chapter 11 Capital Budgeting[6)]

1. Capital Budgeting

1) Definition

Here the Term "capital" refers to fixed assets used in production, while a "budget" is a plan which details projected inflows and outflows during some future period. Thus, the capital budget is an outline of planned expenditures on fixed assets, and capital budgeting is the whole process of analyzing projects and deciding whether they should be included in the capital budget.

2) Importance of Capital Budgeting

A number of factors combine to make capital budgeting decisions perhaps the most important ones that financial managers must make. First, since the results of capital budgeting decisions continue for many years, the decision-maker loses some of his or her flexibility. For example, the purchase of a hotel with an economic life of 40 years "locks in" the firm for a 40 years period. Further, because asset expansion is fundamentally related to expect future sales, a decision to buy a fixed asset that is expected to last 40 years involves an implicit 40-year sales forecast.

6) Adapted from John M. Tarras, 1991. A practical Goide to Hospitality Finace. Van Nostrand Reinhold, New York.

An error in the forecast of asset requirements can have serious consequences. If the firm invests too much in assets, it will incur unnecessarily heavy expenses. If it does not spend enough on fixed assets, two problems may arise. First, its equipment may not be efficient enough to enable it to produce competitively. Second, if it has inadequate capacity, it may lose a portion of its market share to rival firms, and regaining lost customers requires heavy selling expenses and price reductions, both of which are costly.

Timing is also important in capital budgeting-capital assets must be ready to come "on line" when they are needed. Only when a firm forecasts demand properly and plans its capacity requirements a year or so in advance it is possible to maintain or increase its market share of a firm. Effective capital budgeting can improve both the timing of asset acquisitions and the quality of assets purchased. A firm which forecasts its needs for capital assets in advance will have an opportunity to purchase and install the assets before they are needed. If sales increase because of as increase in general market demand, all firms in the industry will tend to order capital goods at about the same time. This results in backlogs long waiting times for assets, and an increase in their prices. The firm which foresees its needs and purchases capital assets early can avoid these problems. Note, though, that if a firm forecasts an increase in demand and then expands to meet the anticipated demand, but sales then do not expand, it will be saddled with excess capacity and high costs. This can lead to losses or even bankruptcy. Thus, Forecast an accurate sales is critical.

Finally, capital budgeting is also important, because asset expansion typically involves substantial expenditures, and before a firm can spend a large amount of money, it must have the funds available -large amounts of money are not generated automatically. Therefore, a firm contemplating a major capital expenditure program should arrange its financing several years in advance to be sure the funds required are available.

3) General Procedure of Capital Budgeting

Capital budgeting projects are created by the firm. For example, a sales representative in a hotel may report that customers are asking for a particular service that the hotel does not have now. The sales manager then discusses the idea with the marketing research group to determine the size of the market for the proposed service. If it appears that a significant market does exist, cost accountants and financial managers will be asked to estimate the costs. If it appears that the service can be served and sold at a sufficient profit, the project will be undertaken.

A firm's growth, and even its ability to remain competitive and to survive, depends upon a constant flow of ideas for new products and services, ways to make existing products and services better, and ways to produce and serve output at a lower cost. Accordingly, a well-managed firm will go into great lengths to develop good capital budgeting proposals.

Conceptually, capital budgeting involves exactly the same six steps that are used in security analysis:

1. First, the cost of the project must be determined. This is similar to finding the price that must be paid for a stock or bond.
2. Next, management estimates the expected cash flows from the project, including the salvage value of the asset at the end of its expected life. This is similar to estimating the future dividend or interest payment stream on a stock or bond, along with the stocks' expected sales price or the bond's maturity value.

3. Third, the riskiness of the projected cash flows must be estimated. For this assessment, management needs information about the probability distributions of the cash flows.
4. Then, given the project's riskiness, management determines the appropriate cost of capital at which cash flows are to be discounted.
5. Next, the expected cash inflows are put on a present value basis to obtain an estimate of the asset's value to the firm. This is equivalent to finding the present value of a stock's expected future dividends.
6. Finally, the present value of the expected cash inflows is compared with the required outlay, or cost; if the PV of the cash flows exceeds the cost, the project should be accepted. Otherwise, it should be rejected. (Alternatively, the expected rate of return on the project can be calculated, and if this rate of return exceeds the project's cost of capital, the project is accepted.)

If an individual investor identifies and invests in a stock or bond whose market price is less than its true value, the value of the investor's portfolio will increase. Similarly, if a firm identifies (or creates) an investment opportunity with a present value greater than its cost, the value of the firm will increase. Thus, there is a very direct link between capital budgeting and stock values: The more effective the firm's capital budgeting procedures are, the higher the price of the stock, and the more value adding will be. And it will result in adding more value.

2. Financing Procedures and Costs

The hotel industry is very management-intensive. Subsequently, there is greater dependence on management for generating a profit for a hotel project. This is especially true in the hotel business, where the lender not only issues loans on the real estate value of the property but also on management's ability to run the property profitably. The role of financing in the hotel industry is pervasive, and it is not uncommon for a hotel project to carry a loan amount up to 75 percent of the value of the property.

As in other chapters, "hotel project" in this chapter refers to hotels, restaurants, clubs, etc., but lender financing plays such an important part in the hotel industry that this chapter emphasizes the hotel industry. Also, many restaurants are leased, and when real estate ownership is involved, borrowing from the lender usually involves shorter-term loans than those for larger hotel projects.

Hotel financing usually involves two different scenarios: a new property or the purchase of an existing property. The financing for an existing property is easier because the major requirement is to obtain financing for part of the purchase price. The financial considerations in building a new building are more complex than those for the purchase of an existing building and will be taken up first in this chapter.

1) Development of a New Property

Financing a new hotel project involves the detailed preparation of a budget to anticipate the total cost of the project Exhibit 6-1 on page 108 illustrates how a typical hotel budget is prepared. This section will focus on the different aspects of obtaining financing for the particular steps in the building process: (1) land acquisition, (2) construction financing, and (3) permanent financing.

(1) Land Acquisition

The developer will first want to secure the land for the hotel development

The developer usually takes out an option to purchase the property over a specified period of time (usually a few months). This allows the developer to inspect the property for building suitability and meet or have changed zoning and government requirements in order to proceed with the project. Once the land has been approved for building, the developer will exercise the right to purchase the property.

Although many factors are taken into consideration at this point about the type of financing available, usually the purchase and financing of raw land are more difficult to obtain then if there was an operating property already on the site. This is because there is a greater risk that the proposed property may never be constructed. If the hotel firm has sufficient assets of its own, it may be able to borrow the money on its own name. On the other hand, the hotel firm may purchase the land by means of a land contract. In this form of financing, the seller of the property finances part of the acquisition price. The developer generally finances the land acquisition over a relatively short period of time, fewer than five years in many cases.

EXHIBIT 11-1 Example of a Construction Budget for a New Mid-Priced 250-Room Hotel Project Cost (000)Omitted

Description	Budget Amount
Land	$900
Building	5,000
Furniture, Fixtures & Equipment	1,500
Total Fixed Assets	$7,400
Pre-Opening	220
Property Taxes During Construction	33
Construction Interest	275
Developer's Fee (5% of Hard Cost)	370
Franchise Commitment Fee	40
Legal & Other	35
Working Capital/Operating Reserve	300
Total Project Cost	$8,673

Also, it is not uncommon for the developer to share an interest in the hotel project if the seller has a very desirable site that he will sell only on condition that he will be given an interest in it. Generally, the developer would rather purchase the land outright and avoid sharing profits with an outside party.

(2) Construction Financing

Once the property has been acquired, the developer secures the necessary construction loan financing to develop the property. Although the land acquisition financing is sometimes included in the construction financing, for the purposes of this chapter the items will be considered separately.

The construction loan is a specialized loan for preparing land for construction, building, and any pre-opening expenses necessary to operate the hotel property. Generally, the developer draws the loan amount in increments from the financial institution as certain parts of the project are completed. This is done to prevent the developer from using the funds for other purposes and to reduce the risk to the lender by matching the funds released to the value of die property. The developer uses the loan proceeds to pay subcontractors working on the project (See Exhibit 11-2 for the types of categories included in the construction of the property.)

Although many lenders issue construction loans, traditionally the commercial banks, and more recently life insurance companies, were the main lenders for construction projects. Savings and loan institutions were involved in construction financing until the recent savings and loan crisis put an end to most of these types of loans.

Construction loans are considered very risky by lenders. At some point, the project may not be completed, and the lender's only recourse is to foreclose on an incomplete building that may be difficult to sell without considerable additional investment in the property. Therefore, the interest rate demanded by the lender is usually higher than that for the permanent financing. The lender may also look for the developer to provide personal guarantees that the loan will be repaid. Interest is usually added to the principal balance, and the total is repaid when the permanent financing is utilized.

As mentioned earlier, construction financing is riskier than other types of financing. As a result, construction lenders may insist that the developer have a commitment from a reputable lender for the permanent financing. This commitment is a promise by the lender that funds will be made available if the developer adheres to the plan and specifications for the building of the hotel project. The construction lender is often the same as the permanent lender for the project.

EXHIBIT 11-2 Types of Construction Categories

1. Architect & Engineering Fees
2. Construction Contract
3. Project Management
4. Elevator
5. Pool
6. Contingency Costs
7. Legal Fees
8. Guest Room Furnishings
9. Operating Equipment
10. Signs
11. Front Office System
12. Telephone System
13. Energy Management System
14. Pre-Opening Operations
15. Pre-Opening Hotel Services

(3) Permanent Financing

The developer of a new property wants to secure the permanent financing at the lowest possible cost. Often, this involves checking with many different lenders and comparing total costs of all types of financing. Frequently, the availability of financing will dictate how much shopping the developer will realistically be able to do. There are many creative forms of permanent Financing available, and this section discusses some of the more common Financing instruments.

The permanent financing or mortgage is activated when all the conditions have been met to operate the hotel project as a going concern. This usually occurs when the hotel project receives its "certificate of occupancy" to do business.

As mentioned, permanent Financing is usually obtained by the developer through a mortgage loan commitment. The lender and developer enter into a contract whereby the lender supplies the mortgage for the property if the hotel project is completed as specified in the commitment contract.

The commitment agreement is a very detailed document that spells out such important items as the amount of the loan, interest rate, terms, full description of the property, and other relevant items.

The lender must investigate the developer and obtain an appraisal and other important, time- consuming items. They will want to recoup these costs by chaining a fee for the loan commitment.

2) Financing Existing Hotel Properties

Every year, many existing hotel properties are sold to individuals and corporations. For example, several hotel firms have sold an entire group of hotels or have restructured and sold most of their operating hotels. If the individual or corporation sells an existing property, the new owners will more likely finance part of the purchase price.

The real estate aspect of hotel property is very important in today's sales. Historically, demand for real estate in this country has risen. The buyer generally contributes equity in the amount of 25-30 percent of the total purchase price, with the balance coming from lenders or the seller or from some combination of the two. One of the often-quoted advantages of hotels has been their ability to raise room rates quickly in response to inflation. This is not the case with office buildings that often have long-term leases. However, this advantage has been offset by the continued oversupply of hotel rooms. In recent years there has been a substantial growth in the number of hotel rooms, to the point that in many markets occupancy rates have been in the 40-50 percent range.

The buyer of an existing property, however, has one major advantage. Knowing the operating history of the property, which can be an indication of future income streams. The seller may carry part or all of the financing of the property if a qualified buyer is unable to secure financing at reasonable rates. Creativity is the key element for financing a hotel project. Often, the hotel manager has the expertise to run a hotel operation but lacks the Financial means to purchase the property. At times likes this, it is very important to be creative in locating sources of capital.

3) Negotiating a Loan

Generally, almost everyone involved in the hotel industry uses debt financing at some point. When the need arises, the hotel executive must focus his or her attention on convincing the lender why money should be loaned to the company. Therefore, it is imperative for the hotel executive to understand the lender's position before granting a loan. Many independent hotel firms have difficulty obtaining financing because of the high failure rate of many independent hotel firms, which results in bad debt for the lending institution. There are many important strategies one should pursue before applying for a loan. This section focuses on how to organize and properly follow the steps for obtaining a loan.

Before entering into negotiations with any financial institution, the executive must understand that a lender makes money from the interest charged on the loan. Unlike the borrower, the lender does not want to be in the hotel business and quite often does not really understand it. Therefore, it is up to the hotel executive to convince the lender not only why this hotel property is so important but also how this property differs from the ones that have failed. Selecting an appropriate lending institution is the first step towards beginning the loan process. The starting point should be contacting those institutions with whom the firm and/or the principal owners of the hotel firm maintain their accounts. However, the executive must be careful where he or she first establishes a banking relationship because lending institutions may differ significantly from one another. Many restaurateurs have been extremely disappointed and frustrated to find out that a financial institution with which they have previously done business now refuses to loan funds due to a very conservative lending policy concerning restaurants. On the other hand, many Financial institutions are quite willing to loan money to a new restaurant. Some Financial institutions may want to loan to a new or expanding hotel venture. For example, a lender may have money available for the particular loan or the hotel industry may be targeted by the lending institution for loans.

A hotel executive should shop for the best loan on the best possible terms. One way of doing this is a referral to a lender by someone whose opinion is respected by the lender. These referrals may be made by the hotel firm's accountant, attorney, or friends who are running successful hotel firms.

Once a lender is approached, he or she will need to know in detail why the hotel executive needs the loan. A hotel firm that approaches a lender with vague needs and dollar amounts is asking to be rejected. The executive must first carefully think through his or her need, because advance preparation is critical to obtaining the loan. The hotel executive should know and ask for the exact amount needed. Although this step requires a detailed analysis, it will save the borrower a great deal of grief in both the short and long run. For example, if the hotel executive asks for too little, either he or she have to approach the lender later to reapply for more money or the lender might notice the inadequate amount and realize the borrower is not fully prepared. Asking for too much in the hopes of "bargaining" for a lesser amount is also a common mistake because this strategy shows a lack of professionalism and accuracy.

The financial plan or loan proposal is the hotel executive's primary selling point for obtaining a loan. Many hotel executives who lack financial sophistication tend to shy away from this very important aspect. If this is the case, the executive should seek the advice of his or her accountant or CPA, who has the proper training and experience in preparing loan requests. Lending officers take financial statements very seriously, and the hotel executive should take the time to prepare them properly and accurately from the beginning.

As previously noted, the lender looks at many criteria when determining whether a loan should be granted. However, the most important factors analyzed are often described as the "four C's" of credit.

1. Character
2. Capacity
3. Capital
4. Collateral

The borrower's character includes hotel experience, honesty, integrity and willingness to pay. The hotel executive should outline for the lender the experiences and special skills of the firm's top management. In many instances, the borrower's track record will be a major factor on how large a loan the hotel firm will be able to obtain.

Furthermore, the hotel executive should describe and identify the hotel firm's product, market, customers, and competitors. This process enables the lender to obtain a more accurate picture of the hotel project that the executive will introduce to the public. This description also helps the lender understand how the hotel executive's prior experience fits into the plans.

The hotel executive should never underestimate personal attributes including self-confidence, manner of presentation, and personal demeanor when negotiating a loan. The relationship between the hotel executive and lender is based on mutual trust. Therefore, it is invaluable for the hotel executive to be able to interact with the lender in the most candid and honest manner possible. If the hotel executive has been turned down for a loan by some other institution, he or she should not try to hide this fact from the lender. Because a potential lender will ultimately know a great deal about the executive, the lender's chances of discovering a previous turndown is quite high. If this information was in fact kept from the lender, he or she might reject the loan on the basis of dishonesty or lack of trust. Trust is also important when the hotel firm faces a crisis and there is serious concern over the possibility of repaying the loan. By alerting the lender to problems as soon as possible, the hotel executive and the lender may have the opportunity to work out a possible solution in lieu of foreclosing on the loan and closing the property.

The capacity of the borrower to pay back the loan is also highly regarded by lenders. Operating a hotel property efficiently and profitably is, of course, a necessity for the loan to be repaid. The ability to repay a loan is demonstrated by showing projected financial balance sheets, income statements, and cash flow statements for generally the first three to five years of operation. Furthermore, because hotel firms generally operate with lower working capital requirements than other types of businesses, the hotel executive must explain this fact to the lender who may have little experience in handling hotel industry loan requests. Another concern for the hotel executive is showing how cash flow will be affected by the seasonality of income, which often varies from season to season due to location, vacation periods, or weather. The lender will be most concerned about how the hotel executive plans to handle shortfalls due to these factors.

As mentioned earlier, in addition to financial statements, the hotel executive should also have prepared the exact amount of the loan requested and be able to explain how the loan proceeds will be utilized. The lender will want a detailed plan outlining how the hotel firm will pay back the loan. It would also be in the hotel executive's best interest to show several different scenarios to help assure the lender that the loan will be paid back even in less than ideal circumstances.

Lenders are also very interested in how much capital the prospective hotel firm and executive possesses with which to pay back the loan if the firm's operations do not live up to expectations. Although in most cases the hotel firm itself obtains the loan, the lender will insist that the principal owners of a smaller hotel company guarantee the loans made to the firm. Additionally, the larger the equity contribution made by the participants, the greater the likelihood of the loan being approved. Lenders like to see a large equity contribution, not only for reducing the risk of a bad loan but also for making the penalty of walking away from a troubled hotel firm more expensive to the participants.

Finally, the lender will insist on collateral for the loan. This often includes liens on the firm's equipment and furniture. However, since lenders realize that most hotel firm equipment has a high rate of depreciation and a low resale value, the lender may also insist on that the principal owners include their personal property as collateral in addition.

After all the requirements of the lender have been met, the hotel executive must still negotiate the terms of the loan. The hotel executive must be cautious because unreasonable restrictions can result in unfavorable consequences. For example, most loan agreements allow the lender to recall the entire amount of the loan if the borrower defaults in any manner from the loan agreement. Although the lender seldom enforces this, it does afford an opportunity to get the delinquent borrower into the office to discuss the problem. The lender may use the recall provision by placing additional restrictions upon the borrower or by renegotiating the entire loan.

Cash controls are other restrictions likely to be imposed by the lender. For instance, the lender may insist that cash balances be maintained at a certain level. As mentioned previously, the borrower must inform the lender about the hotel industry's practice of carrying cash balances smaller than those in most other businesses. Another popular restriction is to insist that the borrower not sell any assets of the hotel firm without permission from the lender. The lender may also stipulate that the hotel firm may not use equipment as collateral for additional loans. Furthermore, the lender may demand that certain debt-to-equity ratios be maintained so as not to leverage the hotel Firm operations beyond levels deemed safe by the lender.

Lenders commonly believe that hotel Firms are a high risk. Thus, it is imperative that the hotel executive spends a great deal of time preparing the loan proposal. From a feasibility study to a less formal preparation of loan documents, the borrower must remember that the goal is to assuage any concerns the lender may have. At the same time, he must allow him or herself the greatest amount of freedom possible in operating the hotel Firm. By spending the time to prepare the loan proposal properly, the executive is in the best possible position for obtaining the required loan.

4) Appraising Hotel Properties

Before a mortgage can be granted by a lending institution, the lender will want an independent third party to appraise the hotel property. The appraisal business is an art, not a science. The appraiser gives an opinion about value, and there is no scientific way of proving that value. Even so, the developer should examine closely the background of the firm conducting the appraisal. Because the hotel industry is so different from other businesses, the appraiser should be experienced in valuing hotel properties.

There has been much controversy about the appraisal profession. One need only look at the savings and loan industry disaster to realize that many loans were made on poor appraisal analysis. A good appraiser will not only be familiar with the hotel industry but will also gather sufficient data to conduct the necessary market and site analysis. All the major assumptions should be analyzed closely for their reasonableness. The appraiser should be able to support the valuation with the data collected.

Once the data has been collected and sorted, the appraiser gives an accurate value of the hotel property. It should be noted that there are fundamental differences in appraising hotels and restaurants. There are, of course, many similarities, but because the dollar value of hotels is usually larger than that of restaurants, this section focuses on hotels. The three basic methods of valuing a hotel property are:

1. Cost approach
2. Sales comparison approach
3. Income capitalization approach

(1) Cost Approach

The cost approach is based on the assumption that a buyer will pay no more for a hotel property than the cost of building another facility. Therefore, a potential buyer should be able to determine a building's worth by estimating the cost to replace that building, less all current depreciation. For purposes of the cost approach, depreciation is defined as any decrease in the value of the building and improvements resulting from physical depreciation, functional obsolescence, and economic obsolescence.

The problem with the cost approach is that the value of the depreciation deduction is subjective. A recently constructed hotel property may be able to use the cost method, but other properties would find this method too subjective to be of much use. Not only does the cost approach method ignore economic factors such as cash flow, but many adjustments have to be made to determine the remaining useful life of die property, making the cost approach method very difficult to use.

(2) Sales Comparison Approach

The sales comparison approach determines the market value of a particular hotel property by analyzing sales of comparable properties. Of course, no two properties are the same, and the appraiser must adjust the valuation by differences in the property. These differences can be perceived subjectively and thus require an appraiser who is very familiar with the local market.

The most common use for the sales comparison approach is for smaller independent hotel properties such as restaurants, where there are fewer and less complex factors to analyze. The more complex properties (such as resort hotels) require more subjective adjustments. This makes valuation by the sales comparison approach difficult. Also, because the hotel industry is so service oriented, a large portion of a property's value is determined by the quality of its management.

Another difficulty with the sales comparison approach is that there are usually only a limited number of sales of comparable properties in the area. Market conditions could have changed dramatically since those sales. Also, the terms of the sale may have influenced the sale of a particular property. For example, the Ace Hotel was sold last year for no money down. The buyer agreed to pay the full asking price in consideration for the seller agreeing to finance 100 percent of the purchase price. Thus, the hotel's selling price would be higher than if the buyer had placed a 20 percent down payment and the seller had agreed to take a money-purchase mortgage on the remaining 80 percent. Unless the appraiser had first-hand knowledge of the terms of the sale, he or she would assume that the property was purchased for its fair market value.

For these reasons, the sales comparison approach is not very useful in evaluating most hotel properties. However, the sales comparison approach can be useful in determining the broad range that hotel properties are sold for in the area. However, this dubious aid is best used when the data needed to make the comparisons is readily available and the appraiser is very familiar with the local market.

(3) Income Capitalization Approach

The income capitalization approach is the most accurate method for obtaining value of a hotel project. As the name suggests, this method of determining value takes the income stream from a hotel operation and applies the appropriate capitalization rate. The theory here is that an investor will only purchase a hotel property for an amount that returns a certain amount of cash on the original investment.

Net operating income is not die same as net income per the income statements. Net operating income is the cash flow from a hotel project after deducting operating expenses but before payments on debt service. An analysis is then made of the debt portion of the hotel property and the anticipated yield on the investment or equity to arrive at the value of the hotel property.

Stabilized Net Income

Ideally, the appraiser analyzes each projected year's operating income. However, to derive net income in this manner is too cumbersome and inaccurate for most hotel properties. So the appraiser anticipates the income that the hotel firm should make after it is fully operational and has established its market. This income is known as the firm's "stabilized net income."

A great deal of expertise is required to analyze many hotel projects, especially hotels. This is due to many factors that come into play when forecasting the net income. For instance, what impact will the local economy have on the occupancy of the hotel? What effect will competitors have if they build additional hotel rooms in the area? How should other factors such as appreciation of underlying real estate be considered? These and other questions must be answered by the appraiser before issuing a report

Capitalization Rate

The selection of the capitalization rate is the key to valuing a hotel property. Simply put, capitalization rate is the percentage by which future cash flow is converted into present value. The capitalization rate for the debt is the mortgage constant which is needed to service the debt. The capitalization rate for the invest mentor equity component is the rate of return acceptable to buyers when compared to other similar investments. For instance, if 30-year U.S. Treasury Bills currently yield 10 percent, one would assume that an investor would want a higher return for the higher risk of operating a hotel property-assuming a constant real estate value.

Viewed from a different perspective, the capitalization rate can be determined by dividing the percentage rate into the stabilized earnings of the hotel project. For example, if the stabilized income for a restaurant is $60,000 for one year, and due to the risk involved a 15% capitalization rate is a reasonable return for the risk involved, then the value of the restaurant would approximately be $400,000, ($60,000 ÷ 15%).

As this example shows, the capitalization rate is vital to obtaining a hotel property's value. The method of selecting the capitalization rate is not cast in stone, as one person may be willing to pay more for a property and take a lower return than someone else. For instance, many foreign buyers of U.S. hotel properties can obtain higher returns in this country than in their own, even though the return accepted in this country is lower than what another U.S. buyer may be willing to pay.

When selecting a discount rate, the appraiser also has to consider such factors as the property's age, location, quality of management, inflation outlook, and other relevant factors.

A simplified example of how a 200-room hotel would be valued utilizing a one-year stabilized net income is shown

Mortgage 70% of Purchase Price	
Equity Contribution 30% of Purchase Price	
Mortgage Rate(20 Year Mortgage)	11.00%
Equity Return Desired	14.00%
Mortgage Constant	12.39%
One year Stabilized Income for the Hotel Property	$3,000,000

The value of the hotel is calculated by weighing the mortgage constant and the equity return desired to arrive at the average rate. The one-year stabilized income ($3,000,000) for the property would then be divided by the average rate (12.87%) to arrive at an approximate value of $23,300,000, as calculated below:

Mortgage Constant	12.39% × 70% = 8.67%
Equity Return	14.00% × 30% = 4.20%
Average Rate	12.87%
Value of Hotel	$3,000,000÷12.87%=$23,310,123 or $23,300,000

Again, it must be emphasized that the above calculation is merely an estimate of value and should not be used in setting the selling price of the property. Numerous other factors influence the property's selling price.

To calculate the earnings at which the hotel project is valued, divide the capitalization rate into 1. For example, a 10 percent capitalization rate means that the hotel firm is valued at 10 times its stabilized earnings (1 ÷ 10% = 10).

5) Summary

Financing hotel projects is an ever-changing area that requires the developer to be constantly alert to financial methods available for constructing or buying a property. The amount and cost of financing a hotel project is one factor that determines whether the project will be profitable or not.

The method of financing a proposed hotel project is more complicated than that for purchasing an existing properly. The hotel developer usually needs to search for an ideal site and then negotiate the loan to purchase the property along with the cost of financing the loan. Also, the developer must obtain construction and permanent financing for the hotel project. Note that the developer may be able to obtain through one lender financing for the entire project from acquisition of land to permanent mortgage.

Existing hotel projects are generally financed by a long-term mortgage. This is easier to obtain because the property has an operating history. Also, there is a greater likelihood that the seller of an existing property will assist in the financing of the purchase price by taking a money purchase mortgage, a land contract, or even a second mortgage position on the property.

No matter what type of financing is available, the borrower wants to obtain it at the lowest possible cost to obtain a loan, the borrower must understand what the lender desires. Generally, the four C's of credit (character, capacity, capital, and collateral) are guidelines in planning for a loan. The lender is primarily interested in knowing how the loan will be repaid. The more confident the lender is in getting paid back, the greater the chances of obtaining a loan. The borrower should be well prepared when seeking a loan, able to answer difficult questions about the proposed hotel business.

Finally, the lender will want an independent appraisal of the proposed or existing hotel property. This will help determine whether there is sufficient value in the property to repay the loan if the borrower fails to make timely mortgage payments. The three accepted appraisal methods are the cost sales comparison, and income capitalization approaches. The cost and sales comparison approaches require too many subjective adjustments to be of much use. The income capitalization approach is much better for valuing a hotel project. The income capitalization approach uses the anticipated or actual stabilized income from a hotel property. The required capitalization rate is obtained and divided into the stabilized income to obtain an approximate value for the property. The value obtained is only the appraiser's best estimate. The developer and lender must realize that appraising is more art than science, and they should carefully examine the appraiser's assumptions.

3. Raising Capital

1) Introduction

It is very difficult for hotel developers to raise the necessary cash to constructor purchase a hotel business. Today, hotel executives must be creative when looking for the financing for a project. Traditional sources are not always available.

The money put into a project by a developer, investor, or limited partner is usually called "equity." The funds borrowed by the hotel business is called "debt". Although it is possible to have a hotel project built with all equity or all debt, the usual method is to combine the two. The developer wants to invest a minimum in the project, and the lending institution generally wants the developer to share substantially in the risk by making a large equity contribution.

Frequently, debt and equity become interchangeable. For instance, a developer may contribute money to a project, but for business reasons he or she may want the contribution to be in the form of debt. On the other hand, a lender may be willing to loan money to a hotel project but wants to participate in the earnings of the project and thus be more like an equity contributor.

However, for legal purposes it is important to distinguish between debt and equity. For example, if a hotel developer has contributed funds to a project mainly in the form of debt, the Internal Revenue Service can reclassify part or all of the debt as equity. Also, debt generally has to be repaid on a schedule while equity return depends on the project generating income.

There are many different sources of financing for a hotel project. These include the traditional sources such as commercial banking, investment banking, and life insurance companies. The individual investor often participates in the hotel industry by investing as a limited partner or taking back a purchase-money mortgage upon the sale of the hotel operation. Institutional funding such as pension funds and Real Estate Investment Trusts(REIT) are playing a bigger role in providing capital for the hotel industry. Finally, government programs such as the Small Business Administration's guaranteed loan programs and direct loans provide needed funds for the development of hotel projects.

This chapter discusses the various sources of capital to discuss how each functions and how each can be a valuable funding source for the hotel industry.

(1) Financial Markets

Business firms, individuals, and government units often need to raise capital. For example, suppose The Sheraton Walkerhill Hotel forecasts an increase in the demand for rooms, and decides to build 100 new rooms. Because Sheraton almost certainly will not have the $200 million or so, necessary to pay for the construction, the company will have to raise this capital from the financial markets. Or suppose Miss. Kim, the owner of a hardware store, decides to expand into appliances. Where will she get the money to buy the initial inventory of TV sets, washers, and freezers? Similarly, if you want to buy a new car that costs $40,000, but you have only $20,000 in savings, how can you raise the additional $20,000? If the city of Seoul wants to borrow $200 million to finance a new sewer plant, or if government needs $200 billion or so to cover its projected 2008 deficit, they too need access to the capital markets.

On the other hand, some individuals and firms have incomes which are greater than their current expenditures, so they have funds available to invest. People and organizations. wanting to borrow money are brought together with those having surplus funds in the financial markets. Note that "markets" is plural - there are a great many different financial markets, each one consisting of many institutions, in a developed economy. Each market deals with a somewhat different type of instrument in terms of the instrument's maturity and the assets backing it. Also, different markets serve different types of customers, or operate in different parts of the country. Here are some of the major types of markets.

1. Physical asset market (also called "tangible" or "real" asset markets") are those for such products as wheat, autos, real estate. Financial asset markets deal with stocks, bonds, notes, mortgages, and other claims on real assets.
2. Spot markets and futures markets are terms that refer to whether the assets are being bought or sold for "on the spot" delivery or for delivery at some future date.
3. Money markets are the markets for debt securities with maturities of less than one year. The New York and London money markets have long been the word's largest, but Tokyo is rising rapidly. Capital markets are the markets for long-term debt and corporate stocks. The KOSPI, which handles the stocks of the Korean corporations, is a prime example of a capital market.
4. Mortgage market deal with loans on residential, commercial, and industrial real estate, and on farmland, while consumer credit markets involve loans on autos and appliances, as well as loans for education, vacations, and so on.
5. World, national, regional, and local market also exists. Thus, depending on an organization's size and scope of operations, it may be able to borrow all around the world or it may be confined to a strictly local, even neighborhood, market.

6. Primary markets are the markets in which corporations raise new capital. If The Shilla Hotel were to sell a new issue of common stock to raise capital, this would be a primary market transaction. The corporation selling the newly created stock receives the proceeds from the sale in a primary market transaction. Secondary markets are markets in which already existing outstanding, securities are traded among investors. Thus, if you decided to buy 1,000 shares of the Shilla hotel stock, the purchase would occur in the secondary market. The KOSPI is a secondary market, since it deals in outstanding as opposed to newly issued stocks and bonds. Secondary markets also exist for mortgages, various other types of loans, and other financial assets. The corporation whose securities are being traded is not involved in a secondary market transaction and thus, does not receive any funds from such a sale.
7. A healthy economy is dependent on efficient transfers of funds from people who are net savers to firms and individuals who need capital. Without efficient transfers, the economy simply could not function: Seoul Power & Light could not raise capital, so Seoul citizens would have no electricity; people visiting Seoul would have no place to stay, so The Shilla Hotel in Seoul would have no guest, and so on. It will obviously, affect the level of employment and productivity, hence our standard of living, would be much lower. Therefore, it is absolutely essential that our financial markets function efficiently - not only quickly, but also at a low cost.

(2) Financial Institutions

Transfers of capital between savers and those who need capital take place in three different ways.

1. Direct transfers of money and securities occur when a business sells its stocks or bonds directly to savers without going through any type of financial institution.
2. Transfers may also go through an investment banking house such as Morgan Stanley, which serves as a middleman and facilitates the issuance of securities. The company sells its stocks or bonds to the investment bank, which in turn sells these same securities to savers. The businesses' securities and the savers' money merely "pass through" the investment banking house. However, the investment bank does buy and hold the securities for a period of time, so it is taking a chance - it may not be able to resell them to savers for as much as it has paid to acquire them. Because new securities are involved and the corporation receives money from the sale, this is a primary market transaction.
3. Transfers can also be made through a financial intermediary such as bank or mutual fund. Here the intermediary obtains funds from savers, issuing its own securities in exchange, and then it uses the money to purchase and then hold a business's securities. For example, a saver might give dollars to a bank, receiving from it a certificate of deposit, and then the bank might lend the money to a small business in the form of a mortgage loan. Thus, intermediaries literally create new forms of capital - in this case, certificates of deposit, which are both safer and more liquid than mortgages and thus are better securities for most savers to hold. The existence of intermediaries greatly increases the efficiency of money and capital markets.

A. Commercial banks, which are the traditional financial "department stores," serve a wide variety of savers and those with needs for funds. Note that commercial banks are quite different from investment banks.

Commercial banks lend money, whereas investment banks help companies raise capital from other parties.

B. Savings and loan association (S&Ls), which have traditionally served individual savers and residential and commercial mortgage borrowers, take the funds from many small savers and then lend this money to home buyers and other types of borrowers.

C. Mutual savings banks, which are similar to S&Ls, accept savings primarily from individuals, and lend mainly on a long-term basis to home buyers and consumers.

D. Credit Unions are cooperative associations whose members have a common bond, such as being employees of the same firm. Members' savings are loaned only to other members, generally for auto purchases, and the like.

E. Pension funds are retirement plans, funded by corporations or government agencies for their workers and administered primarily by the trust departments of commercial banks or by life insurance companies.

F. Life insurance companies take savings in the form of annual premiums, and then invest these funds in stock, bonds, real estate, and mortgages.

G. Mutual funds are corporations which accept money from savers and then use these funds to buy stocks, long-term bonds, or short-term debt instruments issued by businesses or government units.

2) Individual Investors

(1) Individuals

Very few individuals earn a living funding hotel projects. An individual is most likely to be involved in financing a hotel project when he or she is selling a hotel property and helping the seller finance it through a purchase-money mortgage or a land contract.

The circumstances under which a individual helps finance part or all of the purchase price are too numerous to discuss here. Generally a seller who is motivated to sell is more likely to help finance the purchase price than a seller who wishes to sell but does not have to sell. Another source of individual investing in a hotel project is through family members. Parents, grandparents, other relatives, business associates, and friends often loan or invest directly in hotel projects. Care should be taken so that funds contributed are structured properly to avoid future problems to protect everyone concerned. For instance, a relative may wish to invest in another relative's hotel project but does not want to risk more than his or her initial investment In this situation, the hotel project may be organized as a limited partnership to minimize risk of loss to the relative.

(2) Limited Partners and Syndications

Many individuals wishing to invest in the hotel industry simply do not have enough funds or are not willing to risk a large investment on any project. On the other hand, they may find that being a limited partner is a hotel limited partnership is ideal for investing. Because the limited partnership plays such an important role in funding many hotel projects, this section discusses in detail the more important aspects of the syndication process and how it affects the individual investor.

Developers of hotel properties (especially hotels) have for years syndicated or sold equity interest using the limited partnership. The advantage to the developer was that he or she did not need to put in all the money and could share the risk of the project with the investors. The investors received an equity interest in a hotel project to use as a tax shelter. Over time, the hotel project would hopefully appreciate in value so that the investor would receive a large capital gain upon its sale. Many hotels were built in the early- and mid-1980s because they offered excellent tax shelters with good economic potential. Many experts feel that the generous tax rules contributed to the overbuilding of the hotel industry.

(3) Real Estate Investment Trusts

The real estate investment trusts (REITs) is a special form of real estate entity that can be used to invest in the hotel industry. This special entity was created so that many small investors who purchase stock could invest in real estate with a diversified portfolio of properties. The REITs then can either invest in real estate ownership or lend funds in the form of mortgage loans. The REITs sometimes combines the ownership aspect with mortgage lending to form a hybrid trust.

The REITs has a big advantage. If the complicated tax laws are followed, the REITs acts much like a partnership. It is not taxed on any income. Instead, the income is passed through to the individual shareholders, who pay income tax on the income received. REITs requirements are that a significant portion of its assets be maintained in real estate assets, cash, and government securities. In addition, a REITs must distribute 95 percent of its taxable income to shareholders each year.

Many REITs have been formed specifically to invest in the hotel industry. Since the primary purpose of most REITs is investment in income-generating properties, the REIT may be the preferred investment vehicle now that individual tax rates have been reduced and favorable capital gain rates have been eliminated.

3) Government Programs

Frequently, hotel developers want to develop a site as a hotel project but the economics of the project do not justify the financial risk. Often, these projects are in economically disadvantaged areas or the community has been stagnate or declining over the years, increasing the risk of building. Usually, inner city locations come to mind when one thinks of these type of developments. But the scenario can also include hotel developments in impoverished rural areas as well.

Federal, state, and local governments have long realized that in order to improve economically disadvantaged areas, government incentives would be needed to attract developers. Unfortunately, in recent years federal budget deficits have resulted in cuts to government subsidy programs aimed at developing distressed areas. Many programs, although in existence, do not have the impact they once had. However, government financing can still be an effective financing tool for the hotel developer who is willing to spend time locating these incentive programs.

4. Cost of Capital

$$W_0 = DIV_0 + \sum_{i=1}^{n} \frac{DIV_t}{(1+K)^t}$$

$WACC = (W_d \times K_d(1-T)) + (W_p \times K_p) + (W_s \times K_s)$

Required Return = return of capital + return on capital to offset inflation + return on capital to offset perceived risk

$$K_i = K_{rf} + \beta_i (K_m - R_{rf})$$

$$E(K) = \sum_{i=1}^{n} (P_i \times K_i)$$

$K_E = R_{rf}$ + Risk Premium

K

1) Minimizing Cost of Capital

1. Maintaining through time a capital structure acceptable to investor

2. Managing debt-to-equity ratio
3. Wise selection of sources
4. Effective timing in the acquisition of funds
5. Prediction about future tax rates and inflation.

2) Riskiness of Cash Flows

Capital structure - Proportion of different types of capital components
Capital components - Things that on the right hand side of the B/S (ex.: debt. Preferred stock, common stock)

→ Liabilities ⇔ Bond

Equity ⇔ Preferred stock

Common stock

(Ex)

Capital component	amount	weight
Debt	3,600,000	3,600,000/9,000,000 = 0.4
Preferred stock	900,000	900,000/9,000,000 = 0.1
Common stock	4,500,000	4,500,000/9,000,000 = 0.5
Total Liabilities	9,000,000	

* Cost of Capital - weighted average of the cost associated each capital component

3) Marginal Cost of Capital (MCC) - Cost of Capital Applied to the Next Dollar Raised.

- Cost of capital can go up due to flotation costs.
- Flotation cost - cost involved when raising new securities(Legal fee, commission)
- The point at which the MCC changes is called a *"break point"*

5. Determining the Optimal Capital Budgets - Step by Step Procedure

STEP 1

(1) Debt

Par value = \$ 1,000

Coupon payment = \$ 100 per year

Annual payment maturity = 20 years

Market interest rate for similar bonds (YTM) = 10%

Compute Market price = \$1,000

a) Flotation cost = 4% of price for debt up to \$200,000 (net proceed to firm)

b) 8% of price for debt over \$200,000 (net proceed to firm)

(a) Kd for debt up to \$200,000

F/C = 4%, \$1,000 x 0.04 = 40

Net proceed = Price - F.C

= 1000 - 40 = 960

Kd = PV = 960

PMT = -100

FV = -1,000

n = 20

Compound interest = 10.49%

(b) Ks for debt over \$ 200,000

F = 8% of price

1, 000 x 0.08 = 80

Net proceed = 1000- 80= 920

Kd = 920= PV

-100 = PMT

-1000 = FV

20 = N

Compound interest = 11%

(2) Preferred Stock

Dp = 4

Required return for similar stock = 13%

Market price of preferred (VP) = $\frac{4}{0.13}$ = \$30.77 per share

Cost of new (flotation cost) preferred flotation cost

① \$1 for up to 10,000 share

② \$2 for over 10,000 share

① 30.77-1 = 29.77 per share

Total net proceed

= 29.77 × 10,000 = 297,700

② Net proceed = 30,77 - 2 = 28,77 per share

$$Kp = \frac{D_p}{net\ proceed}$$

1. Kp = $\frac{4}{29.77}$ = 13, 44% up to 10,000 share

2. Kp = $\frac{4}{28.77}$ = 13.9 % over 10,000 share

(3) Retained Earning

D = 2.50

g = 7%

Ks = 15%

Cost of retained earning = Ks = 15%

(4) Cost of New Common Stock (CS)

- Flotation cost \$ 3 per share up to \$ 400,000 -①
- Flotation cost \$ 5 per share over \$ 400,000 -②

$$Ke = \frac{D_i}{net\ proceed} + 2$$ Where net proceed = price - flotation costs

$$D_1 = D_n \times (1+g) = 2.5 \times (1.07) = 2.675$$

$$P_0 = \frac{D_1}{ks-g} = \frac{2.675}{0.15-0.07} = 33.4375$$

33.4375 (price) - 3 (flotation cost) = 30.4375

① $Ke = \frac{2,675}{30,4375} + 0.07 = 15.79\%$ for up to \$40,000

② Net proceed = 33.4375 - 5 = 88,4375

$$Ke = \frac{2.675}{28.4375} + 0.07 = 16.41\%$$

for over \$ 40,000 in new CS

STEP 2

MCC change whenever the cost of any capital component changes Break point: The point at which MCC change (stated in total capital dollars, capital budget amount)

- In total capital dollars (capital dollars)
- One MCC, zero BP's
- Two MCC, one BP's
- Three MCC, two BP's

. . .

BP for each capital component = Total amount of one capital component at one cost Fraction of the capital component in the capital structure

(1) Debt

From	To	flotation cost	kd	kd×(1-T)	BP
0	$200,000	4%	10.49%	6.29%	$1500, 000
200,001	∞	8%	11.00%	6.60%	

$$\text{BP for debt} = \frac{200,000}{0.4} = 500,000 \text{ (total capital \$)}$$

(2) Preferred Stock

From	To	Flotation cost	kd
$ 0	$297700	$1	per share 13.44%
$297701	∞	$2	per share 13.90%

$$\text{BP for preferred} = \frac{299,700}{0.1} = 2,977,000$$

(3) Common Stock

RE 100,000

New equity 400,000 F= $3 per share

over 400,000 F= $5 per share

From	to	flotation cost	ks or ke
0	100,000	$0	15%
100,001	500,000	$3	15.79%
500,001	∞	$5	16.71%

$$\text{1st BP for CS} = \frac{100,000}{0.5} = 200,000$$

$$\text{2nd BP for CS} = \frac{500,000}{0.5} = 1,000,000$$

STEP 3

Capital Budget Amount

★★ Cost of capital = Wd x Kd x (1 - T) + (Wp × Kp) + (Ws x Ks)

1) ∅⇒ 200,000 (1st CS BP)

   (0.4) × 6.29 + (1) × 13.44% + (0.5) × 15% = 11.36%

2) 200,001 ⇒ 500,000 (Debt)

   (0.4) × 6.29 + (0.1) × 13.44% + (0.5) × 15.79% = 11.75%

3) 500,001 ⇒ 1,000,000 (2nd CS BP)

   (0.4) × 6.60 + (0.1) × 13.44% + (0.5) × 15.79% = 11.88%

4) 1,000,001 ⇒ 2,977,000 (Preferred stock)

   (0.4) × 6.60 + (0.1) × 13.44% + (0.5) × 16.41% = 12.19%

5) Over 2,977,001

   (0.4) × 6.6 + (0.1) × B.P% + (0.5) × 16.41% = 12.23 %

STEP 4

Marginal Cost of Capital and IOS (Investment Opportunities Schedule)

MCC Schedule

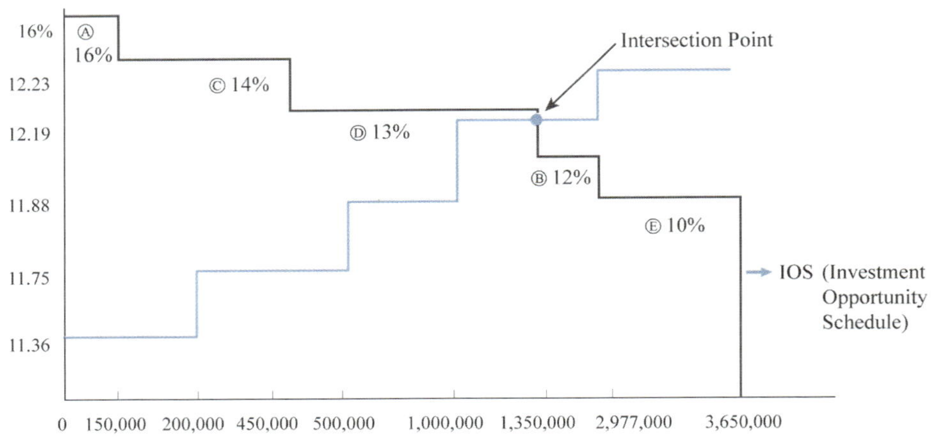

STEP 5

Determine the Optimal Capital Budgets

Liability of investment and their IRR (or Return On Investment) (ROI)
Determine the optimal capital budgets and the corporate cost of capital

① Compute the MCC schedule
② Liability the investment in descending order of return
③ Compute the cumulative budget
④ Determine the "Lowest" (marginal) return
⑤ If marginal return ≧ MCC ⇒ Accept the budget

(Ex)

Project	Budget	IRR
A	150,000	16%
B	800,000	12%
C	300,000	14%
D	900,000	13%
E	1,500,000	10%

Project	Budget	Accumulative Budget	Lowest IRR MCC
A	150,000	150,000	16% > 11.36%
C	300,000	450,000	14% > 11.75%
D	900,000	1,350,000	13% > 12.19%
B	800,000	2,150,000	12% < 12.19%
E	1,500,000	3,650,000	10% < 12.23%

6. Capital Budgeting Decision Rules

1) Measuring Returns on Hotel Projects

Four primary methods are used to rank projects and to decide whether or not they should be accepted for inclusion in the capital budget:

1. Cash on cash return
2. Accounting rate of return,
3. Payback,
4. Net present value,
5. Internal rate of return,

Methods:

Merits of a method depend on whether they are constant with our primary goal

- mutually exclusive ⇒ Rank
- Independent ⇒ minimum requirement

(1) Cash-On-Cash Return

Perhaps the most common method for measuring an investment's rate of return is the simple cash-on-cash method. This is popular because it shows investors the amount of money they will make on the property in relation to their investments each year. Although the time value of money is ignored and oversimplified, the investor is given a quick method of weeding out undesirable hotel projects.

The formula for a cash-on-cash return is determined by dividing the cash flow from a project by the equity investment. (See Exhibit 11-3) The cash-on-cash return can be calculated for the cash flow before taxes or, preferably, for cash flow after income taxes.

The equity investment represents the actual money put up by the owners or investors. The example in Exhibit 11-4 shows how a hypothetical hotel project's operational cash flows. It also shows the subsequent sale of the property as a return on the investors' original investment. Note how the rate of return increases substantially after a few years. This could be the effect of inflationary pressures as well as increased operational efficiencies. Although the return looks rather impressive, it is difficult to know how well the investors or owners are actually doing without applying a discount rate.

Also, the cash-on-cash method makes comparing two projects for the best return difficult. For example, suppose an investor is considering another hotel project. This project may show no cash flow from operations during the first five years, but upon the property's sale at the end of five years, the investor receives an after-tax cash flow from the sale of the property equal to that obtained in Exhibit 11-4($291,000). The return, 242.5 percent, will be the same, but the example in Exhibit 11-6 shows a better investment because the investor would receive cash earlier from the project than in the second example.

EXHIBIT 11-3 Cash-on-Cash Calculation

$$\frac{\text{*Cash Flow}}{\text{Equity Investment}} = \text{Cash-on-Cash Return}$$

EXHIBIT 11-4 Example of a Cash-on-Cash Calculation

Year	Entity Investment	Cash Flow Project Including Sales Proceeds in Years
1	$120,000	0
2		$ 8,000
3		15,000
4		24,000
5		28,000
5(Sale of Project)		216,000
	$120,000	$291,000

$$\text{Cash-on-Cash Return}\frac{291{,}000}{120{,}000} = 242.50\%$$

EXHIBIT 11-5 Example of the Weighted Cost of Capital

	Return Percentage		Percentage of Total	
Debt service	11.76%	×	70%	= 8.23
Equity	13.	×	30%	=3.90
			100	12.13%

As noted earlier, the weakness of the cash-on-cash method is that it does not take into account the time value of money. This is why for a more sophisticated measure of return an investor of owner would use a method such as the internal rate of return that considers the time value of money.

(2) Accounting Rate of Return (ARR)

The ARR model considers the average annual project income (project revenues less project expenses generated by the investment) and the average investment. The calculation of ARR is simply:

ARR = Average Annual Project Income / Average Investment

The average annual project income is the total project income over its life divided by the number of years. Average investment is project cost less salvage value divided by two. The proposed investment is accepted if the ARR exceeds the minimum ARR required. For example, if the minimum acceptable ARR is 40%, a 52% ARR results in project acceptance. The ARR model can be illustrated by using the Hampton Hotel's proposed investment in pizza equipment investment. Let's say total project income over the five-year period is $89,000 ($11,000, $15,000, $17,000, $21,000, $25,000 each year), which results in an average annual project income of $17,800. The average investment is $25,000, determined as follows:

Average Investment = (Project − Salvage)/2
= (50,000 − 0)/2
= \$25,000

The ARR of 71.2% is determined as follows:
ARR = Average Annual Project Income/Average Investment
= 17,800/25,000
=71.2%

Since the project ARR of 71.2% exceeds the required minimum of 40%, if the Hampton Hotel used this capital budgeting model, management would invest in the pizza equipment.

Some managers consider ARR to be useful because it relies on accounting income and, thus, it is easy to calculate and easy to understand. However, these advantages are more than offset by its disadvantages: ARR fails to consider cash flows (considering depreciation) or the time value of money.

(3) Payback Period Method

Payback Period is defined as the expected number of years required for the net revenues of an investment to recover the cost of the investment. The lower the payback is the better. The payback model compares annual cash flows to the project cost to determine a payback period as follows:

Payback Period = Project Cost / Annual Cash Flows

If the calculated payback period is equal to or less than the payback objective, then the project is accepted. The payback model is reasonably popular in the hotel industry because it is conceptually simple. Management simply sets the payback period at the determined length of time required for the operation to get its money back from the project. Also, the payback model is often used as a screening device in conjunction with more sophisticated models, especially in high risk situations. Some operations will not consider evaluating proposed projects using the NPV or IRR approaches unless their initial review using the payback model suggests that the proposed project is viable. The payback period is determined as follows:

A. Set the project cost equal to project cash flows for year 1 through n, where n is the last year (or portion thereof) required for project cash flows to equal the project cost.
B. The payback period equals the number of years of project cash flows to equal the project cost.

For example, the Hampton Hotel invested $50,000 and the estimated cash flows are $18,500, $26,000, $27,500, $31,500, and $35,500 each year. The hotels accept/reject criteria for payback is 3 years. The payback period for the hotel can be calculated as follows:

Project Cost = Project Cash Flows for Years 1, 2, and 2 of year 3.
$50,000 = $18,500 + $26,000 + $5,500
$50,000 = $50,000

The final $5,500 of project cash flows is 2 of the third year's project cash flows of $27,500. Therefore, the payback period is 2.2 years. Since the payback period of 2.2 years is less than the accept/reject criterion of

3 years, based upon the payback model, the Hampton Hotel would invest in the proposed pizza project.

Disadvantages of the payback model that require careful consideration are that it fails to consider either the time value of money or the project flows after the payback period. The latter disadvantage is readily apparent when comparing two mutually exclusive projects (A and B) as follows:

Year	0	1	2	3	4	5
Project A	$10,000	5,000	4,000	3,000	2,000	1,000
Project B	$10,000	3,000	4,000	5,000	6,000	7,000

Payback Period for A: 2.33 years

Payback Period for B: 2.60 years

Excess Cash flow generated beyond payback period of Project A: $5,000

Excess Cash flow generated beyond payback period of Project B: $15,000

Present value of all cash discounted at 15% for the project A: $10,986

Present value of all cash discounted at 15% for the project B: $15,833

Based upon the payback method, project A would be accepted rather than project B, because the payback period of 2.33 years for project is less than 2.6 years for project B. However, the excess cash flow is $10,000 more for project B. The calculation of the present value of all cash flows of $10,986 and $15,833 for project A and B, respectively, is convincing. If this is not readily clear, it will be as we now turn to consider the net present value model.

Payback

Assumption: CF occurs evenly through out the year.

- Payback
= # of year before full recovery + (Unrecovered cost at short of year/CF during that ear)
- Ranking: Shorter, better

Ex)

Minimum requirements: Some arbitrary # of years.

Year	0	1	2	3	4	5
CF's	-500	150	150	150	150	150
cum. CF's	-500	-350	-200	-50	100	250

Payback = 3yrs + (50/150) = 3.33yrs

- **Advantage of payback methods**
    - Simple to use
    - Liquidity of the project

- **Disadvantage of payback methods**
    - Ignore the time value of money
    - Ignore CF's after the payback period
    - Minimum requirement is set arbitrarily

Discounted payback

- Takes into account the time value of money
- Discount all CF's to their PV using the cost of capital

Let WACC = 10%

Year	0	1	2	3	4	5
CF	-500	150	150	150	150	150
PV of CF	-500	136	124	113	102	93
cum. PV OF CF	-500	-364	-240	-127	-25	68

⇒ Discounted payback

$$4+\frac{25}{93}=4.27\,years$$

(4) Net Present Value (NPV) Model

The easiest discounting method is the net present value (NPV) method. The hotel owner or investor selects a rate of return acceptable to him or her. The NPV is most useful in comparing alternative investments in which the cash flows and the timing of the cash flows vary significantly from project to project.

A common way to apply the internal rate of return method in the hotel industry is for the owners or investors to select satisfactory rate of return to their needs. They then apply that discount rate to the hotel project's cash flow projections and derive a present value dollar figure. This present value of the future income is then compared with the initial investment. If the present value is larger than the actual required investment, the project is considered sufficiently attractive to justify the investment.

Both the NPV and IRR models overcome the weaknesses of the previous models in that they consider the time value of money. The new present value approach discounts cash flows to their present value. The new present value is calculated by subtracting the project cost from the present value of the discounted cash flow stream. The project is accepted if the NPV is equal to or greater than zero. If the capital budgeting decision considers mutually exclusive alternatives, the alternative with the highest NPV is accepted and other alternatives are rejected.

<Key Note>

NPV methods of evaluating investment

1) Determine discount rate
2) Compute the PV of the net cash flow
3) Compute the PV of cost outlays required by the investment
4) Subtract the PV of capital outlays from the PV of the net inflow
5) Apply the criteria for acceptance or rejection

    If NPV > 0 accept

    NPV < 0 reject

    NPV = 0 either accept or reject

The advantage of the NPV model over the two models presented previously is the consideration of cash flows and the time value of money. Using the Hampton Hotel's proposed investment in pizza equipment and assuming a discount rate of 15%, the new present value to be $39,491. Therefore, based on the NPV model, the Hampton Hotel should make the proposed investment, because NPV is positive.

* Assumption
  CF's are reinvested on the discounted rate (i.e. the cost of capital)

- Ranking: higher NPV, better
  Minimum requirement: NPV ≧ 0

Ex)

- NPV = Sum of PV
  Using previous ex = -500+136+124+113+102+93 = 68

By calculator,

CF I -500

150

150

150

150

150

i = WACC = 10%

Comp NPV = 68.61

Advantage of NPV

- Takes into account the time value of money
- Look at all CF's
- Discount rate = WACC, we know that
- when NPV ≧ 0, all investors are satisfied
- Reinvestment assumption is "Reasonable".

Examining the Net Present Value (NPV) method

The best way to examine the NPV method is with the following example. An investor wants a rate of return for a hotel project to return at least 14 percent annual average return. Assume that the investor wishes to invest $10,000 in the project. This initial investment is made at Time 0 since the investment takes in the present. The initial investment is then compared against the after-tax cash flow for each year discounted by 14 percent. (See Exhibit 11-6 below.)

Because the present value of discounted cash flow equals $11,093, which is more than the initial investment of $10,000, the investment meets the acceptability criteria. This assumes that all the underlying assumptions relating to the project are realistic. For instance, one major assumption in the example above was that the cash flows in a year occur at the end of the year in question. If this is inaccurate the assumption could result in an error in discounting the cash flows.

Although the above project example meets the investment criteria of 14 percent, the investor or owner does not know the exact yield rate. For that we must use a slightly more sophisticated method known as the internal rate of return (IRR).

EXHIBIT 11-6 Example of Net Present Value (NPV)

14% Rate of Return Desired

Year	Investment	Cash Flow	From Tables Present Value at 14%	Discounted Cash Flow
0	$10,000	0	1.0	
1		0	.877	-0-
2		$3,000	.769	$2,307
3		6,000	.675	4,050
4		8,000	.592	4,736
	Totals	$17,000		$11,093

(5) Internal Rate of Return (IRR)

The internal rate of return (IRR) is a very popular method of measuring the investment analysis of hotel property. Its main advantage is that it gives weight to the time value of money devoted to one project as opposed to alternative projects.

Simply defined the rate of discount, when applied to projected cash flows, will produce a total "present value" equal to the initial investment outlay. Put another way, the IRR is the discount rate that equates all the hotel project's cash inflows to the outflows. Cash flows consist of income from operations plus the sales price at the end of the analysis period.

Exhibit 11-7 below shows the way to find IRR. A 17-percent discount rate with the data yields $10,209. This exceeds the initial investment of $10,000; therefore, the IRR must be greater than 17 percent.

EXHIBIT 11-7

Calculation of NPV of an Income Stream at 17%

Year	Investment	Cash Flow	From Tables PV at 17%	Discounted Cash Flow
0	$10,000	0	1	
1		0	.855	0
2		$3,000	.731	$2,193
3		6,000	.624	3,744
4		8,000	.534	4,272
	Total	$17,000		$10,209

Calculation of NPV of an Income Stream at 18%

Year	Investment	Cash Flow	From Tables PV at 18%	Discounted Cash Flow
0	$10,000	0	1	
1		0	.847	0
2		$3,000	.718	$2,154
3		6,000	.609	3,654
4		8,000	.516	4,128
	Total	$17,000		$9,936

If a discount rate of 18 percent is used (see Exhibit 11-7), the present value of the projected cash flows equals $9,936. This value is less than the initial investment of $10,000; therefore, the IRR is between 17 percent and 18 percent. The actual IRR is 17.75 percent.

Although one can determine the exact IRR for a project through discount tables and interpolation, there is no need to work out the calculations by hand because of the availability of sophisticated calculators and personal computers. This allows the owner or investor more time to actually analyze the project instead of grinding out numbers.

Although the IRR is useful for analyzing hotel investments, it is not perfect. One major assumption of the IRR is that the owner or investor can earn the same rate of return by reinvesting revenues while the project operates. Obviously, this assumption may not hold up in every project considered.

Using the IRR model

The IRR model is a capital budgeting approach that considers cash flows and the time value of money and determines the rate of return earned by a proposed project. In determining IRR, the net present value of cash flows is set at zero and the discount rate is determined. The following assume that a proposed project costs $6,850 and is expected to yield a cash flow stream of $3,000 for three years. The internal rate of return is 15%, determined as follows:

0 = (3,000/1.15*) + (3,000/1.15**) + (3,000/1.15***) − 6,850

Where * is 1, ** is 2, *** is 3.

0 = 2,609 + 2,268 + 1,973 − 6,850

0 = 0

Using the IRR model, a project is accepted if the IRR is equal to, or greater than, the established minimum IRR, which is commonly called hurdle rate by hotel financial managers.

Like NPV model, the IRR model is superior to the ARR and payback approaches because it considers the time value of money. The IRR is also superior to the ARR model because it considers cash flows. When there is a capital budgeting decision involving mutually exclusive projects, results from the IRR model may conflict with the NPV approach. This conflict may occur because of the IRR's assumption that all project cash flows are reinvested at the internal rate of return. Since operations normally invest in the most profitable projects first, one should not assume that other projects would result in the same return. Although the brief illustration of IRR above may have appeared simple, in practice, manual calculations are by trial and error. Various discount rates are tried until the approximate net present value is found to be zero. Alternatively, the IRR can be quickly and easily determined using a computer. In general, the NPV approach is more useful when mutually exclusive projects are considered. On the other hand, many industry financial managers prefer the IRR model because the results are easier to interpret.

IRR

$$NPV = 0 = \sum_{t=0}^{n} CF_t \times \frac{1}{(1+IRR)^t}$$

- Assumption: all CF's are re-invested at the IRR.
- Ranking: higher IRR, better
- Minimum requirement: IRR ≧ WACC (Hurdle rate)
- compute IRR

* Use calculator
⇒ enter all CF's, Comp IRR

Advantages of IRR

- Takes into account the time value of money
- Minimum requirement; all investors are satisfied

Disadvantages of IRR

- Normal CF's (multiple IRR, no solution, and wrong solution)
- Re-investment assumption may not be realistic if the IRR for a project

is exceptional

Practice:

0	1	2	3	4
-400	100	150	200	150

K=12%, m=1

(1) What is NPV? 46.548

(2) What is IRR? 16.9963 ≒ 17%

$$PV_1 = 100 \text{ X } (\frac{1}{1.12})^1 = 89.29$$

$$PV_2 = 150 \text{ X } (\frac{1}{1.12})^2 = 119.58$$

$$PV_3 = 200 \text{ X } (\frac{1}{1.12})^3 = 142.36$$

$$PV_4 = 150 \text{ X } (\frac{1}{1.12})^4 = 95.33$$

446.56 (total PV)

\- 400

46.56 (NPV)

$$46.54 = 600(\frac{1}{1+IRR})^4$$

16.9965%

By Calculator

-400 CF_0

100 CF_1

150 CF_2

200 CF_3

150 CF_4

Comp [IRR] ⇒ 16.9965

IRR < 16.9963 (cutting edge)

By Calculator

-400	CF0
100	CF1
150	CF2
200	CF3
150	CF4
12	I
Comp	NPV = 46.54

Note:

Thinking about the Conflict between IRR & NPV

* Only applied to mutually exclusive project
* Ranking is different under NPV vs. IRR.
* Projects differ in scale and/or timing of CF's

Ex-(difference in scale)

0	1	2	3	4	YEAR
-200	50	100	50	40	Project A
-200,000	40,000	100,000	80,000	40,000	Project B

A & B are mutually exclusive

WACC = 10%

NPV of A = $ 15.52

NPV of B = $ 64.34 > B is better using NPV methods

IRR for A = 14%

IRR for B = 11% > A is better using the IRR methods

⇒ Should use NPV method whenever they are conflict

NPV profile graph of the NPV of a project at different discount rate

$$\text{NPV} = \sum_{t=0}^{n} CF_2 \times \left(\frac{1}{1+k}\right)^t$$

If WACC < crossover rate

Conflict between IRR&NPV

If WACC > crossover rate

IRR B>A NO conflict.

NPV B>A

If WACC = crossover rate

Nap's are the same for A, B and there is no conflict.

(6) Summary

For owners investors to make any type of intelligent investments in hotel projects, they need some way to measure rates of return. The importance of measuring the rate of return takes into consideration not only the return on one project but also how that project compares with other projects investors may be interested in.

Cash flow from the hotel project is a very important component in measuring return on investment. The investor of owner judges the success of the project by how much money is returned over the course of operations and the subsequent sale of the project. The investor or owner may use the simple payback analysis or cash-on-cash method of analyzing the rate of return. These methods provide a quick and easy way to measure return on a hotel project. The biggest disadvantage of these methods is that they fail to consider the time value of money.

"Present value" is simply the premise that a dollar today is worth more than a dollar tomorrow. This concept is easy to apply, but its main application is to determine just how much more that dollar is worth today than tomorrow. For this, the investor or owner must know the projected inflation rate, the likelihood of generating income in the future, and the subsequent collection of funds. The longer in time that one waits for income the greater the risk that money will not be available for collection.

Leverage is a way to use other people's money in such a way that the investor or owner is able to earn a greater rate of return on that money than he or she pays out. If the investor or owner calculates incorrectly or events turn out differently than projected the borrowed funds could cost the hotel project more than the project is earning, thus creating a situation of negative financial leverage.

Appreciation is the most speculative of the various methods used to calculate rates of return. Many successful hotel projects owe their success almost entirely to the appreciation of the property on which the project was located. Also, since the operation of a hotel project is so service oriented, its value often is determined by how well the property is managed.

Before utilizing the time value of money method, the owner or investor must select the appropriate discount rate to use in analyzing the hotel project. "Discounting" consists of assigning the discount rate to the future income projections to arrive at the present value of those income streams. However, arriving at the appropriate discount rate can be rather involved because of the many variables involved. The discount rate is the calculation of what the owner or investor has determined to be an acceptable rate of return taking into consideration such risk factors as future inflation, failure of the project, not meeting debt service, and liquidity risk. Also individuals may differ about what is an appropriate discount rate to use.

The "internal rate of return" offers the advantage of taking into consideration the time value of money. The IRR is the rate of discount applied to projected cash flows that produces a total present value equal to the initial investment outlay. The major assumption used in the IRR is that each year's cash flow can be reinvested at the same rate of return, which may not be realistic in every circumstance.

Practice Questions

Question 1

Carefully explain the process of capital budgeting. That is, discuss the major steps involved in an application of this tool to a specific project. (In your discussion you may "make up" an example if you wish). Further, use the context of this model to explain how changes in interest rates either decrease or stimulate real investment.

Question 2

Are there any similarities and differences in capital budgeting practices between hotel and industrial firms? A CEO was quoted as saying: "Capital budgeting analysis, too often do not anticipate the actions of our competitors, which may reduce the benefits we might otherwise expect. Thus there always is a place for "gut instinct" in the capital budgeting process". How do you respond to this statement using the hotel industry as a context?

Practice Questions

True (T) or False (F)

01 Accounting rates of return do not account for the time value of money.

02 When calculated using cash flows, accounting rates of return understate the true compounded rate of return on a project

03 The payback is the number of periods that a project takes to generate total cash inflows equal to the total cash outflows associated with the investment in the project

04 When a payback does not come out in an exact number of periods, it is expressed as the number of whole periods plus a fraction of the total initial investment.

05 Using the payback method can lead to an emphasis on short-term projects that quickly cover their initial cost.

06 The internal rate of return is the rate of discount that makes a project's net present value equal to the sum of the project's cash flows.

07 An IRR calculated using the equity approach to NPV represents the true financial ROE of the project.

08 The IRR is the true compounded rate of return earned on an investment.

09 An IRR calculated using the WACC approach should be compared with the project's Ke.

10 The IRR criterion is always consistent with the NPV criterion.

11 It is possible for an NPV profile to cross the horizontal axis more than once.

12 The "scale problem" can occur when we use the IRR to evaluate two or more projects that require different levels of investment.

13 The one strength of the WACC approach to NPV is that, given a Ka from corporate headquarters, any manager should be able to estimate the relevant cash flows needed to calculate the NPV.

14 When the WACC approach to NPV is used, interest payments must be added to net income when the project's net cash flow per period is estimated.

15 The WACC approach to NPV implicitly assumes that the leverage ratio will fluctuate over the life of the project.

16 The adjusted present value approach to NPV should be used when the firm's project will be financed with a set amount of debt whose interest and principal payments are known in advance.

▣ Multiple Choices

17 Which of the following is not true of the payback criterion?

a. It ignores the time value of money.
b. It is easy to calculate.
c. It ignores cash flows after the payback period.
d. It is consistent with NPV.

18 When a project's NPV is graphed, the internal rate of return will occur:

a. when $k = 0$.
b. where the NPV of the project is maximized.
c. where the NPV of the project is zero.
d. nowhere; it cannot be determined from the NPV profile.

19 The reinvestment rate assumption is the implicit assumption that the cash flows generated by a project are reinvested at:

a. the project's IRR.
b. the owner's k_a.
c. the owner's k_e.
d. project's accounting rate of return.

20 The present value of a future dividend is affected by the __________ of the dividend.

e. timing
f. riskiness
g. magnitude
h. all of the above

21 In the equity approach to NPV, the correct discount rate is:

a. Ka.

b. Ke.

c. Kd.

d. Kde.

Answers to the Practice Problems:

Answer Keys T, F, T, F, T, F, T, T, F, F, T, T, T, F, F, T, D, C, A, D, B

Chapter 12

Franchising and Management Contracts

Chapter 12 Franchising and Management Contracts[7)]

Franchising has been part of economic system since the 19th century, when Singer Corporation in U.S. introduced it as a way of selling sewing machines. Basically, a franchise is the right to sell someone's product or service. The owner of the business is the "franchisor," and the person who is granted the right to sell the product or service is the "franchisee." Generally, the franchisee pays a one-time initial fee and then a monthly royalty fee based on the gross sales of the franchisee business.

The collector of the royalty fee based on gross sales has an advantage in that both the franchisor and franchisee have a vested interest in the business. The higher the gross sales, the more likely that the franchisee will be more successful; the increased sales mean that the franchisor will receive larger monthly royalty checks. The franchisee can also increase wealth by having a large enough territory to open up more than one outlet. The franchisor benefits again because this expansion increases the loyalty fees that he or she will receive.

Many people mistake entrepreneurial activity with franchising. In franchising, a person buys a proven method of doing business. This is especially true in the hotel industry. People who desire to be their own boss usually will not want to be a franchisee. On the other hand, with the high failure rate among independent hotel firms, a trade of some

7) Adapted from John M Tarras, 1991 A practrical guide to Hospitality Finance. Van Nostrand Reinhold, New York.

independence for a better opportunity to success makes the franchise operation very attractive to many individuals.

There are no guarantees in any business venture. Even though the failure rate for franchises is lower than that for independent operations, many franchises do fail or make insufficient profit to the franchisee for the time and effort put into the business.

Most hotel franchises can be broken down into the restaurant segment and the hotel segment. Both types depend on name recognition, reputation, and a standard method of doing business. Such well-known companies as McDonald's, Wendy's, Holiday Inn, Chi Chi's, Comfort Inn, and others owe their growth to the franchise system.

Any person who wants to obtain a franchise must assess his or her reasons for doing so. Some franchises require that the franchisee actually work in the business and not be merely a passive investor. Other franchises restrict the territory or opportunity to expand beyond a certain limited territory.

1. Types of Franchise

1) Restaurants

The restaurant segment and the hotel segment dominate franchising in the hotel industry.

There are far more restaurant than hotel franchises because it generally costs more to construct a hotel than to open a restaurant.

The restaurant franchising segment is dominated by the fast-food industry. The largest single segment within fast food segment is the hamburger market. This segment has been dominated by McDonald's,

Burger King, Wendy's, and Hardee's. Other important markets include chicken, Mexican food, seafood, steak, sandwich, pancake, ice cream, and yogurt.

Although restaurant franchising has enjoyed tremendous popularity, especially in the past 30 years, there are indications that the restaurant market is becoming saturated. As a result, many franchise companies have folded in recent years, notably the D'lites restaurant chain. Today, restaurants compete not only with themselves but also with other service-oriented businesses such as party stores, supermarkets, and department stores.

To remain competitive, many restaurant franchises now operate within hotels and motels to be closer to demand generators. Another trend is combining two or more franchises in a single building to help reduce real estate and management costs. Many older restaurant franchises are rehabilitating older properties to give them a fresher look to compete with newer franchises.

2) Hotel and Motels

The hotel and motel industry is broken into many segments, with franchising dominating the budget motel segment. In general, the cost of obtaining a hotel or motel franchise is greater than that of a restaurant because of the necessity of building the hotel. Therefore, there are not as many potential investors for hotel and motel franchises as for restaurants.

The most affordable lodging franchises are in the budget hotel segment. Many fill-service hotel chains do not franchise. If they do, they franchise only to certain management companies. The cost of a full-service hotel can run into millions of dollars, which limits the number of potential franchisees. A typical budget motel costs between $10,000 and $20,000 per room, excluding land cost. This means that, depending on the size of the operation, even for a budget motel the total construction cost run between $200,000 and $2.5 million. In addition, the initial franchise fee may cost several thousand dollars. There are many more start-up expenses, such as the cost of furnishing each room, that the franchisee to have sufficient resources prior to opening a hotel.

2. Offering Circular and Contract

1) Offering Circular

The legal relationship between the franchisee and the franchisor is defined in the franchise contract. However, due to widespread fraud in recent years, the Federal Trade Commission(FTC) and several states require that the franchisor provide the prospective franchisee with an offering circular at least 10 days before signing any franchise contract.

The offering circular provides sufficient information to the franchisee to allow him or her to make an intelligent decision about obtaining a franchise. However, the FTC does not review the offering circular for accuracy. The offering circular is not the franchise contract, and important provisions may be left off the document. It is very important for the prospective franchisee to review both the offering circular and the franchise agreement with an attorney who is an expert in franchise law. The following items are required in the offering circular, according to the FTC:

1. Identification of the franchisor and its affiliates. The circular must identify by address the franchisor, addresses of affiliates, and any predecessor companies.

2. The business experience of each of the franchisor's officers, directors, and key management.
3. Any previous bankruptcies involving the franchisor and its officers, directors, and key management. It is much easier to trust someone who has a clean history in business dealing. However, the fact that key personnel have been involved in failed business in the past does not mean this business also will fail. But the franchisee should satisfy him or herself that the reasons for failure were not due to the franchisor's incompetence.
4. Any lawsuits involving the franchisor and its officers, directors, and key management. It is important to analyze the types of lawsuits and their frequency because they may indicate the franchisor's management style. Also, could the lawsuits place the franchisor in financial difficulty?
5. The initial franchise fee and other initial payments to be paid by the franchisee to obtain the franchise. This section states the fee to be paid up front by the franchisee and any other fees required to obtain the franchise. The method of payment is discussed at this point. The manner in which the initial franchise fee may be refunded if the franchise agreement is terminated prior to opening is also defined.
6. The continuing expenses the franchisee will be responsible to pay the franchisor once the business is open. This includes royalties and any other costs such as advertising, equipment, and supplies. This section does not include those expenses that are a normal part of the business operation such as payroll, taxes, and supplies to outside vendors.
7. Any financial assistance available from the franchisor or its affiliates to the franchisee for purchase of the franchise. This does not happen very often. However, several of the more established franchisors do

have programs for assisting qualified minority businesses set up a franchise.

8. The type and quality of goods and services used in the franchise. This includes any requirements about their having to be purchased from the franchisor and any restrictions concerning purchases from the franchisor or its affiliates. In this section, the franchisor must disclose the standards for each product. Generally, it is illegal to require that the franchisee purchase from the franchisor goods and services that can be reasonably purchased from a third party. However, there are exceptions. For instance, a restaurant franchise can require that the franchisee purchase perhaps one brand of soft drink from a third party for consistency among stores. However, a requirement to purchase paper products only from the franchisor may not be legal. Nevertheless, the franchisor may establish standards that the paper products must meet in order to maintain consistency among the franchises.
9. Products or services the franchise is permitted to sell and any restrictions on what may be sold by the franchisee. This section informs the franchisee about what is permissible to sell in the business and the restrictions the franchisor places on the sale of other products or services.
10. Any territory limitations. Each franchise has a certain limited territory in which the franchisee expects exclusivity. If the territory is too small, the franchisee will compete with other franchisees or company stores in an area where there are too few customers to make the territory profitable.
11. Any restrictions on the franchisee in the operation of the business. This is a very detailed list of what is expected of the franchisee in the actual operation of the business. For example, the agreement may

require that the floors of the restaurant be washed every two hours. These restrictions on operation can be quite cumbersome and the franchisee should understand that by agreeing to them he or she is obliged to conform to the agreement.

12. Criteria used for terminating, renewing, and transferring a franchise. This section details conditions that may cause the franchise to terminate, be renewed, and transferred to a third party. It is important to understand what constitutes a termination of the franchise agreement; failure to do so could result in the franchisee losing the franchise. Also, many companies permit regular renewal. However, there is usually an additional cost for renewal and the fees may be substantial. This is especially true if the franchise is very successful.
13. Training programs provided to franchisees. In the hotel business, customer service is very important, and this section must be examined closely for exactly what kind of training will be provided to the franchisee and his or her employees. The service industry is becoming extremely competitive, and the need for a well-trained staff is a must.
14. Any approval necessary for assistance provided in selecting a site for the franchise. The hotel industry is driven by getting customers in the door, and location is extremely important. It is important to know if any assistance is provided to help the franchisee locate a good site. At a minimum, most hotel franchisors require their approval of a site before awarding a franchise.
15. The franchisor's financial statements. The franchisor is required to show the latest financial reports to the franchisee. These include balance sheets and income statements. They should be examined closely to determine the franchisor's financial health. The franchisee should be extremely suspicious of financial reports that have not been audited by an independent certified accountant.

16. Statistical information concerning the franchises. This section contains the raw data on present franchises, the number of terminated franchises, the renewal rate of franchises, the repurchases of franchises, and the projection of future franchises. This data does not name any particular franchisees, but it is intended to give the franchisee an idea of what has been happening in key areas of the franchise. There are almost always franchises that do not work out, so the fact that a small percentage of them have been terminated should not alarm a potential franchisee unduly. However, if more that 20 percent of franchises have been terminated, the franchisee should inquiry more closely about the reasons.
17. The involvement of any celebrities in the franchise. Many franchises use celebrities to pitch for a particular business. However, these celebrities are often not owners but merely paid spokespersons for the franchises. It is a mistake to base an investment on a franchise business because of a celebrity speaking for the franchise.
18. The participation required of the franchisee in the operation of the franchise. Many hotel franchises, especially restaurants, require the franchisee to work full time at the franchise. Many franchisors do not permit the franchisee to operate any business in the same field as the franchise business. For instance, a restaurant franchise may prohibit the franchisee from operating another restaurant franchise.
19. The basis for claimed earnings, if presented. Franchisors very seldom predict what a franchisee will earn in the franchise business. This is to prevent lawsuits by disgruntled franchisees if their earnings do not materialize.
20. A list of the names and addresses of other franchisees so the franchisee can contact them to get their opinions about the franchise business and the franchisor.

Many franchisors have decided that showing projected operating profits that the franchisee may earn is too risky because the franchisee might treat the earnings projections as a guarantee of future earning and involve the franchisor in litigation for misrepresentation if they fail to meet earnings projections. Therefore, most offering circulars do not state any earnings projections.

2) The Franchise Contract

The offering circular is very helpful, but the franchise agreement specifies the legal rights and obligations of the parties. Also, many items are not included in the franchise agreement which had been covered in the franchise contract. The franchise contract is drafted by the franchisor, and thus terms and conditions will favor the franchisor in most instances. This is why it is so important for the franchisee to seek someone with franchise experience to help review and negotiate the franchise contract.

The first step for many franchisees is not actually signing a franchise agreement but rather a purchase agreement. In the purchase agreement, the franchisee puts down a deposit as a good-faith gesture that he or she will execute a franchise agreement in the near future. This deposit is usually required because the franchisee may need assistance locating a suitable site or obtaining a desired lease before the franchise can be obtained. As such, the deposit is usually refundable if the desired location cannot be obtained. However, if the franchisee wants to end the relationship for other reasons, the deposit is usually forfeited as liquidated damages.

3. Franchise Cost and Fees

1) Restaurant Franchise Costs

Many fees are associated with most franchise operations. It is important when evaluating a franchise opportunity to understand all of them. For example, the cost of building the restaurant structure could be hundreds of thousands of dollars. That is why many restaurant franchisees rent rather than build. But even if the franchisee rents, he or she will probably have to spend several thousand dollars on leasehold improvements to bring the property up to the standards of the franchisor. In addition, the franchisee must purchase equipment for the restaurant, and this can easily run into thousands of dollars. The franchisee will also have to purchase an initial inventory supply, incur pre-opening expenses such as hiring and training, and provide sufficient working capital for the operation of the restaurant. Other non-operating costs of obtaining the franchise are:

- Franchise fee. This is the initial franchise fee that is charged to open each operation. This can range from free for a new franchise attempting to get off the ground to several thousand dollars. This fee may be refundable in part if the franchisee is unable to obtain financing. The franchise fee compensates the franchisor for the use of its name and trademarks and to defray the expenses the franchisor incurs in selling franchises, consultation, training, and assistance to franchisees before the opening of each restaurant.
- Royalty fee. After the restaurant is open, it pays a royalty fee based on a percentage of gross sales from the operation. This fee can vary significantly from franchise to franchise, but it is usually in the single digits for most franchises. Established companies such as McDonald's

can command double-digit royalty fees.

- Advertising fees. Most franchisors charge a fee based on gross receipts, usually one to four percent. This fee is usually placed in a special fund that can only be used for advertising and public relations. Often the franchisor contributes to this fund for company-owned stores.
- Local advertising. In addition to requiring the franchisee to pay a fee for national advertising, many franchisors also require the franchisee to spend a minimum amount for local advertising, usually a percentage of gross receipts.
- Renewal fees. Most franchisors charge a renewal fee when the franchise contract expires for the franchisee to retain the franchise.
- Upgrading cost. Most franchisors insist that the franchise be upgraded to remain competitive. Usually, the franchisee is responsible for the entire cost of renovation.
- Transfer fees. The franchisor charges a fee for the transfer of the ownership of an approved franchise. Generally, the fee is lower if the transfer is to an existing franchisee.
- Training costs. Many franchisors provide the initial training for free. Even if there is no charge for training, the franchisee is usually responsible for travel, lodging, and personal expenses.
- Other costs. Other expenses may arise or are contingent upon certain events. For instance, many restaurant franchises require that new franchisees spend a certain amount on the "grand opening" of every store. Also, most franchisors require that if an audit of the books reveals that revenues were understated by more than a certain percentage, the franchisee is required to pay for the audit as well as the royalty shortage.

2) Hotel Franchise Costs

Many expenses common to restaurants also be applied to hotels. The single biggest difference, however, is that hotels and motels are usually constructed and thus renting property is not an option. This makes the hotel franchise a larger business investment. Hotel and motel franchises usually require a minimum number of rooms for each property. The cost to build a hotel could amount to a few thousand dollars per room for budget hotels to hundreds of thousands of dollars per room for luxury properties. The franchisor offers almost no help in financing the construction of these properties. Other likely costs beside normal operating costs in obtaining a franchise are:

- Franchise fee. This initial fee is usually based on a dollar amount per room plus a minimum amount regardless of the number of rooms. This fee covers the cost of training and assistance provided to the franchisees and the cost of quality control inspections and support of the main office staff. For example, a hotel may charge an initial franchise fee of $300 per room and a minimum fee of $40,000.
- Royalty fee. This fee is based on a percentage of gross room revenue, and it varies among hotel chains. Some hotel chains levy a fixed charge per room rather than a percentage of room revenues. The royalty fee is usually two to six percent of gross room revenues.
- Advertising fee. This fee is usually based on a percentage of room revenue, and it supports national and regional advertising. The advertising fee is usually one to three percent of gross room revenues.
- Reservation fee. This fee is charged either at a percentage of room revenue or as a fixed amount per room or reservation. This fee supports the hotel or motel chain's national reservation system. Many lodging

chains require franchisees to purchase or lease reservation equipment.

3) Analyzing Different Franchise Agreements

There is no single method to help the franchisee evaluate one franchise over another. There is always an element of risk in choosing any franchise; the newer the franchise is, the more riskier the investment becomes. In evaluating alternatives, the franchisee must select a method of evaluating the return on the total investment required on discounted return method.

The initial investments by franchisee includes the franchise fees and other start-up costs. Many times, investors make franchise decisions based only on the cost of obtaining the franchise. This is a mistake because some established franchises, such as McDonald's, are expensive to obtain but also offer the closest thing to a guaranteed return as it is in the hotel industry. Another factor that makes evaluation difficult is correctly estimating the support the franchisor provides for the fee charged. The ultimate success of any franchisee depends on the support and financial strength of the franchisor. The franchisee can learn a lot about the franchisor by talking to other franchisees.

The other major cost is the continuing expense associated with the franchise. This includes the royalty fee, advertising fee, and reservation fee. Again, each prospective franchisee should evaluate his or her return on investment after all expenses have been considered. This is difficult to do unless the franchisee reviews the return after total costs are considered. For instance, some franchisors charge a lower-than-average initial franchise fee but then impose a higher-than-average royalty fee.

4. Management Contracts

Management contracts became increasingly popular in the past 10 years. In the past, most hotels were owned and operated by the same company or leased to a hotel operator. However, as hotel financing became riskier and more complicated, lenders began to insist that hotels be professionally managed. Also, the increase in real estate prices in the late 1970s and early 1980s convinced many hotel companies would be more profitable for them to sell hotel properties and enter into long-term management contracts to operate the hotels.

However, criticism has suggested that the new management companies have not operated hotel properties any better than they were in the past. As a result, a new field, "asset management," has evolved in which the owner oversees the operation of the property to ensure that it is run properly. Some hotels are run by the asset managers with the management company merely carrying out the owner's wishes.

A hotel management contract is simply an agreement by the owner or developer and the operating or management company. The owner retains the risk of real estate ownership; the management company, agents for the owner, is responsible for operating the property. In return for operating the hotel property, the management company receives a fee. The fee may be a base fee only, an incentive fee only, or (more likely) a combination of base and incentive fees.

As in any contract between two parties, almost all provisions are negotiable, and the relative strength of the two parties in negotiating process determines which contract provisions will favor which party. Also, the parties must remain flexible in which strategies and tactics are applied in negotiating a contract because what may be effective in today's economy may not work a month later as conditions change.

All sections of the management contract are important and should be dealt with carefully. Some more important provisions are discussed below.

1) Period of the Management Contract

The period or duration of the management contract balances the strength of the management company against that of the owners. The initial term of the management contract could be from one to 50 years, depending on the strengths of the negotiating parties. For instance, an independent management company that manages a few properties is not in the same bargaining position as the Marriot Hotel Management Company and would generally accept a shorter operating term agreement than the Marriot.

The contract may or may not provide for renewal of the management contract provisions. General renewal terms are longer with chain or first-tier management companies than with independent operators or second-tier companies. As with the initial term, the frequency and length of renewal depends on the strength of negotiating parties. Renewal periods may run from one to 10 years.

The duration of management contracts is important because if the management company does a poor job it may be difficult to terminate the contract. Another consideration is when the owners wish to sell the property. The remaining length of the contract may influence the sale price of the real estate. If a prospective buyer wishes to utilize his or her own management company and there is no termination provision in the contract, the buyer may lose interest in purchasing the property because of the time remaining in the contract.

2) Management Fees

The management company expects to be paid for services it renders to the owners. However, the exact form this payment takes is often subject to intense bargaining. Basically, the management contract includes a base-fee provision and an incentive-fee arrangement. However, a management contract may provide for a base-fee arrangement only or an incentive-fee arrangement only.

A typical base-fee arrangement is usually based on a percentage of gross operating revenue and typically consists of between three to five percent of this revenue. The incentive fee, on the other hand, is usually based on gross operating profit, usually net income after fixed charges or on cash flow from the property. The incentive fee could run anywhere from 10 to 25 percent of the net operating profit.

There are many reasons why management contract fees vary greatly from property to property. Following the reputation of the management company, the next consideration is whether the fee structure consists mostly of a basic fee or an incentive fee arrangement. Management companies normally prefer the basic fee on gross revenue to assure themselves a profit no matter how the hotel actually performs. Hotel owners prefer that the operator takes greater risk in the operation of the property and thus prefer to pay the management company on an incentive-fee basis. Therefore, the owner and Management Company must negotiate the fee arrangement to the satisfaction of both parties.

The incentive fee arrangement has to be negotiated so that the hotel property will be able to pay the incentive fee and still be an operating entity. Because a property can generate operating income without necessarily generating a positive cash flow or sufficient rate of return to the owner, the hotel representatives may wish to include a clause in the contract to limit payout of the incentive fee. This limit can relate to minimum cash flow generated by the property, rate of return on the owner's invested capital, or some other mutually agreed-upon limitation.

The management fee, minus the limitation, is due and payable with interest when and if the property reaches the stated objectives or the property is sold. The limit could even be set up so that if the property failed to reach its objective, an incentive fee would be eliminated that year. If that were the case, the management company could bargain for a higher incentive fee rate.

3) Management Company's Responsibilities

Most management contracts grant the management company the exclusive rights to operate the hotel property. This includes the normal operation of the hotel and establishing prices for hotel services. However, the owner may wish to negotiate for provisions that require the management company's consent for major purchases or changes in management. If the owner cannot negotiate these provisions, he or she may at least require final approval for budgeting and capital expenditures to ensure proper appropriation of funds.

At a minimum, the management company should be required to inform the owner of any major policy changes that will affect the property. Thus, many owners establish a reporting system to ensure that the management company is doing everything it has stated it would do.

Financial and other reports must be complete and presented in a timely manner so that the owner can take action if it is necessary. The time period for reporting annual audited profit and loss statements is generally 45 days, although there may be an allowance for up to 120 days. Other important reports that must be received in a timely fashion include daily operating reports and monthly operational and financial reports.

4) Owner's Responsibilities

The owner assumes the risk and rewards of ownership. Thus, it is important for the owner to monitor the management company to ensure that profitability goals are being met. In addition, the owner is usually responsible for providing working capital to the property. The owner must also pay for repairs necessary for the operation of the property.

Although the management company purchases supplies, licenses, and permits for the property, the owner must pay for those supplies.

5) Performance and Termination Clause

Management contracts generally define what shall cause the termination of the management contract for either party. Generally, the owner will want some sort of performance clause included in the contract to measure the effectiveness of the management company. Unless there is a provision for this measurement, the owner usually can remove the management company only if he or she can prove gross negligence- a difficult circumstance to prove.

Much management contract litigation has occurred because owners feel that management companies have not operated their hotels adequately. As with most contracts, the more detailed the contract's definition of adequate performance, the more likely it is that an expensive lawsuit can be avoided. One method of measuring performance is negotiating an acceptable rate of return on the property's assets after the property has operated a few years. This eliminates the start-up variability common to new properties.

Many management contracts do not accurately define what will cause the contract to terminate. Therefore, it may be in the parties' best interest to subject any disagreements to binding arbitration. Arbitration is less expensive and quicker than the civil court system. The parties may then allow the arbitrators to establish the termination payout (if any) that the owner will have to pay the management company.

6) Management Company's Equity Investment

For years, the driving force behind management contract was the profitability of these contracts for the management companies in light of comparatively little risk. Today, many owners require the management company to contribute to the equity of the hotel property in some form. For instance, in the start-up phase of a newly constructed hotel, the management company may contribute equity in the form of working capital, pre-opening expenses, furniture, fixtures and equipment, or as joint ventures or partnerships. These contributions can be structured as dept and be treated as any other loan amount, or the management company could be given preference to payment when cash flow becomes available.

7) Miscellaneous Provisions

Many provisions make up the management contract, and they must be examined carefully by both parties to ensure they accomplish what the parties want. Some common provisions are:

- The management company may implement suitable accounting systems for the property.
- The management company may negotiate, at the owner's request, lease for commercial leases.

- The management company may have the power to make emergency expenditures when necessary to avoid immediate danger to life or property.
- The owner may have the right to select outside accountants and to inspect records at any reasonable time.
- The owner may be required to maintain a minimum ratio of current assets to current liabilities and sufficient cash in the property to fund expense for a specified period of time.
- The owner will obtain all necessary licenses and permits for the property.
- The management company will be reimbursed for any reasonable expenses incurred for the property.
- The owner will provide all insurance coverage for the property.
- The management company will be deemed an independent contractor for the owner under the contract.
- The management company may seek an agreement whereby it will not be held accountable for all losses, costs, expenses, liabilities, or damages arising or alleged to have arisen from any acts or omissions.
- The management contract is binding upon and ensures the benefit of the parties and their respective successors and assigns.
- The contract will be in default if any party files a petition for bankruptcy or consents to an involuntary petition in bankruptcy, or if either party fails to perform under the contract terms.
- Default will occur if the owner fails to pay the management company under the terms of the contract.
- No partnership or joint venture is deemed to have been created by the parties entering into the management contract.

5. Hotel Condominiums

The hotel condominium is a creative financing device often used by hotel developers, especially in resort areas. The hotel condominium is a traditional hotel in that it sells rooms to guests. The main difference from other hotels, however, is the ownership structure. In a hotel condominium several individuals own the rooms instead of a single owner.

The main advantage of the hotel condominium to the developer is that he or she can obtain financing for the project from other than traditional financing sources. The condominium owner usually needs only to obtain construction financing, and the permanent financing is provided by the individual investors.

The hotel condominium is usually managed under a management contract with a reputable firm. The developer or subsidiary of the developer may operate the hotel under a separate management contract. The management contractor receives fees for operating the property and passes on any profits to the individual owners. A reputable management company should be selected because investors may not be willing to invest in the project unless they are reasonably sure the project can return a profit.

Generally, individual investors share room revenues either through the actual individual room rentals or the rental pool.

Under the actual individual room rental method, each unit is given its share of room revenue for each guest who stays in that room. This method works best when the individual rooms are in separate and unique units.

The more common method is shared rental pool. Under this method, guest revenues are pooled, and each owner receives a pro rata share. Often, the method selected is based on the rates of the rooms. Thus, the larger rooms receive a larger portion of the pooled income than the smaller rooms.

Many times, the owner wants to use his or her room at the hotel facility.

Arrangements must be made for when the owner can occupy the unit in the condominium contract. The owner may not be allowed to participate in the rental pool arrangement while occupying the room.

6. Time Sharing

Time sharing is a type of real estate ownership whereby ownership is split among individuals on time basis. The "property interest" of the owner is his or her right to use a particular property for a specified period of time. This interest is usually called a "fee interest time-share." The title to the property is divided into 52 intervals. The purchaser and heirs have the right to use a particular unit for a specified week each year for the life of the property.

The owner purchase the time-share unit for the specified time period, and usually the time-share units are furnished. An annual fee usually covers utilities, taxes, telephones, insurance, cleaning, maintenance, and replacement reserve for the furnishings. This fee is variable and is likely to increase as the cost of maintaining the time-share unit increases.

For the developer, time-sharing units can be very profitable because they sell for several times more than if the units were sold outright to individual buyers. The reason is that for many properties, the parts are greater than the whole. The owner has basically purchased a large segment of his or her total vacation cost and can benefit from any appreciation in his interest.

The negative publicity that time-sharing has had in recent years is due to unscrupulous developers who failed to maintain properties in good condition or who fraudulently took investor's money. This has made the public very wary of time-sharing. Most states have enacted legislation to protect time-share purchases. However, buyers should carefully investigate the reputation and record of any project developer before investing.

7. Summary

Franchising is an important part of economy and is expanding rapidly into international markets. The advantage of the franchise arrangement is that it allows the franchisor to expand rapidly into markets with little capital outlay and offers the franchisee/investor to enjoy a good rate of return based on the proven methods of the franchisor. It is for this reason that franchising is really not an entrepreneurial activity but more of an investment opportunity. Although franchises have been known to fail, the failure rate is lower than that for independent businesses.

There are two types of franchises in the hotel industry: restaurants and lodging. The restaurant franchise market is dominated by the fast-food segment, with the hamburger segment predominant. Other important segments include chicken, Mexican food, seafood, steak, sandwich, pancake, ice cream, and yogurt. Franchising in the lodging industry is represented in all segments, but the budget segment has the greatest number of franchise units. With stiff competition in both the lodging and restaurant segment, many franchisors are attempting to increase profits by placing franchised fast-food establishments within lodging properties.

The franchise agreement is the document that spells out the rights and duties of the franchise and franchisor. It should be reviewed by an expert in franchise law. The franchisor normally charges a fee for the franchisee to have the right to operate the franchisor's business. Whether a franchisee is operating a restaurant or hotel, there is usually an initial franchise fee to cover the cost of setting up franchises by the franchisor. In addition, there is a royalty payable on gross revenue for the right to continue to use the franchisor's products and methods of business. Also, most franchisors charge an advertising fee. A reservation fee is also common for hotels. These fees are in addition to the other normal operating costs that the franchisee incurs in running the business.

When analyzing franchise opportunities, it is important to include all relevant costs in obtaining the franchise. The most important consideration in evaluating different franchises is to estimate as accurately as possible which one has the greatest return on the investment. Too often, potential franchisees base their investments on the cheapest franchise cost but not on the potential return possible from a well-run franchise.

In the past two decades, management contracts have played an ever-important role in the management of hotel properties. As hotel operators discovered that they could make more money with less risk by just operating the hotel properties, the use of management companies has growth tremendously. The management is given the right to run the property as agents for the owners. The owner retains the risk and rewards of owning the hotel.

The management company and the owner negotiate the terms of the management contract based on the strengths of the parties. The first major item to be negotiated is the period or duration of the management contract. Generally; the better the reputation of the management company, the longer the management contract term.

The management company is usually compensated by a combination of basic and incentive fees. The basic fee is often paid as a percentage of gross sales, usually between three and five percent. The incentive fee is usually based on some definition of gross operating profit and is usually deferred if there is insufficient cash flow from the operation in a given year.

There are many areas that must be negotiated between the management company and the owners of a hotel property. Some of the more important negotiation points that should be considered besides the term and fees are the performance criteria, termination clause, and equity investment by the management company.

The management of hotel condominiums represents an opportunity for management companies. A hotel condominium is much like any other hotel, but the ownership is divided among many owners who own individual rooms. Hotel condominiums have been most popular in resort areas and are another form of financing available to developers. Generally, once the hotel is built, the property is managed by a management company, and the owners share the rent by the actual room rental method or the more common pooled rental method.

Time-sharing is another creative method for financing and selling resort properties. Here, a person purchases the right to use a facility for a specified period of time. The title to such a property can be divided into 52 intervals. The time-share owner can swap his or her time with other members or through national organizations with other time-share owners.

The developer of the time-share units has a high profit margin since the individual time periods can be sold for several times more than if the units were sold outright to one buyer. However, due to unscrupulous developers in recent years, many states have begun to regulate time-share developments in order to protect the public.

Appendix A

References

- Adams, D. J., and Kwansa, F. A.(1992). Corporate Performance Appraisal in the International Hospitality Industry. In R. Teare & M. D. Olsen (Eds.), International Hospitality Management, Corporate Strategy in Practice, 275 295. NY: John Wiley & Sons, Inc.
- Andrew, W.P., & Schmidgall, R.S. (1993). Financial Management for the Hospitality Industry. Educational Institute of the American Hotel & Motel Association,East Lansing Michigan.
- Beal, Paul and David A. Troy. "Hotel Feasibility Analysis. Part2." The cornell HRA Quarterly, May 1982, pp.21-27.
- Carey, K. (1992). Optimal hotel capacity: The case of Barbados. Social and Economic Studies, 41(2), 103 26.
- Choi, Jeong-Gil (1997). "A Review of Current Financial Issues facing the International Hotel Industry." The Journal of Hospitality Financial Management, Vol. 5, No. 1
- Choi, Jeong-Gil (2003). Developing an Economic Indicator System (A Forecasting Technique) for the Hotel Industry. International Journal of Hospitality Management
- Choi, Jeong-Gil (2011). Introduction to Hotel Management, Baeksan Publishing Co. Seoul, Korea.
- Coltman, M. (1992) Financial control for your hotel, 1 6.
- Crawford Welch, S., and E. Tse. (1990), Mergers, acquisitions and alliance

in the European hospitality industry. International Journal of Contemporary Hospitality Research 2(1): 10 16.

- Dev, C. S. and M. D. Olsen. (1989), Environmental uncertainty, business strategy and financial performance: An empirical study of the U. S. lodging industry. Hospitality Education and Research Journal 13(3): 171 186.
- Dev, C. S. and S. Klein.(1993), Strategic alliances in the hotel industry. Cornell Hotel Restaurant Administration Quarterly 34(1): 42 45.
- Eyster, James J. The Negotiation and administration of Hotel Management Contracts (Ithaca N.Y:School of Hotel Administration, Cornell University, 1988).
- Friend, I., Hasbrouck, J. (1988). Determinants of Capital Structure. Research in Finance Vol. 7, 1 19.
- Gordon, M.J. (1962). The Investment, Financing, and Valuation of the Corporation. Homewood, IL: Irwin.
- Gu, Z., McCool, A. (1993/1994). Financial conditions and performances: A Sector Analysis of the Restaurant Industry. The Journal of Hospitality Financial Management, 3(1), 1 14.
- Heinkel, R. (1982). A Theory of Capital Structure Relevance under Imperfect Information. Journal of Finance, 37, 1141 1150.
- Herbert B. Mayo, Investment an introduction, Dryden press,(1997),
- John R. Walker, 2002. Introduction to Hospitality, 3rd ed. Prentice Hall
- Martin Richard. “Site Selection: Fundamentals for Success Still Location, Location, and Location.” Nation’s Restaurant News, Nov.24, 1986, p.f7.
- Martin, E. J. (1993). Checking into the hotel market. Institutional Investor, 27(10), Oct., 217.
- Michael M. Coltman (1991). Hospitality Management Accounting, Van Nostrand Reinhold
- Nelson, Richard L. “Checklist: Site Evaluation.” Fast Food, May 1969, pp.118-126.
- Olsen, M. D. & Choi, Jeong Gil (1996).“ The Scale of the International

Hotel Industry A Statistical Analysis", Into the New Millennium: A White Paper on the Global Hospitality Industry, The International Hotel Association, Paris, France, pp. 15 26.

- Olsen, M. D., et al. 1995. Into the New Millenium, a white paper on the global hospitality industry. International hotel and restaurant association, Paris, France.
- Olsen, M. D., West & E. C. Tse. (1998), Strategic Management in the Hospitality Industry, 2nd ed., N.Y.: John Wiley.
- Poitevin, M. (1989). Financial Signaling and the" Deep Pocket"Agreement. Rand Journal of Economics, 20, 26 40.
- Raymond S. Schmidgall (1997), Hospitality Industry Managerial Accounting, American Hotel & Motel Association
- Rushmore, Stephen (1992), Hotel investments: a guide for leaders and owners, New York: Warren Gorham Lamont.
- Rushmore, Stephen and Thomas Arasi, "Stretching Feasibility." Lodging Hospitality, April 1986, p.41.
- Rushmore, Stephen. How to perform an Economic Feasibility Study of a Proposed Hotel/Motel, 1sted., American Society of Real Estate Counselors, 1986.
- Schmidgall, R.S., Geller, A N., & Ilvento, C. (1993). Financial Analysis Using the Statement of Cash Flows. The Cornell H.R.A. Quarterly, February, 47 53.
- Shomir Sil, Pat Obi, Jeong-Gil Choi(2011). Investigation On The Variability of Individual Stock Beta and portfolio size. International Journal of Business, Accounting, and Finance. Vol 5, No 1.
- Siegel, L.Siegel. Franchising (NewYork:JohnWiley&Sons,Inc.,1983).
- Smart, J. Eric. Recreational Development Handbook (Washington,D.C:Urban Land Institute,1981).
- Tarbutton, T. Lloyd. Franchising, The How-To Book (Englewood,N.J. : Prentice-Hall, Inc.1986).

- Tarras, J.M. (1991). A Practical Guide to Hospitality Finance. Van Nostrand Reinhold, NewYork 10003.
- Tarras, John. "Planning a New Property? Study Feasibility." Hotel and Resort Industry, Sept. 1987. pp.66-67.
- Wacker, J. G. (1985). Effective planning and cost control for restaurants: Making resource requirements planning work. Production & Inventory Management, 26(1), First Quarter, 55 70.
- Webster, Bryce. The Insider's Guide to Franchising (New York: American Management Association, 1986).
- White, G.I., Sondhi, A.C. & Fried, D.(1994). The Analysis and Use of Financial Statements. John Wiley & Sons, Inc.
- William P. Andrew&Raymond S. Schmidgall (1993), Financial Management for the Hospitality Industry, American Hotel & Motel Association,
- Wood, D. (1994). Using rooms revenue per available room analysis to forecast rooms revenue. Real Estate Finance Journal, 9(4), Spring, 20 29.

Chapter Appendix B

Glossary

Amortization Reducing debt by the series of periodic payments that make up both an interest and principal component.

Annual percentage rate (APR) The real rate of interest paid by a borrower on a loan. Often there are additional charges or fees charged by the lender that raise the effective rate of interest on a loan.

Appreciation The increase in value of property because of increased desirability of the area.

Balloon note A note that will not be fully paid off over the life of the note but instead will show a large balance at the end of the loan term(balloon).

Capitalization The conversion of future cash flow into present value.

Cash flow The actual cash flow from a hotel project after deducting all the operating expenses and debt service.

Competition analysis A review and study of existing and future hospitality projects that will compete with the hospitality project being considered.

Consultant In the hospitality context, someone who specializes in the hospitality industry and who uses that expertise to advise interested parties.

Demand analysis The study of who will be most likely to be served by the hospitality project and whether there is demand for the proposed hospitality project.

Developer A person or company that builds hospitality projects on vacant land either to be owned by the developer or to be sold to a third party.

Discount rate The percentage by which future cash flows are reduced to calculate a present value.

Equity That part of the investment that represents the owner's of investor's own money.

Feasibility study A report for a hospitality project in a given location, undertaken to ascertain the probable financial success of the project.

Financial risk The risk that the property will not generate sufficient income to service the debt.

Financing costs The total charges involved in the loan process including interest cost.

Franchise A legal relationship between one party (franchisor) who agrees to provide the know-how and/or product and a second party (franchisee) for a fee. The franchisor agrees to assist the franchisee through advertising, promotion, and other advisory service as part of the franchise contract. The franchisee agrees to operate the business according to the terms of the franchise agreement.

Franchisee An individual or company that is given the right to conduct a business concept granted by the franchisor under a franchise agreement.

Franchisor An individual or company that grants a right to someone else to use the business concepts (franchise).

Internal rate of return A finance method that discounts the present worth of future cash flows so that they equal the initial cash investment.

Laventhol & Horwath A consulting firm that specialize in the hospitality industry.

Leverage The use of borrowed funds to attempt to increase the rate of return on a property.

Liquidity risk The risk that property will not be readily convertible to cash when needed.

Loan-to-value ratio The percentage of the total cost of the property that a lender will loan upon.

Loan constant The repayment of the loan with principal and interest repayment is stated as a yearly percentage rate. The percentage rate is based on the monthly payment in relation to the principal originally loaned.

Management contract A contract for operating a hotel property entered into between the owner of the property and a management company. The contract describes the duties and obligations of both parties, including the fee to be paid to the management company.

Management fee The fee paid to the management company to operate a property. This fee usually consists of two parts: the basic management fee (which is usually based on a stated percentage of gross sales) and the incentive management fee (which is usually based on a percentage of net income defined by the parties).

Market analysis An analysis of the area in which the hospitality property will be located. Market analysis takes into account the factors that will influence the construction of a new project.

Mortgage A lien on real estate securing a loan.

Negative cash flow A situation that occurs when cash flow from operations does not exceed expenses.

Net present value The current value of cash proceeds to be received sometime in the future.

Project site and area analysis The specific location where the hospitality project will be located. The suitability of the specific location and immediate area for use as a hospitality business.

Risk of failure The risk that a property will not be profitable due to any number of reasons from poor management to a weak economy.

Risk of inflation The risk that a hotel project will not be able to adjust prices to raising prices due to inflation.

Royalty fee The fee paid by franchisee to the franchisor for the use of the franchise. This fee is usually based on a percentage of gross sales and may include an additional percentage for national advertising.

Time value of money The concept that a dollar today is worth more than a dollar at some point in the future. The dollar is worth more today because the holder can invest it to generate a return and there is a risk that the money may not be collected in the future.

Time-sharing Exclusive ownership for a period of time each year of a vacation condominium. The ownership is shared with other individuals who own other exclusive periods of time throughout the year.

Trademark A symbol protected by law that identifies the commercial operations of a company, including the name of the company, various products, and services.

Uniform system of accounts for hotels A uniform accounting system for hotels developed by the American Hotel and Motel Association to assist preparers present financial report for hotel operations.

Zoning ordinance A legal division of a locality into area (zones) that define what is permissible land use within those area.

Chapter Appendix C

Time Value of Money

$$Discounting: PV = \frac{FV_n}{(1+i)^n} = FV_n = (\frac{1}{i+i})^n = FV_n(PVIF_{i,n})$$

$$Compounding: (FV_n = PV(1+i)^n = PV(FVIF_{i,n})$$

$$Annuity(Future\ Value)$$

$$: FVA_n = PMT\sum_{t=1}^{n}(1+i)^{n-t} = PMT[\frac{(1+i)^n - 1}{i}] = PMT(FVIFA_{i,n})$$

$$Annuity(Present\ Value)$$

$$: PVA_n = PMT\sum_{t=1}^{n}[\frac{1}{1+i}]^t = PMT[\frac{1-\frac{1}{(1+i)^n}}{i}] = PMT(PVIFA_{i,n})$$

$$FVIF_{i,n} = Future\ Value\ Interest\ Factor\ for\ i\ and\ n$$

$$PVIF_{i,n} = Present\ Value\ Interest\ Factor\ for\ i\ and\ n$$

<Table A-1> Future value $FVIF_{i,n}=(1+i)^n$ interest rate(i)

Period (n)	1%	2%	3%	4%	5%	6%	7%	8%	9%	10%
1	1.0100	1.0200	1.0300	1.0400	1.0500	1.0600	1.0700	1.0800	1.0900	1.1000
2	1.0201	1.0404	1.0609	1.0816	1.1025	1.1236	1.1449	1.1664	1.1881	1.2100
3	1.0303	1.0612	1.0927	1.1249	1.1576	1.1910	1.2250	1.2597	1.2950	1.3310
4	1.0406	1.0824	1.1255	1.1699	1.2155	1.2625	1.3108	1.3605	1.4116	1.4641
5	1.0510	1.1041	1.1593	1.2167	1.2763	1.3382	1.4026	1.4693	1.5386	1.6105
6	1.0615	1.1262	1.1941	1.2653	1.3401	1.4185	1.5007	1.5869	1.6771	1.7716
7	1.0721	1.1487	1.2299	1.3159	1.4071	1.5036	1.6058	1.7138	1.8280	1.9487
8	1.0829	1.1717	1.2668	1.3686	1.4775	1.5938	1.7182	1.8509	1.9926	2.1436
9	1.0937	1.1951	1.3048	1.4233	1.5513	1.6895	1.8385	1.9990	2.1719	2.3579
10	1.1046	1.2190	1.3439	1.4802	1.6289	1.7908	1.9672	2.1589	2.3674	2.5937
11	1.1157	1.2434	1.3842	1.5395	1.7103	1.8983	2.1049	2.3316	2.5804	2.8531
12	1.1268	1.2682	1.4258	1.6010	1.7959	2.0122	2.2522	2.5182	2.8127	3.1384
13	1.1381	1.2936	1.4685	1.6651	1.8856	2.1329	2.4098	2.7196	3.0658	3.4523
14	1.1495	1.3195	1.5126	1.7317	1.9799	2.2609	2.5785	2.9372	3.3417	3.7975
15	1.1610	1.3459	1.5580	1.8009	2.0789	2.3966	2.7590	3.1722	3.6425	4.1772
16	1.1726	1.3728	1.6047	1.8730	2.1829	2.5404	2.9522	3.4259	3.9703	4.5950
17	1.1843	1.4002	1.6528	1.9479	2.2920	2.6928	3.1588	3.7000	4.3276	5.0545
18	1.1961	1.4282	1.7024	2.0258	2.4066	2.8543	3.3799	3.9960	4.7171	5.5599
19	1.2081	1.4568	1.7535	2.1068	2.5270	3.0256	3.6165	4.3157	5.1417	6.1159
20	1.2202	1.4859	1.8061	2.1911	2.6533	3.2071	3.8697	4.6610	5.6044	6.7275
21	1.2324	1.5157	1.8603	2.2788	2.7860	3.3996	4.1406	5.0338	6.1088	7.4002
22	1.2447	1.5460	1.9161	2.3699	2.9253	3.6035	4.4304	5.4365	6.6586	8.1403
23	1.2572	1.5769	1.9736	2.4647	3.0715	3.8197	4.7405	5.8715	7.2579	8.9543
24	1.2697	1.6084	2.0328	2.5633	3.2251	4.0489	5.0724	6.3412	7.9111	9.8497
25	1.2824	1.6406	2.0938	2.6658	3.3864	4.2919	5.4274	6.8485	8.6231	10.835
26	1.2953	1.6734	2.1566	2.7725	3.5557	4.5494	5.8074	7.3964	9.3992	11.918
27	1.3082	1.7069	2.2213	2.8834	3.7335	4.8223	6.2139	7.9881	10.245	13.110
28	1.3213	1.7410	2.2879	2.9987	3.9201	5.1117	6.6488	8.6271	11.167	14.421
29	1.3345	1.7758	2.3566	3.1187	4.1161	5.4184	7.1143	9.3173	12.172	15.863
30	1.3478	1.8114	2.4273	3.2434	4.3219	5.7435	7.6123	10.063	13.268	17.449
35	1.4166	1.9999	2.8139	3.9461	5.5160	7.6861	10.676	14.785	20.414	28.102
40	1.4889	2.2080	3.2620	4.8010	7.0400	10.286	14.974	21.725	31.409	45.259
45	1.5648	2.4379	3.7816	5.8412	8.9850	13.765	21.002	31.920	48.327	72.891
50	1.6446	2.6916	4.3839	7.1067	11.467	18.420	29.457	46.902	74.358	117.39
60	1.8167	3.2810	5.8916	10.520	18.679	32.988	57.946	101.26	176.03	304.48

Period (n)	11%	12%	13%	14%	15%	16%	17%	18%	19%	20%
1	1.1100	1.1200	1.1300	1.1400	1.1500	1.1600	1.1700	1.1800	1.1900	1.2000
2	1.2321	1.2544	1.2769	1.2996	1.3225	1.3456	1.3689	1.3924	1.4161	1.4400
3	1.3676	1.4094	1.4429	1.4815	1.5209	1.5609	1.6016	1.6430	1.6852	1.7280
4	1.5180	1.5735	1.6305	1.6890	1.7490	1.8106	1.8739	1.9388	2.0053	2.0736
5	1.6851	1.7623	1.8424	1.9254	2.0114	2.1003	2.1924	2.2878	2.3864	2.4883
6	1.8704	1.9738	2.0820	2.1950	2.3131	2.4364	2.5652	2.6996	2.8398	2.9860
7	2.0762	2.2107	2.3526	2.5023	2.6600	2.8262	3.0012	3.1855	3.3793	3.5832
8	2.3045	2.4760	2.6584	2.8526	3.0590	3.2784	3.5115	3.7589	4.0214	4.2998
9	2.5580	2.7731	3.0040	3.2519	3.5179	3.8030	4.1084	4.4355	4.7854	5.1598
10	2.8394	3.1058	3.3946	3.7072	4.0456	4.4114	4.8068	5.2338	5.6947	6.1917
11	3.1518	3.4785	3.8359	4.2262	4.6524	5.1173	5.6240	6.1759	6.7767	7.4301
12	3.4985	3.8960	4.3345	4.8179	5.3503	5.9360	6.5801	7.2876	8.0642	8.9161
13	3.8833	4.3635	4.8980	5.4924	6.1528	6.8858	7.6987	8.5994	9.5964	10.699
14	4.3104	4.8871	5.5348	6.2613	7.0757	7.9875	9.0075	10.147	11.420	12.839
15	4.7846	5.4736	6.2543	7.1379	8.1371	9.2655	10.539	11.974	13.589	15.407
16	5.3109	6.1304	7.0673	8.1372	9.3576	10.748	12.330	14.129	16.172	18.488
17	5.8951	6.8660	7.9861	9.2765	10.761	12.468	14.427	16.672	19.244	22.186
18	6.5436	7.6900	9.0243	10.575	12.375	14.463	16.879	19.673	22.901	26.623
19	7.2633	8.6128	10.197	12.056	14.232	16.777	19.748	23.214	27.252	31.948
20	8.0623	9.6463	11.523	13.743	16.367	19.461	23.106	27.393	32.429	38.338
21	8.9492	10.804	13.021	15.668	18.822	22.574	27.034	32.324	38.591	46.005
22	9.9336	12.100	14.714	17.861	21.645	26.186	31.629	38.142	45.923	55.206
23	11.026	13.552	16.626	20.362	24.891	30.376	37.006	45.008	54.648	66.247
24	12.239	15.179	18.788	23.212	28.625	35.236	43.297	53.109	65.032	79.497
25	13.586	17.000	21.231	26.462	32.919	40.874	50.658	62.669	77.388	95.396
26	15.080	19.040	23.991	30.167	37.857	47.414	59.270	73.949	92.092	114.48
27	16.738	21.325	27.109	34.390	34.535	55.000	69.345	87.260	109.56	137.37
28	18.580	23.884	30.634	39.204	50.066	63.800	81.134	102.97	130.41	164.84
29	20.624	26.750	34.617	44.693	57.575	74.009	94.927	121.50	155.19	197.81
30	22.892	29.960	39.116	50.950	66.212	85.850	111.06	143.37	184.67	237.38
35	38.575	52.800	72.068	98.100	133.18	180.31	243.56	327.99	440.70	590.67
40	65.001	93.051	132.78	188.88	267.86	378.72	533.86	750.38	1051.6	1469.8
45	109.53	163.99	244.64	363.68	538.77	795.44	1170.5	1716.7	2509.6	3657.3
50	184.56	289.00	450.74	700.23	1083.7	1670.7	2566.2	3927.4	5988.9	9100.4
60	524.06	897.60	1530.1	2595.9	4384.0	7370.2	12335.	20555.	34105.	56347.

<Table A-2> Present value $PVIF_{i,n}=1/(1+i)^n$ interest rate(i)

Period (n)	1%	2%	3%	4%	5%	6%	7%	8%	9%	10%
1	.9901	.9804	.9709	.9615	.9524	.9434	.9346	.9259	.9174	.9091
2	.9803	.9612	.9426	.9246	.9070	.8900	.8734	.8573	.8417	.8264
3	.9706	.9423	.9151	.8890	.8638	.8396	.8163	.7938	.7722	.7513
4	.9610	.9238	.8885	.8548	.8227	.7921	.7629	.7350	.7084	.6830
5	.9515	.9057	.8626	.8219	.7835	.7473	.7130	.6806	.6499	.6209
6	.9420	.8880	.8375	.7903	.7462	.7050	.6663	.6302	.5963	.5645
7	.9327	.8706	.8131	.7599	.7107	.6651	.6227	.5835	.5470	.5132
8	.9235	.8535	.7894	.7307	.6768	.6274	.5820	.5403	.5019	.4665
9	.9143	.8368	.7664	.7026	.6446	.5919	.5439	.5002	.4604	.4241
10	.9053	.8203	.7441	.6756	.6139	.5584	.5083	.4632	.4224	.3855
11	.8963	.8043	.7224	.6496	.5847	.5268	.4751	.4289	.3875	3505
12	.8874	.7885	.7014	.6246	.5568	.4970	.4440	.3971	.3555	.3186
13	.8787	.7730	.6810	.6006	.5303	.4688	.4150	.3677	.3262	.2897
14	.8700	.7579	.6611	.5775	.5051	.4423	.3878	.3405	.2992	.2633
15	.8613	.7430	.6419	.5553	.4810	.4173	.3624	.3152	.2745	.2394
16	.8528	.7284	.6232	.5339	.4581	.3936	.3387	.2919	.2519	.2176
17	.8444	.7142	.6052	.5134	.4363	.3714	.3166	.2703	.2311	.1978
18	.8360	.7002	.5874	.4936	.4155	.3503	.2959	.2502	.2120	.1799
19	.8277	.6864	.5703	.4746	.3957	.3305	.2765	.2317	.1945	.1635
20	.8195	.6730	.5537	.4564	.3769	.3118	.2584	2145	.1784	.1486
21	.8114	.6598	.5375	.4388	.3589	.2942	.2415	.1987	.1637	.1351
22	.8034	.6468	.5219	.4220	.3418	.2775	.2257	.1839	.1502	.1228
23	.7954	.6324	.5067	.4057	.3256	.2618	.2109	.1703	.1378	.1117
24	.7876	.6217	.4919	.3901	.3101	.2470	.1971	.1577	.1264	.1015
25	.7798	.6095	.4776	.3751	.2953	.2330	.1842	.1460	.1160	.0923
26	.7720	.5976	.4637	.3604	.2812	.2198	.1722	.1352	.1064	.0839
27	.7644	.5859	.4502	.3468	.2678	.2074	.1609	.1252	.0976	.0763
28	.7568	.5744	.4371	.3335	.2551	.1956	.1504	.1159	.0895	.0693
29	.7493	.5631	.4243	.3207	.2429	.1846	.1406	.1073	.0822	.0630
30	.7419	.5521	.4120	.3083	.2314	.1741	.1314	.0994	.0754	.0573
35	.7059	.5000	.3554	.2534	.1813	.1301	.0937	.0676	.0490	.0356
40	.6717	.4529	.3066	.2083	.1420	.0972	.0668	.0460	.0318	.0221
45	.6391	.4102	.2644	.1712	.1113	.0727	.0476	.0313	.0207	.0137
50	.6080	.3715	.2281	.1407	.0872	.0543	.0339	.0213	.0134	.0085
60	.5504	.3048	.1697	.0951	.0535	.0303	.0173	.0099	.0057	.0033

Period (n)	11%	12%	13%	14%	15%	16%	17%	18%	19%	20%
1	.9009	.8929	.8850	.8772	.8696	.8621	.8547	.8475	.8403	.8333
2	.8116	.7972	.7831	.7695	.7561	.7432	.7305	.7182	.7062	.6944
3	.7312	.7118	.6931	.6750	.6575	.6407	.6244	.6086	.5934	.5787
4	.6587	.6355	.6133	.5921	.5921	.5523	.5337	.5158	.4987	.4323
5	.5935	.5674	.5428	.5194	.4972	.4761	.4561	.4371	.4190	.4019
6	.5346	.5066	.4803	.4556	.4323	.4104	.3898	.3704	.3521	.3349
7	.4817	.4523	.4251	.3996	.3759	.3538	.3332	.3139	.2959	.2791
8	.4339	.4039	.3762	.3506	.3269	.3050	.2848	.2660	.2487	.2326
9	.3909	.3606	.3329	.3075	.2843	.2630	.2434	.2255	.2090	.1938
10	.3522	.322	.2946	.2697	.2472	.2267	.2080	.1911	.1756	.1615
11	.3173	.2875	.2607	.2366	.2149	.1954	.1773	.1619	.1476	.1346
12	.2858	.2567	.2307	.2076	.1869	.1685	.1520	.1372	.1240	.1122
13	.2575	.2292	.2042	.1821	.1625	.1452	.1299	.1163	.1042	.0935
14	.2320	.2046	.1807	.1597	.1413	.1252	.1110	.0985	.0876	.0779
15	.2090	.1827	.1599	.1401	.1229	.1079	.0949	.0835	.0736	.0649
16	.1883	.1631	.1415	.1229	.1069	.0930	.0811	.0708	.0618	.0541
17	.1696	.1456	.1252	.1073	.0929	.0802	.0693	.0600	.0520	.0451
18	.1523	.1300	.1103	.0946	.0803	.0691	.0592	.0508	.0437	.0376
19	.1377	.1161	.0981	.0829	.0703	.0596	.0506	.0431	.0367	.0313
20	.1240	.1037	.0863	.0723	.0611	.0514	.0433	.0365	.0303	.0261
21	.1117	.0926	.0768	.0633	.0531	.0443	.0370	.0309	.0259	.0217
22	.1007	.0326	.0680	.0560	.0462	.0382	.0316	.0262	.0218	.0181
23	.0907	.0738	.0601	.0491	.0402	.0329	.0270	.0222	.0183	.0151
24	.0817	.0659	.0532	.0431	.0349	.0284	.0231	.0188	.0154	.0126
25	.0736	.0588	.0471	.0378	.0304	.0245	.0197	.0160	.0129	.0105
26	.0663	.0525	.0417	.0331	.0264	.0211	.0169	.0135	.0109	.0087
27	.0597	.0469	.0369	.0291	.0230	.0182	.0144	.0115	.0091	.0073
28	.0538	.0419	.0325	.0255	.0200	.0157	.0123	.0097	.0077	.0061
29	.0485	.0374	.0289	.0224	.0174	.0135	.0105	.0082	.0064	.0051
30	.0437	.0334	.0256	.0196	.0151	.0116	.0090	.0070	.0054	.0042
35	.0259	.0189	.0139	.0102	.0075	.0055	.0041	.0030	.0023	.0017
40	.0154	.0107	.0075	.0053	.0037	.0026	.0019	.0013	.0010	.0007
45	.0091	.0061	.0041	.0027	.0019	.0013	.0009	.0006	.0004	.0003
50	.0054	.0035	.0022	.0014	.0009	.0006	.0004	.0003	.0002	.0001
60	.0019	.0011	.0007	.0004	.0002	.0001	.00008	.00005	.00003	.00002

<Table A-3> Future Value of annuity $FVIFA_{i,n} = \sum_{t=1}^{n}(1+i)^{n-t} = \frac{(1+i)^n - 1}{i}$ interest rate(i)

Period (n)	1%	2%	3%	4%	5%	6%	7%	8%	9%	10%
1	1.0000	1.0000	1.0000	1.0000	1.0000	1.0000	1.0000	1.0000	1.0000	1.0000
2	2.0100	2.0200	2.0300	2.0400	2.0500	2.0600	2.0700	2.0800	2.0900	2.1000
3	3.0301	3.0604	3.0909	3.1216	3.1525	3.1836	3.2149	3.2464	3.2781	3.3100
4	4.0604	4.1216	4.1836	4.2465	4.3101	4.3746	4.4399	4.5061	4.5731	4.6410
5	5.1010	5.2040	5.3091	5.4163	5.5256	5.6371	5.7507	5.8666	5.9847	6.1051
6	6.1520	6.3081	6.4684	6.6330	6.8019	6.9753	7.1533	7.3359	7.5233	7.7156
7	7.2135	7.4343	7.6625	7.8983	8.1420	8.3938	8.6540	8.9228	9.2004	9.4872
8	8.2857	8.5830	8.8923	9.2142	9.5491	9.8975	10.260	10.637	11.028	11.436
9	9.3685	9.7546	10.159	10.583	11.027	11.491	11.978	12.488	13.021	13.579
10	10.462	10.950	11.464	12.006	12.578	13.181	13.816	14.487	15.193	15.937
11	11.567	12.169	12.808	13.486	14.207	14.972	15.784	16.645	17.560	18.531
12	12.683	13.412	14.192	15.026	15.917	16.870	17.888	18.977	20.141	21.384
13	13.809	14.680	15.618	16.627	17.713	18.882	20.141	21.495	22.953	24.523
14	14.947	15.974	17.086	18.292	19.599	21.015	22.550	24.215	26.019	27.975
15	16.097	17.293	18.599	20.024	21.579	23.276	25.129	27.152	29.361	31.772
16	17.258	18.639	20.157	21.825	25.657	25.673	27.888	30.324	33.003	35.950
17	18.430	20.012	21.762	23.698	25.840	28.213	30.840	33.750	36.974	40.545
18	19.615	21.412	23.414	25.645	28.132	30.906	33.999	37.450	41.301	45.599
19	20.811	22.841	25.117	27.671	30.539	33.760	37.379	41.446	46.018	51.159
20	22.019	24.297	26.870	29.778	33.066	36.786	40.995	45.762	51.160	57.275
21	23.239	25.783	28.676	31.969	35.719	39.993	44.865	50.423	56.765	64.002
22	24.475	27.299	30.537	34.248	38.505	43.392	49.006	55.457	62.873	71.403
23	25.716	28.845	32.453	36.618	41.430	46.996	53.436	60.893	69.532	79.543
24	26.973	30.422	34.426	39.083	44.502	50.816	58.177	66.765	76.790	88.497
25	28.243	32.030	36.459	41.646	47.727	54.865	63.249	73.106	84.701	98.347
26	29.526	33.671	38.553	44.312	51.113	59.156	68.676	79.954	93.324	109.18
27	30.821	35.344	40.710	47.084	54.669	63.706	74.484	87.351	102.72	121.10
28	32.129	37.051	42.931	49.968	58.403	68.528	80.698	95.339	112.97	134.21
29	33.450	38.792	45.219	52.966	62.323	73.640	87.347	103.97	124.14	148.63
30	34.785	40.568	47.575	56.085	66.439	79.058	94.461	113.28	136.31	164.49
35	41.660	49.994	60.462	73.652	90.320	111.43	138.24	172.32	215.71	271.02
40	48.886	60.402	75.401	95.026	120.80	154.76	199.64	269.06	337.88	442.59
45	56.481	71.893	92.720	121.03	159.70	212.74	285.75	386.51	525.86	718.90
50	64.463	84.579	112.80	152.67	209.35	290.34	406.53	573.77	815.08	1163.9
60	81.671	114.05	163.05	237.99	353.58	533.13	813.52	1253.2	1944.8	3034.8

Period (n)	11%	12%	13%	14%	15%	16%	17%	18%	19%	20%
1	1.0000	1.0000	1.0000	1.0000	1.0000	1.0000	1.0000	1.0000	1.0000	1.0000
2	2.1100	2.1200	2.1300	2.1400	2.1500	2.1600	2.1700	2.1800	2.1900	2.2000
3	3.3421	3.3744	3.4069	3.4396	3.4725	3.5056	3.5389	3.5724	3.6061	3.6400
4	4.7097	4.7793	4.8498	4.9211	4.9934	5.0665	5.1405	5.2154	5.2913	5.3680
5	6.2278	6.3528	6,4803	6.6101	6.7424	6.8771	7.0144	7.1542	7.2966	7.4416
6	7.9130	8.1152	8.3230	8.5355	8.7537	8.9775	9.2068	9.4420	9.6830	9.9299
7	9.7830	10.089	10.405	10.730	11.067	11.414	11.772	12.142	12.523	12.916
8	11.859	12.300	12.757	13.233	13.727	14.240	14.773	15.327	15.902	16.499
9	14.163	14.776	15.416	16.085	16.786	17.519	18.285	19.086	19.923	20.799
10	16.722	17.549	18.419	19.337	20.304	21.321	22.393	23.521	24.709	25.959
11	19.561	20.655	21.814	23.045	24.349	25.733	27.199	28.755	30.404	32.150
12	22.713	24.133	25.650	27.271	29.002	30.850	32.823	34.931	37.180	39.581
13	26.211	28.029	29.984	32.089	34.352	36.786	39.404	42.219	45.244	48.497
14	30.095	32.393	34.883	37.581	40.505	63.672	47.103	50.818	54.841	59.196
15	34.405	37.280	40.418	43.842	47.580	51.660	56.110	60.965	66.261	72.035
16	39.199	42.753	46.672	50.980	55.717	60.925	66.649	72.939	79.850	87.442
17	44.501	48.884	53.739	59.118	65.075	71.673	78.979	87.068	96.022	105.93
18	50.396	55.750	61.725	68.394	75.836	84.141	93.406	103.74	115.26	128.12
19	56.939	63.440	70.749	78.969	88.212	98.603	110.29	123.41	138.16	154.74
20	64.203	72.052	80.947	91.025	102.44	115.38	130.03	146.63	165.42	186.69
21	72.265	81.699	92.469	104.77	118.81	134.84	153.14	174.02	197.85	225.03
22	81.214	92.503	105.49	120.44	137.63	157.41	180.17	206.34	236.44	271.03
23	91.148	104.60	120.20	138.30	159.28	183.60	211.80	244.49	282.36	326.24
24	102.17	118.16	136.83	158.66	184.17	213.98	248.81	289.49	337.01	392.48
25	114.41	133.33	155.62	181.87	212.79	249.21	292.10	342.60	402.04	471.98
26	127.99	150.33	176.85	208.33	245.71	290.09	342.76	405.27	497.43	567.38
27	143.08	169.37	200.84	238.50	283.57	337.50	402.03	479.22	571.52	681.85
28	159.82	190.70	227.95	272.89	327.10	392.50	471.38	566.48	681.11	819.22
29	178.39	214.58	258.58	312.09	377.17	456.30	552.51	669.45	811.52	984.07
30	199.02	241.33	293.19	356.79	434.75	530.31	647.44	790.95	966.71	1181.9
35	341.59	431.66	546.68	693.57	881.17	1120.7	1426.4	1816.7	2314.2	2948.3
40	581.83	767.09	1013.7	1342.0	1779.1	2360.8	3134.5	4163.2	5529.8	7343.9
45	986.64	1358.3	1874.2	2590.6	3585.1	4965.3	6879.2	9531.6	13203.	18281.
50	1668.7	2400.0	3459.5	4994.5	7217.7	10436.	15089.	21813.	31515.	45497.
60	4755.1	7471.6	11762.	18535.	29220.	46057.	72555.	114189.	179494.	281737.

<Table A-4> Present value of annuity $PVIFA_{i,n}=\sum_{t=1}^{n}\frac{1}{(1+i)^t}=\frac{1-\frac{1}{(1+i)^n}}{i}=\frac{1}{i}-\frac{1}{i(1+i)^n}$

interest rate(i)

Period (n)	1%	2%	3%	4%	5%	6%	7%	8%	9%	10%
1	0.9901	0.9804	0.9616	0.9615	0.9524	0.9434	0.9346	0.9259	0.9174	0.9091
2	1.9704	1.9416	1.9165	1.8861	1.8594	1.8334	1.8080	1.7833	1.7591	1.7355
3	2.9410	2.8839	2.8286	2.7751	2.7232	2.6730	2.6243	2.5771	2.5313	2.4868
4	3.9020	3.8077	3.7171	3.6299	3.5460	3.4651	3.3872	3.3121	3.2397	3.1699
5	4.8534	4.7135	4.5797	4.4518	4.3295	4.2124	4.1002	3.9927	3.8897	3.7908
6	5.7955	5.6014	5.4172	5.2421	5.0757	4.9173	4.7665	4.6229	4.4859	4.3553
7	6.7282	6.4720	6.2303	6.0021	5.7864	5.5824	5.3893	5.2064	5.0330	4.8684
8	7.6517	7.3255	7.0197	6.7327	6.4632	6.2098	5.9713	5.7466	5.5348	5.3349
9	8.5660	8.1622	7.7861	7.4353	7.1078	6.8017	6.5152	6.2469	5.9952	5.7590
10	9.4713	8.9826	8.5302	8.1109	7.7217	7.3601	7.0236	6.7101	6.4177	6.1446
11	10.368	9.7868	9.2526	8.7605	8.3064	7.8869	7.4987	7.1390	6.8052	6.4951
12	11.255	10.575	9.9540	9.3851	8.8633	8.3838	7.9427	7.5361	7.1607	6.8137
13	12.134	11.348	10.635	9.9856	9.3936	8.8527	8.3577	7.9038	7.4869	7.1034
14	13.004	12.106	11.296	10.563	9.8986	9.2950	8.7455	8.2442	7.7862	7.3667
15	13.865	12.849	11.938	11.118	10.380	9.7122	9.1079	8.5595	8.0607	7.6061
16	14.718	13.578	12.561	11.652	10.838	10.106	9.4466	8.8514	8.3136	7.8237
17	15.562	14.292	13.166	12.166	11.274	10.477	9.7632	9.1216	8.5436	8.0216
18	16.398	14.992	13.756	12.659	11.690	10.828	10.059	9.3719	8.7556	8.2014
19	17.226	15.679	14.324	13.134	12.085	11.158	10.336	9.6036	8.9501	8.3649
20	18.046	16.351	14.877	13.590	12.462	11.470	10.594	9.8181	9.1285	8.5136
21	18.857	17.011	15.415	14.029	12.821	11.764	10.835	10.017	9.2922	8.6487
22	19.660	17.658	15.937	14.451	13.163	12.042	11.061	10.201	9.4424	8.7715
23	20.456	18.292	16.444	14.857	13.489	12.303	11.272	10.371	9.5802	8.8832
24	21.243	18.914	16.935	15.247	13.799	12.550	11.469	10.529	9.7066	8.9847
25	22.023	19.524	17.413	15.622	14.094	12.783	11.654	10.675	9.8266	9.0770
26	22.795	20.121	17.877	15.983	14.375	13.003	11.826	10.810	9.9290	9.1609
27	23.560	20.707	18.327	16.330	14.643	13.210	11.987	10.935	10.027	9.2372
28	24.316	21.281	18.764	16.663	14.898	13.406	12.137	11.051	10.116	9.3066
29	25.066	21.844	19.188	16.984	15.141	13.591	12.278	11.158	10.198	9.3696
30	25.808	22.397	19.600	17.292	15.373	13.765	12.409	11.258	10.274	9.4269
35	29.409	24.999	21.487	18.665	16.374	14.498	12.948	11.655	10.567	9.6442
40	32.835	27.356	23.115	19.793	17.159	15.046	13.332	11.925	10.757	9.7791
45	36.095	29.490	24.519	20.720	17.774	15.456	13.605	12.108	10.881	9.8628
50	39.196	31.424	25.730	21.482	18.256	15.762	13.801	12.233	10.962	9.9148
60	44.955	34.761	27.676	22.623	18.929	16.161	14.039	12.376	11.048	9.9671

Period (n)	11%	12%	13%	14%	15%	16%	17%	18%	19%	20%
1	0.9009	0.8929	0.8850	0.8772	0.8696	0.8621	0.8547	0.8475	0.8403	0.8333
2	1.7125	1.6901	1.6681	1.6467	1.6257	1.6052	1.5852	1.5656	1.5465	1.5278
3	2.4437	2.4018	2.3612	2.3216	2.2832	2.2459	2.2096	2.1743	2.1399	2.1065
4	3.1024	3.0373	2.9745	2.9137	2.8550	2.7982	2.7432	2.6901	2.6386	2.5887
5	3.6959	3.6048	3.5172	3.4331	3.3522	3.2743	3.1993	3.1272	3.0576	2.9906
6	4.2305	4.1114	3.9975	3.8887	3.7845	3.6847	3.5892	3.4976	3.4098	3.3255
7	4.7122	4.5638	4.4226	4.2883	4.1604	4.0386	3.9224	3.8115	3.7057	3.6046
8	5.1461	4.9676	4.7988	4.6389	4.4873	4.3436	4.2072	4.0776	3.9544	3.8372
9	5.5370	5.3282	5.1317	4.9464	4.7716	4.6065	4.4506	4.3030	4.1633	4.0310
10	5.8892	5.6502	5.4262	5.2161	5.0188	4.8332	4.6586	4.4941	4.3389	4.1925
11	6.2065	5.9377	5.6869	5.4527	5.2337	5.0286	4.8364	4.6560	4.4865	4.3271
12	6.4924	6.1944	5.9176	5.6603	5.4206	5.1971	4.9884	4.7932	4.6105	4.4392
13	6.7499	6.4235	6.1218	5.8424	5.5831	5.3423	5.1183	4.9095	4.7147	4.5327
14	6.9819	6.6282	6.3025	6.0021	5.7245	5.4675	5.2293	5.0081	4.8023	4.6106
15	7.1909	6.8109	6.4624	6.1422	5.8474	5.5755	5.3242	5.0916	4.8759	4.6755
16	7.3792	6.9740	6.6039	6.2651	5.9542	5.6685	5.4053	5.1624	4.9377	4.7296
17	7.5488	7.1196	6.7291	6.3729	6.0472	5.7487	5.4746	5.2223	4.9897	4.7746
18	7.7016	7.2497	6.8399	6.4674	6.1280	5.8178	5.5339	5.2732	5.0333	4.8122
19	7.8393	7.3658	6.9380	6.5504	6.1982	5.8775	5.5845	5.1362	5.0700	4.8435
20	7.9633	7.4694	7.0248	6.6231	6.2593	5.9288	5.6278	5.3527	5.1009	4.8696
21	8.0751	7.5620	7.1015	6.6870	6.3125	5.9731	5.6648	5.3837	5.1263	4.8913
22	8.1757	7.6446	7.1695	6.7429	6.3587	6.0113	5.6964	5.4099	5.1486	4.9094
23	8.2664	7.7184	7.2297	6.7921	6.3988	6.0442	5.7234	5.4321	5.1668	4.9245
24	8.3481	7.7843	7.2829	6.8351	6.4338	6.0726	5.7465	5.4509	5.1822	4.9371
25	8.4217	7.8431	7.3000	6.8729	6.4641	6.0971	5.7662	5.4669	5.1951	4.9476
26	8.4881	7.8957	7.3717	6.9061	6.4906	6.1182	5.7831	5.4804	5.2060	4.9563
27	8.5478	7.9426	7.4086	6.9352	6.5135	6.1364	5.7975	5.4919	5.2151	4.9636
28	8.6016	7.9844	7.4412	6.9607	6.5335	6.1520	5.8099	5.5016	5.2223	4.9697
29	8.6501	8.0218	7.4701	6.9830	6.5509	6.1656	5.8204	5.5093	5.2292	4.9747
30	8.6938	8.0552	7.4957	7.0027	6.5660	6.1772	5.8294	5.5168	5.2347	4.9789
35	8.8552	8.1755	7.5856	7.0700	6.6166	6.2153	5.8582	5.5386	5.2512	4.9915
40	8.9511	8.2433	7.6344	7.1050	6.6418	6.2335	5.8713	5.5482	5.2582	4.9966
45	9.0079	8.2825	7.6609	7.1232	6.6543	6.2421	5.8773	5.5523	5.2611	4.9986
50	9.0417	8.3045	7.6572	7.1327	6.6605	6.2463	5.8801	5.5541	5.2623	4.9995
60	9.0736	8.3240	7.6873	7.1401	6.6651	6.2491	5.8819	5.5553	5.2630	4.9999

Chapter Appendix D

Index